The
EQUIP
Program

Teaching
Youth to
Think
and Act
Responsibly
through a
Peer-Helping
Approach

John C. Gibbs

Granville Bud Potter

Arnold P. Goldstein

Research Press
2612 North Mattis Avenue
Champaign, Illinois 61821

Sarah's Problem Situation: From "A Comparison of Social Skills in Delinquent and Nondelinquent Adolescent Girls Using a Behavioral Role-Playing Inventory" by L. R. Gaffney and R. M. McFall, 1981, *Journal of Consulting and Clinical Psychology*, 49, 959–967. Copyright 1981 by the *Journal of Consulting and Clinical Psychology*. Adapted by permission.

George's Problem Situation: From *Dilemmas for Applied Use* by A. Colby and B. Speicher, 1973, unpublished manuscript, Harvard University, Cambridge, Massachusetts. Copyright 1973 by the authors. Adapted by permission.

Leon's and Reggie's Problem Situations: From *Moral Dilemmas at Scioto Village* by D. W. Meyers, 1982, unpublished manuscript, Ohio Department of Youth Services, Columbus. Copyright 1982 by the author. Adapted by permission.

Juan's Problem Situation: From *Dilemma Session Intervention with Adult Female Offenders: Behavioral and Attitudinal Correlates* by H. H. Ahlborn, 1986, unpublished manuscript, Ohio Department of Rehabilitation and Correction, Columbus. Copyright 1986 by the author. Adapted by permission.

Copies of this book may be ordered from the publisher at the address given on the title page.

Cover design by Doug Burnett
Composition by Tradewinds Imaging
Printed by McNaughton & Gunn

ISBN 0–87822–356–8
Library of Congress Catalog Number 95–68367

For a safer, more positive world

Contents

Part 1

Motivating and Equipping Youths to Help One Another Think and Act Responsibly

Part 2

The EQUIP Program

Appendix A

Appendix B

Figures and Tables

Preface

EQUIP is a new, highly effective program that motivates and equips young people to help one another. The EQUIP program had its beginning in November of 1986: Gibbs and Potter had each accepted an invitation to colead a workshop on juvenile offenders as part of a conference on youth organized by the Ohio State University Commission on Interprofessional Education and Practice. Gibbs knew only that his prospective coleader was an Ohio Department of Youth Services professional known for his work with incarcerated adolescents. Reciprocally, Potter knew only that Gibbs was a psychology professor at The Ohio State University known for similar work.

When they met to begin planning the workshop, Gibbs and Potter shared their experiences, successes, and frustrations. Gibbs had become noted as an expert on applying a theory of moral development to delinquents. In essence, that theory proposed that antisocial adolescents "had some growing to do" in their moral judgment and that such growth would diminish their antisocial behavior. Gibbs had developed group treatment techniques for improving moral judgment (e.g., Gibbs, Arnold, Ahlborn, & Cheesman, 1984) but had not found much evidence for accompanying behavioral improvement. Perhaps that was, after all, not surprising—in general, the juveniles with whom Gibbs had worked at several Ohio Department of Youth Services facilities and at the Clearbrook School in Columbus (a public middle school for antisocial juveniles) did not seem motivated to change. The juveniles' participation in group discussions was often halfhearted and sometimes downright resistant. Gibbs still believed in approaches seeking to equip antisocial youths with much-needed maturity and skills, but he sensed with some frustration that such approaches would have little impact on behavior without individual and group motivation to change.

Potter, too, had applied a theory to group work with antisocial youths. Much of his experience had been at Maumee Youth Center in Liberty Center, Ohio, where staff and administration were dedicated to implementing peer group approaches, such as Guided Group Interaction (McCorkle, Elias, & Bixby, 1958) and Positive Peer Culture (Vorrath, 1974; Vorrath & Brendtro, 1985). Indeed, as a staff member and administrator since 1967, Potter had helped to innovate, implement, and refine these techniques. Through his experiences at Maumee and other institutions—for instance, several Ohio Department of Youth Services facilities—Potter had come to believe in the power of these techniques to motivate change through the medium of a positive group influence. Yet Potter, too, sensed that something was missing. These approaches, which did so much to *motivate* youth to help one another, did little to *equip* them to help one another once they desired to do so. Because group members were deficient in positive helping skills, their efforts to help sometimes degenerated into name-calling, harassment, screaming, hostility, and physical conflict. Indeed, it was not uncommon for the staff leading the groups to exhibit similar degeneration as they attempted to remedy these degenerated group situations. Potter had on his own attempted to provide positive tools—for example, by devoting group time to communication skills training. But he also was left with the sense that his approach was insufficient.

During Gibbs and Potter's workshop planning, the obvious struck: Each had something to offer the other; their equipping and motivating approaches were complementary. Why not combine the two approaches—that is, motivate *and* equip youths to help one another? The proposed workshop began to take on a multicomponent theme. During workshop preparation, Gibbs and Potter's attention was drawn to the relevant work of a leader in the field, Arnold Goldstein at Syracuse University. Goldstein's then-forthcoming multicomponent psychoeducational program *Aggression Replacement Training: A Comprehensive Intervention for Aggressive Youth* (Goldstein & Glick, 1987) offered extensive training and practice in the replacement of aggression and anger with interpersonally responsible and skilled behavior. Particularly gratifying to Gibbs was the inclusion of moral education within this comprehensive program. Aggression Replacement Training appeared just in time to expand the content of Gibbs and Potter's workshop. At this point, then, EQUIP was multicomponent in two senses: First, it helped youths develop skills in order to render the mutual help group approach more effective (in other words, it combined skills training with mutual help approaches). Second, the skill development was itself multifaceted, focusing on moral judgment, anger management (including the correction of thinking errors), and social skills.

The theme of the workshop (Gibbs & Potter, 1987) was that conduct-disordered youths will help one another effectively once they are both *motivated* through a positive group context and *equipped* with specific skills for giving mutual help. The idea seemed intuitively appealing and was well received at the workshop by helping professionals in psychology, education, law, and social work. Why not see if such a multicomponent program would work? Fortunately, Potter was then superintendent of the Buckeye Youth Center, a juvenile correctional facility in Columbus, and in that capacity could provide an opportunity to implement EQUIP. The program was developed and refined over the next 2 years at this site.

Meanwhile, in December 1988, Gibbs and Potter invited Goldstein to join the EQUIP enterprise. In this book, much of the material on anger management skills, social skills, and program administration has been adapted from Goldstein's work (Goldstein, 1988; Goldstein & Glick, 1987). Goldstein and Glick's Aggression Replacement Training approach (as adapted by Gibbs and Potter) was an important contribution, permitting youth group members to bolster their "positive culture" and help peers more effectively. Reciprocally, the group context with its motivating potential could enhance the effectiveness of Aggression Replacement Training. After all, one of Goldstein's graduate students, Steve Litwack (1976), had found that juveniles were better motivated to acquire skills when they expected to use them later to help other adolescents. And Goldstein and Glick had acknowledged that "the peer group is an exceedingly powerful force in shaping and maintaining behavior" (p. 242).

Beginning in April 1989, an evaluation of the EQUIP program as established at the Buckeye Center was conducted by an Ohio State University graduate student, Leonard Leeman. Leeman's study (Leeman, 1991; Leeman, Gibbs, & Fuller, 1993), using control groups, showed EQUIP to be effective both in dramatically improving institutional conduct and in cutting the recidivism rate by better than half, a year after participating youths were released.

In recent years, we have conducted a number of workshops presenting EQUIP to a variety of organizations and personnel—teachers, school psychologists, forensic psychologists, child care workers, line staff, administrators, social workers, and other helping professionals. At the end of many workshops, participants have told us that they had seen the need for something like EQUIP at their institutions and had even attempted to do similar "equipping" work on their own—much as Potter himself had been doing before EQUIP! Like Potter's, however, their individual efforts were ultimately insufficient. Our workshops offered inspiration but not the full substance they needed. Now, with the publication of this book, we can offer helping professionals systematic, comprehensive guidelines for implementing the multicomponent EQUIP program.

We are indebted to many individuals and institutions for helping us translate our vision into this volume. Preeminent thanks must go to George Bennett and Barbara DeVoss, excellent social work professionals from whom—and from whose youth groups— we have learned so much in our effort to make EQUIP meaningful and useful to this population. We also appreciate the kindness and extensive cooperation shown us by (among others) Jerry Agee, Leila Reece and Mal Baumgartner, then of the Buckeye Youth Center; Sister Alena Bernert, Steve Dubros, Debbie Harrison, Carol Johnson, and

Sister Monica Nowack of the Rosemont Center; Nick Boase, Louis Mazzoli, and John Taracko, then of the Clearbrook School; and Evelyn Farmer, then of the Training Center for Youth—all located in Columbus. Psychologist SaraJane Rowland of the Ohio Department of Youth Services was especially kind in sharing with us her constructive reactions to our work, as well as her own work as she enriched it from other sources. Sharon Shumsky was kind enough to send us the entire California Department of the Youth Authority (1994) victim awareness manual. We also thank Cheri Walter for sending us the Ohio Department of Youth Services (1990) victim awareness manual, to which SaraJane Rowland contributed substantially. For providing constructive comments on chapter drafts, our heartfelt thanks go to Kevin Arnold, David Berenson, Lowell Gibbs, Sophia Gibbs, S. Viereck Gibbs, Valerie Gibbs, Debbie Harrison, Ron Huff, Molly Laird, Leonard Leeman, Tom Lickona, Andrew Martin, Tony Panzino, Stanton Samenow, Sue Simonian, Karen Steiner, Ann Swillinger, Jean Tucker, Mike Vasey, and Charles Wenar.

In the course of implementing EQUIP, first at the Buckeye Youth Center and then at the Training Center for Youth, we took numerous field trips to observe and learn from relevant treatment models already in operation. In this connection, we also appreciate the kindness and extensive cooperation of the late Mary Bachmann at Maumee Youth Center; Vicki Agee, then at Paint Creek Youth Center in Bainbridge, Ohio; and Bill Wasmund, then at the United Methodist Children's Home in Columbus. Without the help of so many good people, there simply would not have been EQUIP.

PART 1

Motivating and Equipping Youths to Help One Another Think and Act Responsibly

CHAPTER 1

EQUIP: Introduction and Description

EQUIP is a new treatment program for young people with antisocial behavior problems. In the EQUIP program, such youths become motivated and equipped to help one another in groups. For the past 40 years, "self-help" group programs in schools and residential facilities have sought—with mixed success—to motivate antisocial youths to help one another. Our thesis is that these youths will help one another *effectively*—and in the process help themselves—only if they and their group are equipped with certain skills and techniques.

This book provides all the material needed for understanding and implementing the EQUIP program. In this chapter, we develop the rationale for EQUIP, introduce its basic features and components, and describe a recent study documenting its effectiveness. This chapter lays the groundwork for the book as a whole and for the rest of part 1, which concerns the techniques (chapter 2) and skills (chapters 3 through 5) needed for motivating and equipping antisocial youths to help one another. The chapters in part 2 address program-level considerations, including procedures for program implementation and maintenance (chapter 6), principles for developing a positive staff culture (chapter 7), and ways in which EQUIP might be adapted or expanded (chapter 8). Certain of the assessment instruments mentioned throughout the book are found in the appendixes.

THE PEER-HELPING APPROACH

Although people have been motivated to help one another in groups for thousands of years, the modern self-help—or more properly, *mutual* help—group originated in 1935 with the founding of Alcoholics Anonymous. Such groups quickly proliferated. In recent years, approximately 500,000 peer or mutual help groups have emerged, involving over 12 million Americans (Hurley, 1988; Wuthnow, 1994). Like Alcoholics Anonymous, many of these group programs (e.g., Gamblers Anonymous) address the struggle against an addictive behavior. Other groups are composed of individuals facing stressful or painful situations (e.g., single parenthood, heart disease, widowhood, murder of a child). Still other groups (e.g., Al-Anon) aim to provide help for friends and relatives of the person with the problem.

Beginning in the 1940s, mutual help groups began to be applied to individuals who regularly victimize others and society. In a psychiatric hospital setting in Great Britain, Maxwell Jones (1953) innovated techniques for cultivating what he called a "therapeutic community" among sociopathic patients. At about the same time, Lloyd McCorkle, F. Lowell Bixby, and others adapted and applied similar techniques to delinquent boys in New Jersey (McCorkle, Elias, & Bixby, 1958), in an intervention they termed "Guided Group Interaction." These techniques were subsequently refined by Harry Vorrath and Larry Brendtro (1974), who modified the guided group interaction approach and renamed it "Positive Peer Culture," or PPC, to depict its intended goal. The revised edition of Vorrath and Brendtro's book *Positive Peer Culture* (1985) is the most articulated description available of the principles and procedures of such a program. A similar statement with regard to severely antisocial adolescents is Vicki Agee's (1979) *Treatment of the Violent Incorrigible Adolescent.* Positive Peer Culture (PPC) and other mutual help derivatives (e.g., Hickey & Scharf, 1980) have proliferated in various schools and residential facilities (correctional settings, group homes) and have engendered a professional society, the National Association of Peer Group Agencies.

The Challenge of a Negative Youth Culture

Antisocial youths represent a formidable challenge for the peer-helping approach. Unlike most mutual help groups, which are initiated voluntarily by participants, mutual help groups for antisocial youths are initiated by adults and typically meet with initial resistance. After all, antisocial youths already have in place a "culture," and it is a negative one, not given to helping others. Its themes are that "drug use is cool, sexual exploitation proves manliness, and you have to watch out for number one" (Brendtro & Wasmund, 1989, p. 83). In correctional settings, the negative youth culture is "characterized by opposition to institutional rules and goals, norms against informing authorities about rule violations, and the use of physical coercion as a basis of influence among inmates" (Osgood, Gruber, Archer, & Newcomb, 1985, p. 71).

Mutual help programs applied to antisocial youths must transform this self-centered and harmful culture into one characterized by caring and provision of constructive help for peers. The thesis of PPC and similar programs is that such transformations are possible because antisocial youths would like to be able to feel genuinely good about themselves and can learn that helping others is one way to do it. Caringly confronting and providing help to others means that one is making a difference for the better in the world and hence has a solid basis for self-respect. "In reaching out to help another, a person creates his own proof of worthiness; he is now of value to someone" (Vorrath & Brendtro, 1985, p. 6). The youths and those they help in the group become more positive, and the group culture changes (Harstad, 1976). Furthermore, their own thought and behavior become more responsible—after all, they are not only helping others in the group but are being helped themselves. As group members are helped to become more responsible, they thereby gain a further basis for experiencing self-respect and for meriting the respect of others. Changed adult offenders in an intensive, year-long group program described the appeal of self-respect in terms of being "clear" in their thinking about life with other people and having an "inner peace" or inner sense of being "clean" (Yochelson & Samenow, 1977, p. 425).

Evaluations of Mutual Help Programs

Evaluations of mutual help programs have yielded a mixed picture. Outcome evaluation studies of PPC and related programs have been conducted in schools (public and alternative), juvenile correctional facilities or detention centers, private residential facilities, and community group homes. Many of these studies have found guided mutual help programs to be effective in improving self-concept or self-esteem (Atwood & Osgood, 1987; Martin & Osgood, 1987; Vorrath & Brendtro, 1985; Wasmund, 1988). Gottfredson (1987) noted in connection with a controlled study of PPC in Chicago that schools in which guided peer programs operated became "safer over time, schoolwide reports of negative peer influence went down, and schoolwide belief in conventional rules went up" (p. 710). Hence, there is some support for the claim that such positive groups "deliver the teacher from an embattled 'me against them' position" (Carducci, 1980, p. 157), reducing management problems and permitting learning to take place. On the other hand, the trustworthiness of other results was generally undermined by serious methodological flaws, such as the absence of a control group. Significant reduction in recidivism was less likely to be found in the more rigorously controlled studies (Garrett, 1985; Gottfredson, 1987).

This mixed picture is perhaps not surprising in light of other research indicating that PPC programs often do not operate as intended. To investigate problems and program needs as seen by participants, Brendtro and Ness (1982) surveyed 10 schools and facilities using mutual help programs. Cited as a problem at 9 out of 10 centers was "abuse of confrontation" (e.g., "harassment, name-calling, screaming in someone's face, hostile profanity, and physical intimidation"; p. 322). Similarly, Yochelson and Samenow (1976) note that offenders often use confrontation in such groups to build themselves up by controlling or exerting power over someone else. One group required a member "to hang a toilet seat around his neck on which was painted the inscription 'I am crapping on people with my behavior' " (Vorrath & Brendtro, 1985, p. 108). Even worse, Harstad (1976) reported an incident in which a peer group beat to death a defiant group member. Such excesses are presumably not what Vorrath and Brendtro had in mind when they praised the "zeal" of formerly antisocial youths in helping others or suggested that the not-yet-reformed group member must be made "uncomfortable" (p. 13).

The intended constructive spirit of confronting and helping fellow group members may also be undermined in other ways. Yochelson and Samenow (1976, 1977) found that in therapeutic community or milieu therapy groups for criminals at Saint Elizabeths hospital in Washington, D.C., confrontation was used not only to exert power but also to impress the therapist and hence gain early release. "Helping" mainly meant keeping quiet about a fellow group member's rule violation or lying on behalf of a group member to help him cover up a crime. The criminals defined their basic problem not as antisocial behavior but rather as confinement and unsatisfactory institutional conditions; hence, to them, solving their problem meant not reforming conduct but rather regaining freedom. The group meetings became gripe sessions or "snow jobs" at best, criminal operations at worst.

It might be argued that evaluations of the peer-helping approach might be more consistently favorable if institutions more often implemented and operated mutual help programs as intended. Yet the widespread abuse of confrontation and "helping" may signal a problem deeper than that of insufficient staff training. Although Vorrath and Brendtro (1985) have railed against abuses, one can argue that the abuses are to some extent inevitable when insufficient attention is accorded to the limitations of the help providers. Indeed, in an important critique, Cleveland schoolteacher Dewey Carducci (1980) argued that the effectiveness of mutual help programs for antisocial juveniles is undermined from the outset by the juveniles' limitations. Vorrath and Brendtro's claim that PPC youths "demonstrate great skill in helping the student . . . to understand and work toward a resolution of his problems" (p. 92) warrants skepticism. Where would such "great skill" originate? More realistic is Agee and McWilliams' (1984) position:

> The violent juvenile offender, with his long history of sabotaging attempts at intervention and poor interpersonal relationships, would seem to be about as likely to benefit from a therapeutic community as a schizophrenic. The vital difference is that while the interpersonal skills of the violent juvenile offender are characteristically poor, the majority of them *can be taught the behaviors necessary to be therapeutic with each other.* (p. 286, emphasis added)

Not only violent juvenile offenders but all juvenile offenders must be properly motivated and properly equipped if they are to remedy their limitations and help their peers. It is fair to conclude that the peer-helping approach has underestimated the challenge represented by antisocial youths with their limitations and negative youth culture.

LIMITATIONS OF ANTISOCIAL YOUTHS

The limitations widely evident among antisocial youths can be characterized as three socially problematic "Ds": social skill *deficiencies*, social developmental *delays*, and social cognitive *distortions*. Carducci's (1980) analysis of the limitations of youths with antisocial behavior problems touches upon all three of these Ds. We feature Carducci's analysis as an introduction to more extensive depictions of the Ds in chapters 3 through 5.

Social Skill Deficiencies

With regard to social problems or conflicts, Carducci asserts that antisocial youths "do not know what specific steps, on their part or the part of the owner of the problem, will result in its being solved" (1980, p. 158). Carducci offered this case illustration from his PPC classroom:

> Tyrone, a 15-year-old Black youth from the inner city . . . asked to go to the library. As customary, he was accompanied by the other two members of his triad [in an adaptation of PPC, students are grouped in triads who work together, teach and support one another, and check one another's behavior]. He asked the . . . librarian if she had a book entitled, "The Autobiography of a Pimp," and she immediately became

angry; hostile words were exchanged, culminating in Tyrone's exclaiming, "Fuck your damn library!" and storming out of the classroom. (p. 161)

Clearly, Tyrone's response does not reflect the skills necessary to deal constructively with the librarian's anger.

Sociomoral Developmental Delays

Carducci writes that the antisocial juvenile is "frequently at a stage of arrested moral/ethical/social/emotional development in which he is fixated at a level of concern about getting his own throbbing needs met, regardless of effects on others" (1980, p. 157). Carducci is referring to the two main aspects of sociomoral developmental delay: (1) immature or superficial moral judgment and (2) pronounced egocentric bias. Superficial moral judgment and pronounced ego-centric bias are normal features of early childhood. Asked to distribute fairly items such as candy bars, young children typically confuse fair-ness with their own desires—for example, judging that they should get the most candy bars because they want to have them (Damon, 1977). Sociomoral developmental delay and its remediation are dis-cussed more fully in chapter 3.

Primary Cognitive Distortions

If the growing child's egocentric bias persists, it tends to become consolidated as a primary cognitive distortion (i.e., inaccurate or ratio-nalizing attitude, thought, or belief concerning one's own or others' social behavior; Gibbs, 1993). The self-serving nature of a primary cognitive distortion is often illustrated in clinical writings on offenders. Samenow (1984) quoted a 14-year-old delinquent as saying, "I was born with the idea that I'd do what I wanted. I always felt that rules and regulations were not for me" (p. 160). Yochelson and Samenow (1976, 1977) termed this egocentrically biased sense of entitlement to whatever one desires "ownership" (to be distinguished from the PPC use of this term to refer to the acceptance of responsibility for one's problem behavior).

Primary cognitive distortions constitute the first category (Self-Centered) in Gibbs and Potter's (1992) typological model of cognitive distortion. As we will discuss in more detail in chapter 4, this thinking error involves according status to one's own views to such a degree that the legitimate views of others are disregarded. We believe that pronounced egocentric bias and primary cognitive distortions are the basic problem of the irresponsible or antisocial individual (e.g., Gibbs, 1987, 1991). Accordingly, learning to take the viewpoint of others is a prominent treatment theme throughout the EQUIP program.

Secondary Cognitive Distortions

Gibbs and Potter's (1992) model identifies three categories of secondary distortion, which serve to support primary distortions. These are Minimizing/Mislabeling, Assuming the Worst, and Blaming Others. In brief, Minimizing/Mislabeling means depicting antisocial behavior as acceptable and causing no real harm. Assuming the Worst means gratuitously attributing hostile intentions to others or assuming that improvement in self or others is impossible. Carducci (1980) characterized Blaming Others as "the defense mechanism of [externalization] . . . in which [youths] blame others for their misbehavior" (p. 157). More complete descriptions of the thinking errors appear in chapter 4.

EQUIP: DEEPENING MUTUAL HELP AND PROVIDING REMEDIAL EQUIPMENT

Despite Vorrath and Brendtro's (1985) warning against hybrid programs, both Carducci (1980) and Agee and McWilliams (1984) advocate combining PPC with a training or teaching—we would say "equipping"—component. EQUIP remediates the three Ds we noted and renders the mutual help meeting more profound by requiring group members to report their underlying cognitive distortions or thinking errors. The cognitive distortions are studied in alternative meetings called *equipment meetings*, which also address group members' deficiencies in social skills and anger management and delays in sociomoral development. Equipment meetings are introduced after the mutual help group is established. The equipment meetings are based on coordinated curriculum components that deal with moral education, anger management and correction of thinking errors, and social skills. Although the three components are the subjects of separate chapters in this book, they are presented in alternation throughout the EQUIP course. Although the leaders of both mutual help meetings and equipment meetings use Socratic questioning and other indirect techniques, the group leader's role is much more prominent in equipment meetings. This distinction is reflected in a difference in terminology: We often refer to the group leader for the mutual help meetings as the "coach" and to the leader for the equipment meetings as the "equipper."

The group engaging in mutual help and equipment meetings should be moderately small: not fewer than six nor more than nine members. Vorrath and Brendtro (1985) argue that nine is the ideal size, although other group therapists recommend a somewhat smaller number (Rose & Edleson, 1987; Yalom, 1985). The consensus is that therapeutic potential declines precipitously with youth groups outside the six-to-nine range. (An important exception is dyadic or "pair" therapy, as developed by Selman and Shultz, 1990.) Groups of five or fewer can readily become complacent and predictable, whereas groups larger than nine can become unwieldy and superficial. When larger groups—twelve or more youths—already exist, they should be divided (if possible) into separate EQUIP groups of six or more.

Vorrath and Brendtro (1985, pp. 76–106) provide extensive guidelines concerning format, length, and seating arrangements that are especially helpful for mutual help meetings. Agee (1979, pp. 49–62) also provides helpful guidelines in many of these areas. Strategies for preparing and developing the EQUIP groups are described in chapter 2.

Remediating Cognitive Distortions: The Deeper Mutual Help Meeting

In EQUIP, as in guided group interaction or PPC programs, mutual help meetings are adult-guided but youth-run. Meetings last 1 to 1½ hours and take place five times a week (typically on weekdays). In EQUIP, one or two of these meetings each week are replaced by equipment meetings.

Mutual Help Meeting Format

We recommend a five-phase format for the EQUIP mutual help meeting: introduction, problem reporting, awarding the meeting, problem solving, and summary. The introduction is an addition to the traditional four-part PPC format. A helpful discussion of the latter four phases is found in Vorrath and Brendtro (1985). The phases proceed as follows.

Introduction. The group leader (or coach) begins each meeting with reflections from the previous meeting, evaluations of the group's progress, encouraging comments, and challenges. These introductory comments should take no longer than 5 minutes.

Problem reporting. During this phase, each member reports on the problems he or she has had since the last session or on another problem not yet brought to the group's attention. Group members may need to be reminded that a complaint about the institution or failure to get one's way cannot be reported as a problem. The reporting group member is responsible for stating all problematic incidents clearly and briefly; any important problems not mentioned should be brought up by the group. The group member describes his or her problems in terms of a standard vocabulary of "problem names." In EQUIP the mutual help meeting is deeper because each member reports not only a problem but also an underlying cognitive distortion or "thinking error." Problem reporting typically takes around 15 minutes, depending on the size of the group.

Awarding the meeting. After listening to each member's report of problems, the group decides who needs help most that day. Once the members reach a consensus, they award the meeting to that individual. Deciding who is to "have the meeting" generally takes about 5 minutes.

Problem solving. During the problem-solving phase, group members actively try to understand and resolve the problem of the member awarded the meeting. Once the equipment meetings have started, the group will be aided in this process by having learned certain skills. The group member should commit to a plan for implementing the proposed problem solution, as well as to a time line for reporting on the progress of the implementation. The problem-solving phase may last up to an hour if the group has progressed efficiently through the earlier phases.

Summary. During this phase, the coach summarizes the meeting's accomplishments and suggests ways in which subsequent meetings can be more effective. The summary generally takes about 10 minutes.

Problem Names and Thinking Errors

Throughout the mutual help meeting, group members and the leader use two sets of standard terms to designate social problems and thinking errors. Group members first use the 12 problem names compiled by Vorrath and Brendtro (1985) for PPC. These names, along with definitions of the problems provided by EQUIP group members, are shown in Table 1.1. Using this vocabulary in problem reporting helps keep the group's attention appropriately focused on behaviors that have harmed others and/or the reporting group member. The very use of the vocabulary may stimulate an awareness of the extent of one's antisocial behavior: We recollect the reaction of a youth who was among those in a living unit selected to

TABLE 1.1
Positive Peer Culture Problem Names

1. LOW SELF-IMAGE

   Has poor opinion of self. Often feels put down or of no worth. Quits easily. Plays "poor me" or perceives self as victim even when victimizing others. Feels accepted only by others who also feel poorly about themselves.

2. INCONSIDERATE OF SELF

   Does things that are damaging to self. Tries to run from problems or deny them.

3. INCONSIDERATE OF OTHERS

   Does things that are damaging to others. Doesn't care about needs or feelings of others. Enjoys putting people down or laughing at them. Takes advantage of weaker persons or those with problems. Has poor manners, is sloppy.

4. AUTHORITY PROBLEM

   Gets into major confrontations with those in authority, often over minor matters. Resents anyone telling him or her what to do or even giving advice. Won't listen. Even when complying, glares, sulks, or curses.

5. EASILY ANGERED

   Quickly takes offense. Is easily frustrated or irritated; throws tantrums.

6. AGGRAVATES OTHERS

   Threatens, bullies, hassles, teases, or uses put-downs. "Pays back," even when others didn't mean to put him or her down.

7. MISLEADS OTHERS

   Manipulates others into doing his or her dirty work; will abandon them if they are caught.

8. EASILY MISLED

   Prefers to associate with irresponsible peers, is easily drawn into their antisocial behavior. Is willing to be their flunky—hopes to gain their approval.

9. ALCOHOL OR DRUG PROBLEM

   Misuses substances that can hurt him or her. Afraid he or she won't have friends otherwise. Is afraid to face life without a crutch.

12

10. STEALING

   Takes things that belong to others. Doesn't respect others.
   Is willing to hurt another person to take what he or she wants.

11. LYING

   Cannot be trusted to tell the truth or the whole story. Twists the
   truth to create a false impression. Denies everything when he or
   she thinks it is possible to get away with it. Finds it exciting to
   scheme and then get away with a lie—in other words, to "get
   over" on people. May lie even when there is nothing to be gained.

12. FRONTING

   Tries to impress others, puffs him- or herself up, puts on an act.
   Clowns around to get attention. Is afraid to show his or her true
   feelings.

---

begin an EQUIP group. The youth had read the problem list aloud
to peers and attending staff. After a meditative pause, the youth
looked up and exclaimed in revelation, "We do all these things!"

   Once each of the problems has been named, the group and the
leader also use terms for the four cognitive distortions or thinking
errors described earlier—Self-Centered, Minimizing/Mislabeling,
Assuming the Worst, and Blaming Others—in order to deepen self-
awareness and make the problem analysis more penetrating. Complete definitions of the four thinking errors are provided in Table 1.2.
The thinking errors can usually be discerned as leading to the problems just named. The cognitions are labeled *errors* for a reason: The
group members' explanations are not "different" or "right for them"—
they are *wrong* or *inaccurate*. In Glasser's (1965) terms, they are at vari-
ance with "the tangible and intangible aspects of the real world" (p. 6).
The therapeutic advantage is clear: Wrong or inaccurate thinking invites
correction, whereas thinking considered merely "different" may not.

   The thinking errors are powerful tools that the group can use to help
its members achieve accurate thinking. For example, they help the
group to get a handle on the defensive explanations and diversionary
maneuvers commonly heard during mutual help and equipment
meetings. To illustrate, we have identified in brackets and italics the
thinking errors in the diversionary explanations of a group member
whose comments reveal an Alcohol or Drug Problem (perhaps
accompanied by Low Self-Image, Easily Misled, and other problems):

   As a group begins to work with this person, he will advance
   a number of seemingly plausible explanations. (1) It's really

TABLE 1.2

Cognitive Distortions

1. SELF-CENTERED

According status to one's own views, expectations, needs, rights, immediate feelings, and desires to such an extent that the legitimate views, etc., of others (or even one's own long-term best interest) are scarcely considered or are disregarded altogether.

2. MINIMIZING/MISLABELING

Depicting antisocial behavior as causing no real harm or as being acceptable or even admirable, or referring to others with belittling or dehumanizing labels.

3. ASSUMING THE WORST

Gratuitously attributing hostile intentions to others, considering a worst-case scenario for a social situation as if it were inevitable, or assuming that improvement is impossible in one's own or others' behavior.

4. BLAMING OTHERS

Misattributing blame for one's harmful actions to outside sources, especially to another person, a group, or a momentary aberration (one was drunk, high, in a bad mood, etc.), or misattributing blame for one's victimization or other misfortune to innocent others.

---

not a problem; I can stop any time I want [Minimizing/ Mislabeling]. (2) I just do it because my friends do [Blaming Others]. (3) Research says drugs are not harmful [Minimizing/ Mislabeling]. (4) All adults use drugs like tobacco and alcohol [Minimizing/Mislabeling]. (5) I just want to enjoy myself. What's wrong with that [Minimizing/ Mislabeling]? (6) It's my life; I can do what I want with it [Self-Centered]. (Vorrath & Brendtro, 1985, p. 98)

The group's problem reporting and problem solving, then, would include identifying the group member's issues at the surface level (Alcohol or Drug Problem, etc.) and at the underlying cognitive level (Self-Centered, Minimizing, etc.). Requiring a deeper level of problem reporting makes it harder for youths to minimize problems, externalize blame, or engage in mindless or mechanical verbalization (the second most frequently cited problem with PPC; Brendtro & Ness, 1982, p. 313).

Identifying both surface problems and thinking errors helps the group dig deeper to the source of antisocial behavior. An incident from one EQUIP group of incarcerated juvenile offenders illustrates the way in which examination of the thinking errors can add depth and power to a mutual help meeting. One youth, Mac, reported resisting and yelling profanities at a staff member who, in accordance with institutional policy, had attempted to inspect his carrying bag. The designation of Mac's behavior as an Authority Problem was easy enough. Identification of the underlying thinking error required some discussion but was very helpful. Mac explained that the bag had contained something very special and irreplaceable—photos of his grandmother—and that he was not going to let anyone take the photos from him. In seeking to identify underlying thinking errors, the group learned important further information: Mac thought only of safeguarding his photos. He did not for a moment consider the staff member's perspective—she was only carrying out institutional policy concerning inspection for contraband. Nor did he consider that she was not abusive and that he thus had no reason to assume that the photos would be confiscated. Generating the surface behavior identified as Authority Problem, then, were Self-Centered and Assuming the Worst thinking errors. Mac's anger at staff for his subsequent disciplinary write-up was identified as an Easily Angered problem and attributed to a Blaming Others thinking error (after all, objectively speaking, Mac had only himself to blame for the write-up). In general, groups must be cautioned against "overloading" problem labels upon a group member; fortunately, Mac accepted this additional problem labeling constructively.

As Mac, with the help of his peers, learned the vocabulary terms for his irresponsible thinking and acting (along with certain constructive skills, described later), his anger dissipated considerably. Perhaps most important, he began to regret his verbal assault on the staff member. We believe that Mac's remorse was therapeutically crucial: He could now see the unfairness of his behavior toward the staff member, empathize with her, and attribute blame to himself. Identification and correction of Mac's thinking errors permitted this therapeutic breakthrough of remorse. Over the course of subsequent sessions, Mac's Authority and Easily Angered problems manifested themselves less frequently.

Remediating Deficiencies and Delays: Equipment Meetings

The goal of the equipment meeting is to "equip" the group with needed skills and resources for helping its members. Equipment meetings are held once or twice each week, replacing mutual help meetings on those days and providing not only training in important skills but also some variety in the daily group sessions. The meetings are called "equipment" meetings not only because they provide much-needed tools for mutual help but also because there is nothing "sissy" or weak about getting equipment.

The group consists of its members, so equipping the group means providing direct help to group members with deficits in social or anger management skills, cognitive distortions, and delays in moral development. In the EQUIP program, however, the emphasis is on how the group can *be helpful* rather than on how the group or its members *need help*. The group is also cautioned against substituting power plays or grandstanding for genuine caring and is urged to be open in problem reporting and receptive to constructive criticism. Equipment meetings are generally not introduced until the group has developed sufficiently to be receptive.

HOW THE EQUIP COMPONENTS WORK TOGETHER

The benefit that the group derives from the equipment meeting is illustrated with the earlier case of Mac, the youth who verbally attacked a staff member because of Self-Centered and Assuming the Worst thinking errors. Helping Mac to identify and correct his thinking errors was only one aspect of problem solving; social skills were also important. Specifically, the social skill Expressing a Complaint Constructively was helpful in resolving the situation (see chapter 5). The group had learned and practiced this skill during previous equipment meetings. With some prompting from the leader, group members reminded Mac of the four steps involved in the skill:

Step 1: Identify the problem. How are you feeling? What is the problem? Who is responsible for it? Did you contribute—or are you contributing—to the problem in any way?

Step 2: Plan and think ahead. To whom should you express your complaint? When? Where? What will you say (see step 3)?

Step 3: State your complaint. In a calm, straightforward way, tell the person the problem and how you feel about it. If you've contributed to the problem, mention how you may be partly at fault and what *you* are willing to do.

Step 4: Make a constructive suggestion. Tell the person what you would like done about the problem. Ask the other person if he or she thinks your suggestion is fair. If the other person

makes a constructive suggestion, say that you appreciate the
suggestion or that it sounds fair.

Step 1 of this skill was especially helpful to Mac in that it required him
to correct his Self-Centered thinking error—that is, to recognize how he
had contributed to the problem he experienced with the staff member.

A similar social skill was helpful for Tyrone, the student described
earlier who stormed out of the library (Carducci, 1980). Tyrone's peers
and teacher were able to help him discuss the problem. He and his
peers then role-played a constructive encounter with the librarian
using a social skill similar to Expressing a Complaint Constructively.
After several practice trials, in which Tyrone's peers helped him
improve his wording and manage his tone of voice and body language,
he was able to express calmly his hurt and anger, apologize, explain
that he meant no offense, and make a constructive suggestion—that
he would be more respectful if the librarian wouldn't assume the worst
about his intentions. (To help clear up any remaining hard feelings,
he could even have asked her how she felt about his suggestion.)
"Although they still do not understand or like each other very much,
the librarian and Tyrone are able to conduct their mutual business
without incident, and Tyrone is neither aggressive nor obsequious
with her" (p. 161).

In addition to the social skill equipment, certain anger management tools were helpful for Mac and could also have been for
Tyrone. These techniques—for example, taking deep breaths, counting backward, and thinking ahead to the undesirable consequences
of losing control—will be discussed in chapter 4. Finally, moral education (see chapter 3) contributes to the maturity of the group's
moral reasoning with members such as Mac or Tyrone. Having gained
equipment to remedy all three Ds (distortions, deficiencies, delays),
the group was able to help Mac effectively.

EVALUATION OF THE EQUIP PROGRAM

Although vivid and encouraging, case illustrations do not provide
adequate evaluation of an intervention program's effectiveness. The
effectiveness of the EQUIP program has been evaluated in a systematic and controlled outcome study (Leeman et al., 1993). The study
was conducted at a medium-security correctional facility maintained
by the juvenile corrections department of a Midwestern state. Participating as subjects were 57 male juvenile offenders, aged 15 through
18, who were incarcerated at the facility. The subjects were randomly
assigned either to the EQUIP experimental unit or to one of two

control groups (a simple passage-of-time control and a control that received a motivational message). The experimental treatment initiative was introduced by the study's authors to institutional staff; interested staff members (youth leaders, social workers, supervisors, and a teacher) were trained in the EQUIP program methods and subsequently conducted the program.

The treatment program was conducted at a living unit located in one wing of the facility building. The unit had the same design as other units in the institution, providing a dormitory, a living area, a "quiet room" (for studying, etc.), and a staff office. The quiet room was used as the meeting room for the experimental (EQUIP) group. EQUIP groups met daily, on weekdays, for 1 to 1½ hours. Three of the five daily sessions were regular mutual help meetings; two of the five were equipment meetings devoted to teaching the EQUIP curriculum.

Outcome measures for the study addressed both institutional and postrelease conduct. Institutional misconduct (and certain mediating processes such as social skills, as discussed in chapter 5) were assessed through both self-report and archival measures. Experimental as well as control group subjects completed both pretest and posttest self-report questionnaires. The questionnaire (adapted from Gold, 1970) asked whether or how often in the past month the subject had damaged something, been involved in a fight, defied staff, or taken drugs. Archival measures of institutional misconduct were based on disciplinary incident reports and unexcused school absences. The postrelease archival measure consisted of information on parole revocation and/or institutional recommitment.

EQUIP was found to stimulate substantial institutional and postrelease conduct gains. Institutional conduct gains were highly significant for the EQUIP group, relative to the control groups, in terms of self-reported misconduct, staff-filed incident reports, and unexcused absences from school. These results corroborated informal observations and comments by institutional staff that the EQUIP unit was dramatically easier to manage than other units: There were substantially fewer instances of fights, verbal abuse, staff defiance, and AWOL attempts. Interestingly, the control subjects approached the low-frequency levels of the EQUIP groups on incident reports and unexcused absence during the final month of their incarceration (see Figures 1.1 and 1.2). Possibly, members of the control group were on their best behavior just before their release dates to avoid risking disciplinary action and delay in their release.

The most notable finding was that the EQUIP program's impact was evident 12 months after subjects' release. The recidivism rate for EQUIP participants remained low and stable, whereas the likelihood of recidivism for the untreated subjects climbed. Specifically, the EQUIP group's recidivism rate was 15% at both 6 months and 12 months after release. In contrast, the mean recidivism rate for the control groups was 29.7% at 6 months and climbed to 40.5% at 12 months; the latter difference, between 15 and 40.5%, was statistically significant. In other words, the EQUIP youths were about a third as likely to recidivate.

Overall, the Leeman et al. (1993) study showed the EQUIP group treatment program to be highly effective: Antisocial adolescents' conduct significantly improved during incarceration, and the lower recidivism rate would suggest that this improvement was maintained during the year following release from the institution.

FIGURE 1.1

**Mean Incident Report Frequencies by Month
for Experimental and Control Groups**

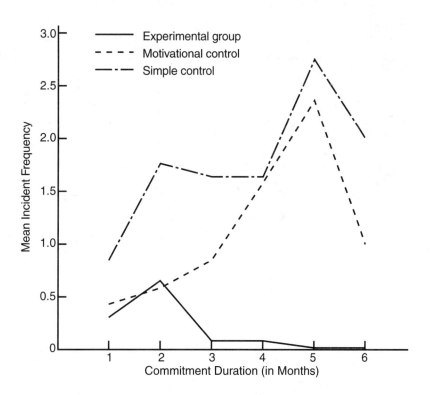

FIGURE 1.2

Mean Frequency of Unexcused Absences from School by Month for Experimental and Control Groups

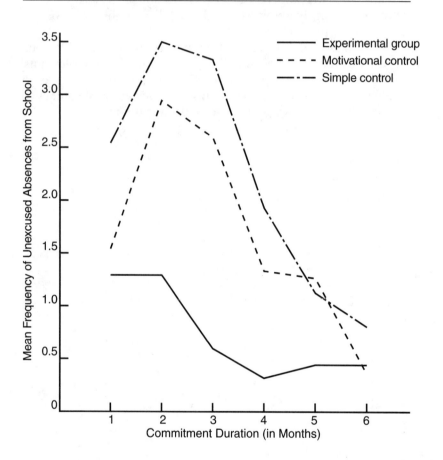

CHAPTER 2
Developing a Positive Youth Culture

This chapter will discuss principles, procedures, and techniques for cultivating a positive, caring youth culture. As noted in chapter 1, antisocial youths pose a formidable challenge to the mutual help approach; they have already in place a culture that is not even neutral but is in fact negative. The thesis of the mutual help approach is that this negative culture can be transformed into a positive one because the antisocial juvenile senses that something is missing. Left unfulfilled by a self-centered life-style, such young people at times desire a genuine basis for self-respect. They find it as they begin to be of value to others, helping them in sincere and thoughtful ways. The group evolves from power plays and "fronting" operations into genuine caring, and the group members achieve responsible thought and behavior.

As indicated in chapter 1, our assessment of the mutual help approach is that it has underestimated the challenge posed by antisocial youths. Although the thesis that many antisocial youths can get "hooked" on helping others is tenable, cultivating the conditions for genuine helping is not easy. It requires remediation of the limitations of antisocial youths as well as special techniques for fostering group development. In this chapter, we describe ways to develop a positive group as adapted from PPC and other sources as well as our own experience. We believe that one particular factor—the equipment meetings—makes a crucial contribution to the ability of antisocial young people to develop an authentic, mutually caring, responsible group.

SELECTING AND PREPARING THE GROUP

Strictly speaking, principles and procedures for selecting and preparing the group are part of program implementation and hence are treated in chapter 6. Clearly, however, the attributes of group members and the way the program is introduced to them bear heavily on subsequent group development, so we mention them here. Briefly, juveniles selected to start a core group should be relatively popular with negative peers and yet amenable to positive appeals—in other words, strong enough to resist the delinquent norms against cooperating with adults or institutions. In an incarcerative facility, one must expect even these youths to be motivated first mainly by the desire to "score points" with staff and perhaps gain early release from the institution. At least they will cooperate, however. The thesis is that in time their helping behavior will become more genuine, motivated increasingly by self-respect.

As the program is introduced to the core members, emphasis is on the points that they are being given an opportunity to help others and, in the process, to help themselves, that the "problems" for group attention will not be complaints but instead irresponsible ways of acting and thinking, that the "help" must be responsible and not a show or a power play, and that members must not only give constructive criticism but also have the courage to receive such criticism—in other words, to open up to the group and be worthy of the trust of others who dare to disclose problems. Of course, these basic points have little impact until they are repeated by the group leaders in concrete contexts, but their presentation at the outset does contribute moderately to the quality of the group.

STAGES OF GROUP DEVELOPMENT

Techniques for cultivating a positive youth culture are best discussed in relation to the milestones or stages of group development. Several writers (Vorrath & Brendtro, 1985; Tuckman & Jensen, 1977) have described four stages of group development: forming, storming, norming, and positive youth culture. First, in the "forming" stage, group members generally act in a tentative or uncertain manner, seek information, and proceed cautiously (perhaps "casing" the program). Group members are likely to be untrusting, so the leader must repeatedly encourage disclosure. Second is the "storming" stage, in which group members are less tentative; they openly disagree and test limits by attempting to subvert or divert the program. Group members' advice to one another may consist of shows or power plays, and the advice givers often do not apply their advice to themselves. During this phase, the group leader must frequently inveigh against misusing the group meeting as a gripe session. In the third or "norming" stage, many—but not all—group members become more genuine about responsible change, try not to let the group down, and in a humble and thoughtful way express their disapproval of irresponsible behavior. Although negative group members (or "negative leaders," to be discussed) still have influence, they can no longer set the dominant tone. Virtually unanimous, constructive group participation is the hallmark of the final stage, positive youth culture: "a strong, cohesive, clique-free group that embodies a value system of mutual caring and concern" (Vorrath & Brendtro, 1985, p. 47).

FACILITATING PROGRESS THROUGH THE STAGES OF GROUP DEVELOPMENT

A group of initially irresponsible, antisocial youths will not progress through these stages of group development without the application by staff, the group leader, and the group itself of many facilitative techniques and activities. Certain activities or techniques are used by the same party (e.g., the group leader) throughout the stages of group development. Other activities are used throughout but by different parties—for instance, basic mutual help techniques that are applied increasingly by the youths themselves. Still other activities are geared to particular stages of group development. We will discuss the following facilitators of a positive youth culture:

Basic mutual help techniques

The life story meeting

"Ask, don't tell"

Expanded use of the problems and thinking errors log

Equipment meetings

Redirection of the negative leader

Formats for expressing support

Vocational and community service projects

Faith-building activities

Basic Mutual Help Techniques

Four basic mutual help techniques that foster development toward a positive youth culture are reversing, confronting, checking, and relabeling.

Reversing

Perhaps the most formidable barrier to change encountered in work with antisocial youths is their secondary cognitive distortion of Blaming Others. The self-protective value of externalizing blame is illustrated by Redl and Wineman (1957), who, upon asking an aggressive child about a transgression, would encounter "a barrage of moral indignation stirred up like a dust cloud to hide or confuse" (p. 180):

> Thus, for instance, when we would try to pin a youngster down into telling us about some of the most . . . extreme and atrocious behavior he afforded at school that day, he would, sensing what was coming, harp on another item where either another youngster jostled him, or where some time ago the teacher accused him wrongly of something of minor importance. . . . In short, the youngster would skillfully pick up any such issue and now become the accuser . . . [especially,] that we do not pay enough attention to the youngster's . . . having suffered an unfairness or injustice. (pp. 180–181)

As long as obfuscation and projection of blame allow violent and other antisocial youths to avoid feeling accountable for their behavior, little can be accomplished in any treatment program. Hence, Vorrath and Brendtro (1985) stress the importance of shifting the responsibility back to the young people themselves, a technique they refer to as *reversing*. To the adolescent who says, "I got in trouble because both of my parents are alcoholics and don't care about me," Vorrath and Brendtro suggest a rejoinder such as "Do you mean that all people with parents who have problems get in trouble?" (p. 39).

Harstad (1976) contributes other illustrations of reversing:

Youth: It's all you assholes that are causing my problems!

Worker: You know, Bob, it's going to be great when you feel good enough and strong enough about yourself that you do not have to put other people down or blame them.

Youth: I only got into trouble because the guys I hang around with did.

Worker: You mean that you were the "flunky" of your gang and had no will of your own? (pp. 111–112)

Related to reversing is the practice of pointing out that the irresponsible person made choices that contributed to the current "problems" of which he or she complains, that others from far worse homes nonetheless made responsible choices, that the person has victimized others more than he or she has been victimized, and that offering excuses is a way of escaping responsibility (Yochelson & Samenow, 1977, p. 200). Group leaders should also insist that group members accept total responsibility for their problems. Yochelson and Samenow advocate maintaining the position that offenders must assume full responsibility for their share of a situation, whether or not others contributed to it. They give the following example:

> There was the beginning of antagonism in the group. C1 claimed that C2 was ignoring him and not even saying "hello" in the morning. C2 maintained that C1 was unfriendly and unresponsive. Actually there was evidence of both. Operationally to achieve a result, each had to consider himself totally to blame. By assuming full responsibility, each criminal had to focus on his changing, not on excuses. (pp. 193–194)

Confronting

Reversing is often used in conjunction with *confronting*—making individuals aware of the effects of their actions on others. In this spirit, Yochelson and Samenow (1977) recommend that change agents (i.e., group leaders) respectfully but forthrightly challenge antisocial individuals to put themselves in others' positions and to understand the "chain of injuries" (p. 223) resulting from every crime, even if the challenges induce discomfort. Agee and McWilliams (1984) contrast this technique with therapeutic styles emphasizing unconditional affirmation or support: "If by some miracle you could provide for every need and desire of the youths at all times, they would still attempt to escape. . . . They prefer criminal excitement to the stress and pressure of critically examining their behavior and changing it" (p. 290). Similarly, Glasser (1965) cautions against wrongly concluding that

> a delinquent child broke the law because he was miserable, and that therefore our job is to make him happy. He broke the law . . . because he was irresponsible. The unhappiness is not a cause but a companion to his irresponsible behavior. (p. 30)

The therapist's—and the mutual help group's—"job" is to provide not permissive support but instead caring confrontation that exposes the discrepancy between a member's words and his or her actions:

> Instead of being guilt-ridden and overly anxious, many youth (particularly delinquents) do not experience enough guilt and so may need to become more anxious in order to be motivated to change. They must come to feel uncomfortable and ill at ease each time they hurt themselves or others. . . .

As the youth is awakened to his lack of concern for self
and others, he is already becoming a better human being.
(Vorrath & Brendtro, 1985, p. 13)

Checking

In situations where full-fledged confronting may not be necessary or feasible (e.g., in a classroom), *checking* may be used. Whereas
reversing and constructive confronting usually require extensive
modeling by the group leader, group members typically begin
quickly to learn and use checking. Briefly, a "check" is a cue or
reminder. When a group member begins to show a problem, a peer
reminds him or her to get back in control by saying, "Check yourself." Peers can also give nonverbal cues if verbal cues would be
inappropriate. As Agee (1979) describes it, the aim of checking is

to build an "early warning system" in each youth's cognitive
process. . . . [Antisocial youths] do not become anxious
early enough in the acting out sequence to be able to stop
their behavior (that is, they become anxious when pulling
the trigger, not when planning the crime). Constant early
warnings will hopefully train the [antisocial youth] to be
able to say "check yourself" to himself. (p. 77)

Training group members in verbal self-regulation is a major
thrust of the EQUIP curriculum (see chapter 4). Emphasized in that
chapter are "think ahead" and "TOP" (think of the other person and
the pain your actions have caused other people), phrases that youths
can use along with "check yourself."

Relabeling

The youth culture cannot be therapeutic unless the giving and receiving of help are perceived in positive terms. In the culture of antisocial
youths, however, quite the opposite is true: Unless helping means fighting to rescue a fellow gang member, giving or getting help is often
viewed as weak, dumb, or sissy. Positive words such as *strong, cool, smart,*
or *sophisticated* are explicitly or implicitly applied to antisocial behavior
instead. The notion that helping others—or letting others help you—
is weak, whereas hurting others is strong, probably reflects the Self-
Centered and Minimizing/Mislabeling thinking errors of antisocial
youths.

Correcting this distortion is crucial to the development of a positive culture. The development of skills for identifying and correcting
Self-Centered thinking errors (e.g., reversing for Blaming Others)

should help to some extent. Vorrath and Brendtro (1985) suggest that the coach redirect—but not attack—antisocial youths' desire to be strong. Strength or maturity should be associated with helping or accepting help ("Who is big enough to admit that they could use help from someone else?") in order to "make caring fashionable" (p. 21). Instead of attacking a group member's show of strength (e.g., "You're not as strong as you pretend to be"), the coach recognizes the youth's strength but links it to helping: "Somebody as strong as you will really be able to become a great group member; helping takes strength" (p. 23). Vorrath and Brendtro term this strategy *relabeling* and give other examples pertaining to what in EQUIP are considered cognitive distortions (especially Minimizing/Mislabeling):

> If the delinquent youth perceives criminal types as cool, mature, smart, and masculine, then we might counter this view [in EQUIP terms, Mislabeling] by noting that many 50-year-old criminals are locked in cages because they act like babies and must be watched all the time. . . . If "truancy" has an exciting quality to it, we ought to give this problem a label that sounds less mature, perhaps "playing games of hide and seek." If delinquent youth [Mislabel] their mass rape of a girl [as] cool, then we should relabel this act as "messing over [an innocent] person." If stealing is seen [Mislabeled] as slick, then it should be relabeled as "sneaky and dumb." If a youth gets some rewards from his tendency to act in violent ways, then the attractiveness of such behavior can be diminished when it is relabeled as "having a childish temper tantrum" or "acting like a hothead." . . . Likewise, if the group under the guise of helping is possibly communicating a veiled threat (e.g., "You had better change or we will be climbing on your back"), staff can question the intent by posing new labels: "Does that mean hurting or helping?" (p. 23)

As the group leader's modeling and explicit encouragement continue, the youths should begin to pick up the cues. The leader should see the group employing reversing, confronting, checking, and relabeling with increasing frequency. All of these techniques are critical for inducing personal accountability among the youths and facilitating development of the group beyond the forming and storming stages.

The Life Story Meeting

The life story meeting is a variant of the mutual help meeting in the tradition of PPC. This activity facilitates development toward a positive youth culture by fostering a closeness based on mutual personal sharing. As Vorrath and Brendtro (1985) write, "The very act of sharing oneself is of great value, for the student is now invested in others: 'I have told you about myself; so now I am a part of you.'" (p. 15). A life story meeting takes place when the group grants a new member's request to be awarded the meeting in order to reveal his or her personal history—an account of the way he or she has related to family, peers, school, and community, with emphasis on past "problems" or instances of viewing things irresponsibly, making irresponsible choices, and harming self and others. A new group member shares his or her life story within a few weeks of joining the group, after other members have shared their life stories with the new member. Established members may share their life stories in abbreviated form, either outside the regular meeting time or at the start of meetings they themselves have been awarded.

Besides facilitating group development, the life story helps the group see how the new member views him- or herself and others and hence what behavior problem and thinking error themes from the past are likely to be current trouble spots requiring problem solving. The purpose of hearing a life story is *not* to ask "why" questions in order to help the sharer achieve insight into the origin of problems. As Yochelson and Samenow (1977) observe, "Long ago, we discovered that asking why yields only self-serving rationalizations" (p. 170). A sharer who feels encouraged to provide excuses will also feel absolved from accepting responsibility for harmful behavior.

Even if they are not encouraged with "why" questions, group members may be self-serving in sharing their life stories. They may "cite the broken home, the drinking father, and so forth, without mentioning any of the mitigating factors that helped to stabilize their homes. Nor will they mention that a brother or sister confronted by the same problems managed to surmount them" (Yochelson & Samenow, 1976, p. 123). Although the group should allow the member telling a life story to talk freely, they should ask for clarification, specification, or elaboration at key points where it appears the teller is being deliberately confusing, diversionary, vague, or minimizing.

The group should also ask the teller to recollect his or her thoughts during important past events. Often the thoughts fit into a broad pattern of criminal thinking. Yochelson and Samenow (1977) describe an offender at a group meeting who, without group probing, would not have divulged homicidal thinking about his father-in-law. The offender

> went into great detail about going fishing. He described
> everything he did, right down to the colors and stripes of

the fish he caught. Then he made passing references to his father-in-law's being taken to the hospital and his own remaining at the hospital for many hours. However, there was not a word about [his] thoughts during all those hours. . . . [The offender] emphasized details about a situation that did not bring out thinking errors. [Without the group's probing] he [would have] failed to disclose his [homicidal] thinking [at the hospital]. (p. 192)

Sharing life stories enables the group (and the coach) to diagnose each member's particular profile of problems. As noted in chapter 1, problem identification in the traditional PPC format consists exclusively of the assignment of problem names (Table 1.1). In the EQUIP format, by contrast, the group arrives at a dual diagnosis: one or more "surface" or behavioral problems paired with one or more underlying cognitive distortions. The combined behavioral-cognitive problem identification following appropriate probing permits a more penetrating analysis. So equipped, the group can reveal the truth in a way that commands respect from the youth and can lead to genuine change.

"Ask, Don't Tell"

Cultivating a trusting but challenging (i.e., therapeutic) group culture is crucial in EQUIP because the vehicle for treatment is the group, not the mutual help meeting coach or even the equipment meeting equipper. Although the group leader (coach or equipper) should not be passive or uninvolved—especially in the early mutual help meetings, when the procedures must be taught—the leader should remember that his or her primary role is to cultivate the group: to guide or stimulate, not to inject statements or instructions. Group members must be involved and empowered as "owners" of the treatment process. As Yalom (1985) states, "It is important that the group begin to assume responsibility for its own functioning. If this norm fails to develop . . . the members are dependent upon the leader to supply movement and direction, and the leader feels increasingly fatigued and irritated by the burden of making everything work" (p. 126).

The group must be stimulated, then, to grow to the norming stage of group responsibility for positive change in its members. To foster the development of that norm, both group leaders—the coach and the equipper—should ask questions. By nature, questions require the listener to think. The questioning style is characterized by Lickona (1983) as the "ask-don't-tell method of reasoning with kids" (p. 302). Vorrath and Brendtro (1985) depict the value of the ask-don't-tell method:

> While several group members all talk simultaneously, a
> highly perceptive comment from one youth goes unnoticed.
> The group leader does not tell the group, "you shouldn't all
> be talking at once," or make any other directive comment.
> Rather, he only needs to ask, "Did the group hear Ronald's
> question?" (p. 73)

In a typical mutual help meeting, the coach may find it necessary to intervene with guiding questions perhaps a half-dozen times. Vorrath and Brendtro provide diverse examples. If a group member claims that he can handle his problems without the group's help, the coach might ask, "Is John saying that accepting help from others makes him feel small?" (p. 99) and follow the question with encouragement (e.g., "The group should look forward to the time John will trust the group enough to accept help"). If a highly verbal, attention-seeking group member is beginning to dominate the meeting with power plays, the group leader might simply ask, "How many members are in the group?" or "Is the group letting one member take control?" If the group is vicariously enjoying the fantasy of a member's "war stories" (i.e., sensationalized accounts of exploits), the coach might ask, "Is John trying to make his troubles sound exciting?" (p. 100).

If an aggressive group member is intimidating other members who are trying to help him, the coach can ask, "Why does the group let Tom push them around?" or "Can Tom get help if nobody dares to be honest with him?" (Other techniques for dealing with negative group members are discussed later in this chapter.) In this connection, Vorrath and Brendtro (1985) mention a nonquestioning but still group-referential technique termed "predicting possible outcomes": "Once the group deals with Tom it will be interesting to see if the members will become afraid of him again or if he will get mad and show his easily angered [and in EQUIP terms, Self-Centered] problem[s], or if he will withdraw and sulk [and blame the group for his problems]" (p. 101). By anticipating and labeling these possible outcomes, the coach alerts the group to prepare to deal with them.

"Ask, don't tell" should be applied to fronting behavior, a problem especially evident in early group stages. A certain amount of fronting is to be expected; fortunately, we have seen "helping" in the service of ulterior motives gradually grow into genuine caring. A youth who shows no such growth after several weeks should be challenged. To deal with the persistently fronting group member, the coach may ask a challenging or clarifying question—for example, "When is Sam going to start working for the group instead of [trying to impress] staff?" (Vorrath & Brendtro, 1985, p. 113) or "Does the group think Ron is really serious?" (p. 101). The leader may also challenge the group—for example, "How long will the group let Ron get away with his Fronting and Inconsiderate of Self problems?"

As for any technique, the ask-don't-tell method must be applied properly. The coach's appeals should be to the group so that members are encouraged to communicate with one another rather than with the coach. Vorrath and Brendtro (1985) even recommend that a new coach *always* address a group member (at least one who has been awarded a meeting) indirectly through the group—for example, "Is the group interested in finding out why George feels he always has to be high on drugs?" (p. 73).

If the coach typically uses certain pronouns *(you, I, we),* the group will not develop. Specifically, *you* (e.g., "Do you see . . . ?") used frequently tends to encourage direct two-way conversations between group members and the coach. *I* (e.g., "I was really disappointed . . .") tends to draw attention to the coach and hence encourages the entire group to front—that is, to say whatever might sound good to the coach. *We* (e.g., "We weren't very constructive today") weakens the group as distinct from the coach and thereby undermines the group's empowerment and development of responsibility.

Lickona (1983) suggests that proper questions are those that stimulate youths to consider positive, constructive, prosocial alternatives. For instance, the leader might ask a dilatory group, "What do group members need to do to make this a helpful meeting today?" Improper questions are those that attempt to shame ("Can't the group act better than a bunch of 2-year-olds today?"), embarrass ("What kind of impression would that give anyone visiting this group?"), or intimidate ("Do you know what I'm going to do if I catch any of you doing that?"). Such questions direct group attention toward pleasing others or avoiding detection and punishment rather than toward acknowledging that certain actions are harmful or unfair to others. Where punishment must be enforced, the appeal should not be personally threatening but should instead be objective and information oriented (e.g., "Does the group remember what the consequence is when a group member's practice work isn't done?").

The style and tone of the questions are also important. The coach's questions should be simple and brief, asked one at a time (asking several questions at once can be confusing). The questioner should maintain a normal volume and speak in a respectful rather than a threatening or demanding tone of voice. In this connection, Lickona (1983) notes an added dividend of the ask-don't-tell method: If the leader has become angry or distressed at a turn of events in the meeting, asking a question (even an "I" question; "Why am I upset right now?") lets him or her regain emotional control as the responsibility for talking shifts immediately to the group. Furthermore, the question doesn't put the group on the defensive as a statement might, and it gives the group a chance to acknowledge and correct the unfairness or harmfulness of their actions.

An action—or inaction—particularly unfair to the group is that of the nonparticipatory group member, a problem that can persist beyond the forming stage of group development. The group member who is so inactive as to fall asleep during a meeting should be awakened by the group. Incidentally, such nonparticipation can be a pose; in our experience, the ostensible dozer sometimes reveals that he or she has in fact been listening and is more aware of group proceedings than anyone had suspected. Nonetheless, the coach should use the ask-don't-tell technique to encourage the group to challenge the sleeper: "What kind of problem is José showing by pretending to sleep here? Is he being Inconsiderate of Self? Inconsiderate of Others? Is José Assuming the Worst that he won't be able to succeed in the group?" and "Is José being Self-Centered and unfair when he is intentionally silent and so makes the other group members have to work harder?" The nonparticipation problem is also addressed under our discussion of expanded use of the problems and thinking errors log.

The ask-don't-tell method can be overused. Lickona's advice is to "ask questions when it feels natural to do so, and make a direct statement when it feels natural to do that" (1983, p. 322). Indeed, avoiding direct statements altogether would virtually preclude the teaching that needs to take place. Vorrath and Brendtro's "predicting possible outcomes" technique, described earlier, is one example of appropriate coach input that takes the form of statements rather than questions. Statements are also made during the introduction and summary phases of the mutual help meeting. Still, Lickona advocates extensive use of the ask-don't-tell method and suggests that a direct challenge from the youth (e.g., "Never mind the questions—just give it to us straight!") be met forthrightly (e.g., "I'm asking questions because I want the group to think about this, to come up with the best judgment"). In this connection, second author Potter has often used his summary time at the end of a mutual help meeting to provide a helpful metaphor: "Does the group want to be given a fish or learn how to fish?" In both mutual help meetings and equipment meetings, the group must be challenged to learn *how* to fish—to help one another. Used to an appropriate degree, the ask-don't-tell method is an excellent tool for cultivating youths' autonomy and sense of responsibility for providing mutual help.

Expanded Use of the Problems and Thinking Errors Log

In the early days of a group's mutual help meetings, nonparticipation by many members is typically a problem. Ironically, the group members with the longest offense histories—those who need the most help—are often the very ones who claim "nothing happened" and attempt to "pass" during problem reporting. We have seen the value of the ask-don't-tell technique in stimulating the group to seek participation from such members. But "ask, don't tell" is not a panacea; these group members may still participate only minimally, with long silences and pseudocontributions.

What if minimal participation continues, week after week, to be a widespread problem in the group? In effect, the question is, How does the coach deal with group developmental delay? In the next section, we will recommend initiating equipment meetings for a group stalled after 4 weeks in the storming stage. Here we are concerned with earlier delay, at the forming stage—prolonged, widespread, minimal participation by group members. We do not recommend initiating the equipment meetings this early because they would fall flat in such an undeveloped group. However, one resource from the EQUIP curriculum—the Problems and Thinking Errors log (Figure 4.3)—may be helpful. The log is a structured vehicle that guides young people in observing and documenting their own problem behaviors and thinking errors. When inadequate participation persists, we recommend having the group start completing the log, even before the equipment meetings are introduced, and using the log as the basis for problem reporting. Furthermore, we propose expanding the use of the log with such a group. The group should be instructed that if they don't have a standard problem to record, they should record any event, action, or conversation in connection with which they can also record a thinking error. (After all, the criminal thought today may lead to the crime tomorrow, given the right circumstances.) Failing that, they should simply write down any noncomplaining stream of thought pertaining to their goals or to other people.

To be able to do such reporting, group members need special training. The proposed expanded use of the log corresponds to a technique called "phenomenologic reporting" (Yochelson & Samenow, 1976, 1977) used in group therapy with adult offenders. Participants are instructed to take notes as if they could consult special closed-circuit, soundtrack television cameras in their minds, cameras that can see their thoughts and videotape them continuously. The mind-camera can immediately make a videotape or computer printout of the raw data of thinking: "stray thoughts, recurrent ideas, inner debates, and incipient criminal ideas" (Yochelson & Samenow, 1977, p. 168), with the emphasis on thinking errors. A participant's notes are to be like this printout, except that the reporting should be ordered chronologically or by subject matter (e.g., thinking about peers, staff, relatives, future plans) and should omit extraneous details (e.g., what type of pie was served with dinner).

When this technique is used with a mutual help group, members are responsible for bringing their log-based notes to each meeting and for reporting from those notes within the time constraints of the session. Probing questions by the group and the leader promote more comprehensive reporting. In the Yochelson-Samenow group, one passing thought in a participant's report may reveal a criminogenic thinking pattern and hence serve as the discussion theme for the entire meeting. In an EQUIP group, the coach should use the ask-don't-tell technique as much as possible to focus group discussion on the criminogenically significant thoughts of the member who has the meeting.

Use of the EQUIP Problems and Thinking Errors log, expanded in a manner similar to phenomenologic reporting, may jump-start a stalled group. Unless they have been mentally dead for the past 24 hours, group members can scarcely claim that "nothing happened"!

Equipment Meetings

As we will see in chapters 3 through 5, the perspectives, skills, and maturity gained through the equipment meetings contribute powerfully to the development of a positive youth culture. However, if the equipment skills are to be learned well, the equipment meetings should not be introduced until the group is sufficiently developed. Litwack (1976) found that delinquents who were informed that they would first be learning social skills and then using those skills to help others learned those skills more effectively. The chicken-or-egg dilemma is that, although the EQUIP curriculum presupposes a developed and receptive group, an advanced stage of group development is unlikely to be achieved unless the developing group is given the tools for attaining it. The problem is serious because delay in introducing the curriculum entails a risk that the unequipped group will become frustrated in their helping attempts and resort to the coercive behaviors they know all too well.

With this dilemma in mind, we suggest beginning the EQUIP curriculum course no sooner than 2 weeks—but no later than 4 weeks—after a full-size EQUIP group has begun to have daily mutual help meetings. By the end of the fourth week of mutual help meetings, the average group should have progressed to the norming stage, an indication that it is sufficiently mature to take seriously and appreciate the equipment meetings. If even by this time the group still has not progressed to the norming stage, the equipment meetings should be initiated anyway. We have seen the EQUIP curriculum enable groups to achieve responsible norms and values.

The mutual help group should be prepared from the outset for the introduction of the equipment meetings. The message should not be that the group is helpless without those meetings but that the equipment provided in the meetings will make the group much more effective in helping its members. A sports analogy can be very helpful: The mutual help coach can note the importance of skill development and practice for any successful team and point out that the same applies to the EQUIP group. Teams that take practice seriously and practice hard tend to be winners.

Redirection of the Negative Leader

The greatest impediment to the development of a positive youth culture is often the influence of an actively resistant group member who attempts to lead the group in a negative direction. A group of antisocial youths typically has one or more members who are not only irresponsible but also highly skilled at conning, controlling, and directing others. These individuals' extensive offense histories reflect a long-standing, entrenched, pervasively criminal way of living and thinking. If unchecked, the determined negative leader can keep a group in the storming stage indefinitely. Yet that youth can be seen as a potential asset because the group will also be amenable to his or her strong influence if it is exercised in a positive direction. Just as caring for or wanting the best for someone can be relabeled as showing strength, the influence of the negative leader can be redirected toward positive group leadership.

To redirect the negative leader, Vorrath and Brendtro (1985) suggest avoiding any direct attack during group time because the likely result would be a rallying by the leader's followers or assistants and hence an even more formidable barrier to group development. Rather, the most effective strategy—apart from a special outside-of-group confrontation coordinated by the treatment team (see Vorrath & Brendtro, 1985, pp. 110–111)—is to attack the leader's base of support by confronting the assistants and holding them accountable for the leader's hurtful behavior. The assistants should be reminded that EQUIP separates the problem from the person and that the negative leader is still someone worthy of their help.

Use of the cognitive distortion and problem vocabulary can strengthen appeals to the assistants: Are they Minimizing the harm the leader's behavior is doing the group or Mislabeling it as smart or cool or strong? Are they Assuming the Worst—that they are helpless to confront the leader's Self-Centered attitude or to insist that the leader accept responsibility for his or her harmful actions instead of Blaming Others? The coach should identify the Minimizing/Mislabeling character of the assistants' perception of the negative leader, relabel the assistants' loyalty as an Easily Misled problem, and make clear that true caring about the negative leader would mean showing the strength to stand up to his or her manipulation by insisting on positive behavior. And the Easily Misled problem is also more broadly construed as an Inconsiderate of Self problem (insofar as loyalty amounts to a failure to identify and correct thinking errors) and an Inconsiderate of Others problem (insofar as the negative leader is not being helped to identify and correct thinking errors). The vocabulary tools gained in EQUIP, then, help group members redirect the negative leader. Nevertheless, they should be cautioned that efforts to redirect will not be quick or easy; the leader will probably not give up cognitive distortions and negative behavior without a fight.

In addition to depriving the negative leader of his or her support, the coach should provide opportunities for the leader to become involved with the group in a positive way. Once the youth demonstrates the ability to exert positive leadership, staff can appeal to this evidence of competence, continuing to support the new positive role until it becomes established. Then the coach has an ally with considerable expertise

> in dealing with other youth of similar background. He will acquire considerable knowledge about those in his group, and other members will not find it easy to deceive him. The best expert on defending, excusing, and shifting the blame is the person who himself used these procedures. Nobody can deal better with the con artist than another con artist. (Vorrath & Brendtro, 1985, p. 7)

In addition, that ally has great credibility within the group:

> Strong and reforming youth present to those not yet committed to change a particular challenge whose influence cannot readily be dismissed. The new member in a group knows that their reforming peer has experienced many of the same problems, and his word has to be given special credibility. Criticism cannot be viewed as it would be if it came from an adult or from a "square" peer. (Vorrath & Brendtro, 1985, p. 8)

The coach cannot succeed in redirecting the negative leader unless the youth acquires the skills necessary to think and act responsibly and maturely—to become an assertive but not aggressive helper in the group. For this reason, equipment meetings will play a crucial role in the redirection of the negative leader.

A negative leader or any other group member who is on the verge of becoming physically assaultive may require physical restraint by staff, with verbal assistance from the group. If physical intimidation or danger persists, staff may need to follow up in a private conference, conveying the unequivocal message that the youth will not be permitted to continue intimidating peers or adults. Once the other group members learn that staff are not afraid to place demands on the hostile person, they will feel more confident and be able to deal with that person as well.

The intractably hostile group member who continues to undermine the group in serious ways may require removal from the group for a limited time. A temporary time-out is an appropriate, fair consequence following logically from behavior that abuses others: Because respecting others is a ground rule of social life, those who break this essential rule must lose their social opportunities until the social abuse stops. A youth who has committed an assault in a community setting could face arrest and criminal charges; perhaps especially to avoid such charges, the youth may return to the group and begin to participate in a more positive way. The time-out period can be used as a teachable moment for the group: What are the logical consequences of abusing others? Is helping a group member sometimes more like a marathon than a dash?

Formats for Expressing Support

A group member need not be a negative leader to engage in behavior incompatible with a positive culture. Indeed, that behavior may not even be intentionally or overtly hostile. For example, immature group members tend to be insecure or emotionally unstable and hence are at risk for Low Self-Image and Easily Misled behavior problems. If immature group members are to become active and consistent contributors to a positive group, it is crucial for the coach to provide and model for the group expressions of at least qualified approval and emotional support. The approval is "qualified" in part as a precaution against the tendency of irresponsible individuals to overgeneralize any positive comments as a blanket approval covering even their antisocial behavior (Yochelson & Samenow, 1976).

To maintain a balance between criticism and approval, we suggest a "sandwich" style of constructive criticism, in which a critical comment is preceded and followed by supportive ones—for example, "Vincent has been identifying other problems [support]—why won't he recognize his Easily Angered problem [criticism]? He's strong enough to do that [support], and the group can help." Vorrath and

Brendtro (1985) call a simpler version the "punch and burp" message—"That was childish behavior [criticism]. You are much more mature than that [compliment]" (p. 111). Similarly, Agee (1979) suggests giving "a pat and a swat at the same time . . . [e.g.,] 'You are too valuable [pat] to continue doing stupid things to yourself [swat]' . . . hurting others hurts oneself" (p. 37).

Goldstein (1993) suggests a strategy for supporting immature group members during social skills training—having them ease into role-playing by first playing supporting or "coactor" roles for other group members, with the leader providing reassurance (e.g., "You can do it"; "Take it one step at a time"; "The group will help you as you go along"). Reticent individuals thus get accustomed to speaking in front of the group while the spotlight is still on someone else before moving on to their own role-plays. Assertive skills such as Expressing a Complaint Constructively, detailed in chapter 5, may be especially important for such youths to become assets to the group.

Support is especially important following periods of therapeutic gain, when some types of juvenile offenders tend to "fall apart":

> They are so accustomed to misery, and so frightened by good feelings, that they are almost forced to do something to sabotage the situation when they are doing well. During these periods, the [severe juvenile offenders] need strong encouragement and reminders of their tendencies to "make mountains out of molehills." Even more than most adolescents, they exaggerate each crisis and become convinced that they are doomed [in EQUIP terms, Assuming the Worst]. During these times, they can be reminded of incidents they have handled well [a pat], of how they overreacted to the last crisis [a swat], and of the therapist's [in EQUIP terms, the coach's] assurance that just because they have been sliding does not mean that they have to . . . slide clear to the bottom [correcting Assuming the Worst]. Obviously, they need enormous support during these periods. Support does not include rationalization for their behavior, however, but is more in the line of "You made a mistake—what have you learned this time?" (Agee, 1979, p. 115)

The immature group member presents not only a challenge but an opportunity for the leader to model constructive expressions of support under trying circumstances, particularly in equipment meetings. (Mutual help meetings offer fewer such opportunities because of the need to leave room for group initiatives.) For example, the equipper can engage the member who resists doing a role-play by using a variation of the skill Dealing Constructively with Someone Angry at You (see chapter 5). Goldstein (1993) reports good results with this technique, which he calls "empathic encouragement." The basic steps are as follows.

Step 1: Listen openly and actively.

Step 2: Express your understanding of the resistant group member's feelings and thinking, and express acceptance of the parts (if any) with which you can honestly agree.

Step 3: Express your honest disagreement with the other parts and suggest that resolution of these areas be postponed.

Step 4: Urge the group member to try, in the meantime, to engage in the equipment exercise.

One alternative to empathic encouragement is simply to ignore the resistant behavior, in the hope that ignored or unrewarded behavior will extinguish. Ignoring the behavior may be appropriate if it is minimally disruptive—for instance, whispering (especially if the content is helpful information such as explanation of group expectations to a new member). The behavior may have to be challenged as an Inconsiderate of Others problem if it continues.

Vocational and Community Service Projects

As the positive youth culture develops, a curious phenomenon can occur: Although the group can become a community of genuine caring and mutual concern during group meetings in the presence of staff, the established delinquent culture of threats, put-downs, and manipulation can persist back in the living and recreation areas when staff are not around. Participant-observer studies indicate that youths can sometimes maintain such dual lives with little discomfort and that even a high-quality treatment team can be unaware of the persistence of the delinquent culture (Polsky, 1962; Rose, 1991).

Even when the caring group carries the positive culture from the group meeting to other facility settings, the prosocial behavior of group members may not continue after release. Vorrath and Brendtro (1985) point out that the positive group can be a mere "greenhouse" (p. 119): beautiful within its limited sphere but unrelated or irrelevant to the real world. If positive behavior is to be maintained and generalized, responsible functioning must be *practiced*. The role-play and practice of social skills (chapter 5), for example, is of vital importance. The more the practice, the greater chance that an athletic team will make the leap from great practice games to a victory when the big game finally arrives—and the greater chance that the youth will successfully meet the challenges of the real world when the release date finally arrives!

To foster the authenticity of group caring throughout the facility and beyond—and to provide a broad base for self-respect—Vorrath and Brendtro (1985) recommend providing opportunities for young people to be competent, productive, and useful in the institution and the community. One such opportunity is work activities while still in the institution. Agee and McWilliams (1984) assert that it is "as important for the youths to learn how to relate while washing dishes as it is while telling their innermost secrets in group therapy" (p. 288). Yochelson and Samenow (1977; pp. 400–408, 509–511) provide a helpful discussion of work experiences as an excellent arena for learning responsible behavior. Vorrath and Brendtro recommend not only work activities but also community service and related projects, such as helping at a community day-care center, assisting in Special Olympics events, helping children with developmental disabilities, earning money to provide food for needy families, and visiting shut-in citizens.

In addition to reinforcing positive behaviors and feelings, service projects can provide a context for juvenile offenders to become more aware of how their actions have been harmful to others (cf. victim awareness programs, discussed in chapter 8). For example, at Maumee Youth Center in Liberty Center, Ohio, delinquents with histories of drug trafficking have learned first-hand how drugs ruin lives as they have prepared and served meals at a community center for homeless people.

Vorrath and Brendtro (1985) offer a number of excellent suggestions for introducing service learning projects, such as encouraging the group to see the project as their initiative and labeling the project as requiring strength ("This will be a tough job"). They conclude with the caveat that, although service learning offers personal development to the participants, its spirit must be genuinely altruistic if the activities are not to degenerate into "yet another kind of narcissism" (p. 122). Similarly, Yochelson and Samenow (1977) warn, "The danger of the good deed is that it reinforces the criminal's belief that he is not a criminal" (p. 301). Hence, work and community service projects should be undertaken only by groups in the positive youth culture stage of development, or at least those well into the norming stage.

Faith-Building Activities

The equipping curriculum increasingly encourages soul-searching questions: What kind of person do I want to be? What kind of impact do I want to have on others and the world? and What do I want my life to amount to? As the group develops toward a positive culture, group members may increasingly seek a spiritual meaning and direction for the positive moral values that they are developing. Ideally, the institution can offer faith-building opportunities for these youths. The Annsville Youth Center in New York State offers a religious program that

> attempts to expose the adolescent to the notion of a loving God and to help him respond freely to that God according to his own conscience. Chaplains work closely together to give the youth the experience of God's love and to help the youth understand what moral response God expects of them in this life. The chaplains have an initial interview with each youth soon after he is admitted to the facility. At this interview they seek to establish a good rapport with the youth and to demonstrate their approachability and future availability for personal and confidential counseling. The youth attend weekly religious education classes at which they are exposed to the beliefs of various religious traditions such as Christianity, Judaism, Buddhism, Hinduism, and Islam. The classes are also used to try to inculcate in the youth sound spiritual and moral values. Youth also have the opportunity to attend religious services at various local churches of their own choice. . . . The Annsville religious program aims at giving the youth a knowledge and experience of a loving God, so that when they leave Annsville they will possess the spiritual and moral capacity to lead productive and happy lives. (Goldstein & Glick, 1987, p. 292)

Like community service activities, opportunities for spiritual development are most constructively used by youths who are well along in the change process (Yochelson & Samenow, 1976, pp. 297–308; 1977, pp. 517–520). Group members' spiritual development then contributes to the depth and authenticity of the positive youth culture.

CHAPTER 3

Equipping with Mature Moral Judgment

As we noted in chapters 1 and 2, the limitations of antisocial youths tend to hamper their efforts in guided peer programs to help one another change. Our solution to this problem is to bolster such programs by equipping young people—that is, by remedying their limitations. One fundamental limitation is moral developmental delay or immaturity. In this chapter we will outline the cognitive-structural theory of moral development and delay, discuss previous programs that have attempted to remediate this delay, and provide EQUIP's "equipment" for remediating this limitation of antisocial youths.

MORAL DEVELOPMENT AND DELAY

Cognitive-structural or cognitive-developmental theory (e.g., Kohlberg, 1984) posits a primary role for cognition in the motivation of moral or antisocial behavior. *Cognition* here refers to basic patterns or "structures" of mature or immature thought (in the present case, moral judgment). According to this theory, antisocial behavior is attributable at least in part to sociomoral developmental delay—that is, the persistence beyond early childhood of (1) immature or superficial moral judgment and (2) a pronounced degree of "me-centeredness" (Lickona, 1983) or egocentric bias. Cognitive-structural interventions attempt to provide social perspective-taking opportunities that address both of these aspects of sociomoral developmental delay.

Delay as Prolonged Immaturity in Stage of Moral Judgment

In cognitive-structural theory, moral development involves a "construction" of progressively mature moral meaning. Kohlberg contended that this constructive process results in an identifiable, cross-culturally standard sequence of stages of moral judgment development and maturity (see Colby & Kohlberg, 1987; Gibbs, 1995; Kohlberg, 1971, 1984; for a review of pertinent research, see Walker, 1988). Kohlberg's Stages 1 through 4 are adapted and used in Gibbs, Basinger, and Fuller's (1992) neo-Kohlbergian typology, which classifies the adapted stages into levels of developmental maturity and immaturity. Stages 1 and 2 represent immature or superficial moral judgment; an adolescent or adult evidencing exclusively or predominantly these stages should be considered developmentally delayed in moral reasoning. Stages 3 and 4, representing mature or profound moral judgment, should define the cognitive-structural norm for any culture. The adolescent or adult who has constructed moral meaning at these levels may hold, for example, that one should keep a promise to a friend to preserve the trust on which the friendship is based or because mutual respect is the basis for any relationship. Mature or profound moral understanding pertains to a broad spectrum of culturally pervasive moral norms and values, such as telling the truth, refraining from stealing, helping others, and saving lives.

The superficiality of immature moral judgment is most evident in Stage 1, which reflects "the natural tendency of young children to embody . . . moral notions in concrete places or events" (Damon, 1988, p. 15). Stage 1 morality entails a physicalistic understanding of moral authority (e.g., "The father is the boss because he's bigger"; Kohlberg, 1984, p. 624) or of the moral worth of a human life (one of the subjects in Kohlberg's longitudinal study suggested that saving the life of more than one person is especially important because "one man has just one house, maybe a lot of furniture, but a whole bunch of people have an awful lot of furniture," p. 192). Similarly, keeping a promise might be justified by appeal to physical consequences (otherwise the person "will beat you up"). Perceptually impressive features of a situation (e.g., size, objects, or actions), then, tend to capture the young child's attention or imagination; these features are central to the child's reasons for obeying authority, saving a life, keeping a promise, or adhering to other moral prescriptions.

Stage 2 reasoning goes beyond physicality to interrelate psychological perspectives, but even this stage can still be characterized as superficial. Kohlberg (1984) described the Stage 2 perspective as

> pragmatic—to maximize satisfaction of one's needs and desires while minimizing negative consequences to the self. The assumption that the other is also operating from this premise leads to an emphasis on instrumental exchange. . . . For example, it is seen as important to keep promises to insure that others will keep their promises to you and do nice things for you, or . . . in order to keep them from getting mad at you. (pp. 626–628)

With the advent of Stage 3, moral judgment advances beyond superficiality to a mature understanding of moral norms and values.

Stage 3 entails an interrelating of pragmatic perspectives sufficient to bring about an understanding of the mutuality or trust that underlies mature interpersonal relationships. Kohlberg (1984) suggested that "Stage 3 reciprocity [allows] one to understand reciprocity as going beyond concrete notions of equal exchange to maintaining relationships, mutuality of expectations, and sentiments of gratitude and obligation" (pp. 628–629). This progression in moral judgment from instrumental exchange ("You scratch my back, I'll scratch yours") to a mutuality of expectations was also found by Piaget (1965/1932), whose study of moral judgment was seminal for Kohlberg's work. Piaget characterized the progression as a transition from "reciprocity as a fact" to "reciprocity as an ideal" or "do as you would be done by" (p. 323).

Stage 3 moral judgment does not represent full moral-cognitive adequacy or maturity for members of a society more complex than a small community. As individuals move beyond local communities to universities or complex work settings, they increasingly deal with strangers and relate to people who have diverse or heterogeneous values. As a result of this experience and the reflection it stimulates, the appreciation of the need for mutual trust (Stage 3) expands into an appreciation of the need for commonly accepted, consistent standards and interdependent requirements (Stage 4; cf. Edwards, 1975, 1982; Mason & Gibbs, 1993a, 1993b). As a subject in Kohlberg's longitudinal study said, "You've got to have certain understandings in things that everyone is going to abide by or else you could never get anywhere in society, never do anything" (Colby et al., 1987, p. 375). In the absence of commonly accepted understandings, such as the responsibility to respect others' rights and to contribute to society, not only will society never advance, but (in the words of another of Kohlberg's longitudinal subjects) "chaos will ensue, since each person will be following his or her own set of laws" (p. 375).

In sum, then, the child progresses in moral judgment from a relatively superficial (physicalistic, pragmatic) level to a more profound and mature level entailing insight into the psychological meaning and functional bases of interpersonal relationships (mutuality of expectations) and society (commonly accepted standards, interdependencies, and other understandings). This age-related progression has been found in longitudinal studies (Colby, Kohlberg, Gibbs, & Lieberman, 1983; Page, 1981; Walker, 1989) and in cross-cultural research. In a review of Kohlbergian moral judgment studies in 27 countries, Snarey (1985) concluded that Kohlberg's Stages 1 through 4 are "represented in a wide range of cultural groups" (p. 218). Key characteristics of the stages are presented in Table 3.1.

TABLE 3.1

Stages in the Development of Moral Judgment

IMMATURE MORALITIES: STAGES 1 AND 2

Stage 1—Power: "Might Makes Right"

Morality is whatever big or powerful people say that you have to do. If you are big or powerful, whatever you say is right, and whatever you want to do or get is fair.

If you don't get punished for what you did or no one powerful saw it, whatever you did was okay. It is wrong if you do get punished; the punishment is mainly what makes it wrong.

Physical damage or other obvious injury—but not psychological suffering—is noticed and acknowledged to be wrong.

Individuals tend to spout clichés ("You should never tell a lie") without understanding and disregard them unless a powerful person (who can detect and punish) is present.

CRITIQUE

A Stage 1 individual doesn't understand the moral reasons for rules, has trouble with reciprocity if it requires taking more than one perspective at a time, and attributes a superficial perspective to someone physically powerful.

Stage 2—Deals: "You Scratch My Back, I'll Scratch Yours"

Morality is exchange of favors ("I did this for you, so you'd better do that for me") or of blows (misunderstanding of the Golden Rule as "Do it to others before they do it to you" or "Pay them back if they've done it to you").

You should ask or figure, "What's in it for me?" before you help or obey others.

The main reason for not stealing, cheating, and so on is that you could get caught.

Individuals may assert that nobody (even those in legitimate positions of authority) should "boss anybody around"; that people should mind their own business; that because everybody has his or her own point of view as to what's right, everybody should have the right to think and do whatever he or she wants.

Individuals may suggest that you should "fix things" or "get even" if somebody gets more than you do.

Stage 2 individuals have trouble understanding the ideal of mutuality in a relationship. Also, they tend to be self-centered: better at detecting how others are unfair to them or don't do things for them than at seeing how they are unfair to others or don't do things for others.

MATURE MORALITIES: STAGES 3 AND 4

Stage 3—Mutuality: "Treat Others as You Would Hope They Would Treat You"

In mutual morality, the relationship itself becomes a value: trust and mutual caring, although intangible, are real and important.

People can really care about other people, can have trust in them, can feel part of a "we."

You should try to understand if your friend is acting hostile or selfish.

You should try to make a good impression so that others understand that you are a well-intentioned person and so that you can think well of yourself.

CRITIQUE

Stage 3 thinking entails caring about the mutuality of relationships and even the preciousness of human life. However, Stage 3 thinkers can care so much about what others think of them that they turn into "moral marshmallows" in difficult situations.

Stage 4—Systems: "Are You Contributing to Society?"

This morality involves interdependence and cooperation for the sake of society: Society can't make it if people don't respect others' rights and follow through on their responsibilities.

Honoring your commitments is a sign of character.

If you are in the position of a judge, teacher, or some other social authority, you should uphold consistent and fair standards (but also consider extenuating circumstances).

In difficult situations, retaining integrity and self-respect may mean becoming unpopular.

CRITIQUE

Stage 4 thinking entails appeals to respect for rights and responsibilities as the basis for society, and even for *ideal* society. Stage 4 societal morality expands more than replaces Stage 3 interpersonal morality.

Kohlberg (1984) emphasized the mediating role of social inter-action in moral judgment development:

> If moral development is fundamentally a process of the restructuring of modes of role-taking, then the fundamental social inputs stimulating moral development may be termed "role-taking opportunities." . . . Participation in various groups . . . [stimulates] development. . . . The child lives in a total social world in which perceptions of the law, of the peer group, and of parental teaching all influence one another. . . . Various people and groups . . . [stimulate] *general moral development.* . . . The more the social stimulation, the faster the rate of moral development. (pp. 74–78)

As children enter adolescence, they normally have enjoyed suffi-cient role- or perspective-taking opportunities to construct at least a Stage 3 understanding of human social life. Those who have lacked such opportunities are left with a superficial or pragmatic worldview (e.g., Stage 2); such developmentally delayed youths are prone to behavior that is antisocial—and potentially dangerous, given the size, strength, independence, sexual impulses, and ego capabilities of adolescents. As might be expected, controlled comparisons of delin-quent or conduct-disordered children or adolescents with normal peers (Bear & Richards, 1981; Blasi, 1980; Campagna & Harter, 1975; Chandler & Moran, 1990; Gavaghan, Arnold, & Gibbs, 1983; Jennings, Kilkenny, & Kohlberg, 1983; Nelson, Smith, & Dodd, 1990; Trevethan & Walker, 1989) indicate that, at least on production measures, delin-quent or conduct-disordered youths on the average demonstrate delay in the development of moral judgment (attributable mainly to a considerably higher usage of Stage 2 reasoning). In a study analyz-ing moral judgment delay by area of moral value, Gregg, Gibbs, and Basinger (1994) found delay in *every* area. The area of greatest delay concerned the reasons offered for obeying the law. Nondelinquents generally gave Stage 3 reasons—for example, people's mutual expec-tations of adherence to the law, the selfishness of lawbreaking, and the resulting chaos, insecurity, or loss of trust in the world. In con-trast, the delinquents' reasoning generally concerned the risk of get-ting caught and going to jail.

Delay as Persistent and Pronounced Egocentric Bias

Another aspect of the sociomoral developmental delay of antisocial youths is the persistence into adolescence of a strong "me-centeredness" (Lickona, 1983) or egocentric bias. That bias is a natural feature of thought and behavior in early childhood. Damon (1977) found that young children's reasoning on distributive justice tasks confuses fairness with their own desires. For instance, a child may assert, "I should get it because I want to have it" (p. 75). Lickona characterized the general orientation of the young child as "whatever I want is what's fair!" (p. 91).

Piaget (1965/1932) and Flavell, Miller, and Miller (1993) suggested that egocentric bias is pronounced in early childhood because interchanges with peers and others have not yet prompted children to "de-center" in attention from their own very salient needs, desires, or impulses. (Note, however, that in the presence of a highly salient adult authority figure, the child may momentarily "re-center" on the adult; Stage 1 moral judgment pertains precisely to such circumstances. Young children also respond empathically on occasion, especially in response to physically salient distress cues; Hoffman, 1978.) Case (1991) argued that egocentric bias and other "centerings" in early childhood may be to some extent inevitable, given working memory limitations that affect the young child's ability to consider multiple perspectives.

With continued experience in social perspective taking and maturing of working memory, egocentric bias and other centration tendencies normally decline. In a study of the development of children's reasons for obedience, Damon (1977) found later reasons to be "less egocentric . . . the self's welfare is still important, but at these later levels self-interest is increasingly seen in the context of the welfare of everyone in the relation" (p. 221). Although egocentric bias tends to decline with age, it may never disappear completely. Flavell et al. (1993) pointed out that, even as mature adults, "we experience our own points of view more or less directly, whereas we must always attain the other person's in more or less indirect manners. . . . We are usually unable to turn our own viewpoints off completely, when trying to infer another's" (p. 181). "Not turning one's own viewpoint off completely" is an understatement in the case of antisocial adolescents, whose egocentric bias generally has remained at the pronounced levels characteristic of childhood.

Egocentric bias is perhaps especially evident in spontaneous Stage 2 moral judgment, as Lickona (1983) pointed out:

> Especially when Stage 2 is first breaking through, kids' energy tends to go into asserting *their* needs and desires and making the world accommodate them. They have a supersensitive Unfairness Detector when it comes to finding all the ways that people are unfair to them. But they have a big blind spot when it comes to seeing all the ways they aren't fair to

others and all the ways parents and others do things for
them. (p. 149; cf. Redl & Wineman, 1957, pp. 153–154)

Even after Stage 2 has "broken through," the very nature of its
pragmatic egoism virtually invites egocentric bias: After all, self-interested exchanges are readily subvertible to self-interested *advantages* if
the opportunity arises. The Stage 2 thinker may evaluate obeying the
law and not stealing as important, but the value is basically contingent on the individual's calculations and interests. Stage 2 thinking
may support not stealing from someone if that person has done one
favors or is likely to detect the theft and retaliate; by the same token,
that thinking may support stealing if the other person has *not* done
one any favors lately or if the chance of detection is low. Incarcerated juvenile felons in our intervention groups, when reflecting on
their shoplifting and other offenses, have recollected that their thoughts
at the time concerned whether they could get what they wanted and
get away successfully. Spontaneous references to the victims of the
offenses were totally absent.

Egocentric bias may be present even where "ego" relates to immediate friends and relatives. Moral judgment may be age appropriate
in the immediate, familiar context but delayed where the context for
moral reasoning includes acquaintances or strangers. Such a contex-
tual distinction may characterize delinquents' moral judgment concerning the value of life. Two "life value" questions on the Sociomoral
Reflection Measure–Short Form (Gibbs et al., 1992; see Appendix A)
are especially pertinent to this issue. Question 7 asks respondents,
"How important is it for a person (without losing his or her own
life) to save the life of a stranger?" Gregg et al. (1994) found that male
delinquents' responses revealed particular delay in moral reasoning
on this question (in addition to the previously noted delay in reasoning concerning the importance of obeying the law). The following
were typical Stage 2 responses to question 7: "If you hardly know
them, then who cares?" "That would be stupid, to help someone you
don't know" and "It doesn't matter, you won't see them again." In contrast, on question 6, pertaining to saving the life of a friend, male
delinquents did not evidence delayed moral judgment at a statistically significant level in comparison with the control group (male
and female delinquents combined, however, showed significant
delay on all questions). The implication is that some delinquents are
capable of age-appropriate moral judgment in some areas but exhibit
delay largely because they exercise mature reasoning only in a restricted
social sphere. Contributing to the developmental delay, then, is the
narrowness of the valued social world; juvenile offenders tend to be
either "me-centered" or "me-and-my-few-friends-centered."

MORAL-COGNITIVE INTERVENTIONS

Interventions addressing the sociomoral developmental delay of antisocial youths have used mainly the Kohlbergian stages as the frame of reference for development. As noted earlier, a disproportionate percentage of antisocial youths show immaturity in sociomoral reasoning, especially egocentrically biased Stage 2, or pragmatic, morality. Accordingly, the treatment rationale is straightforward. To the extent that antisocial behavior results from a delay in moral judgment development, the treatment of antisocial youths should entail remediation of the developmental delay.

In theoretical terms, moral judgment–delayed youth need an enriched, concentrated "dosage" of social perspective-taking opportunities to stimulate them to catch up to an age-appropriate level of moral judgment. In the context of either a macrointervention or a microintervention program, young people are given opportunities to consider the perspectives of others vis-à-vis their own. In the macrointervention, or Just Community, program, attempts are made to restructure the institution (school or correctional facility) in accordance with principles of democracy and justice, such that subjects (students or inmates) participate as much as is feasible in the rule-making and enforcement processes that affect institutional life (e.g., Duguid, 1981; Hickey & Scharf, 1980; Higgins, 1995; Kohlberg & Higgins, 1987; Power, Higgins, & Kohlberg, 1989). The narrower microintervention program focuses on peer group discussion of relevant sociomoral dilemmas or problem situations as a stimulus for perspective-taking experiences. Subjects must justify their problem-solving decisions in the face of challenges from more developmentally advanced peers and from group leaders (e.g., Gibbs et al., 1984).

In the strict sense, EQUIP is mainly a micro- rather than a macrointervention program: The peer group engages in mutual help but is not granted a role in making rules or policy for the entire school or facility. Nonetheless, an effective EQUIP program requires institutional support and involvement at all levels, as well as a staff culture that could be called a Just Community (where therapeutic and other staff decisions are achieved in a fair and democratic manner; see chapter 7). Furthermore, the EQUIP peer group may plan group activities, set rules for cottage living or classroom conduct, and assist in the monitoring of compliance with those rules. Finally, the peer group has one direct opportunity to promote Just Community conditions at the institution through a social skill exercise, Expressing a Complaint Constructively, with which staff are encouraged to cooperate (see chapter 5).

The most impressive study to date of the remediation of moral developmental delay has been Arbuthnot and Gordon's (1986) microintervention, a 4-month program entailing small-group discussions. This program involved antisocial juveniles as identified by teachers. The subjects showed gains not only in moral judgment but also in behavior (in terms of disciplinary referrals, tardiness, and grades), both on short-term assessments of conduct made 2 or 3 weeks after the intervention and on 1-year follow-up posttests, relative to a randomly assigned, passage-of-time control group. Several differences between the experimental and control groups increased on the follow-up assessment. Similarly, changes in classroom conduct (in terms of absenteeism and teachers' ratings) did not reveal significant improvement for the experimental group relative to the controls until the 1-year follow-up, suggesting a possible sleeper effect. We found a similar sleeper effect. Although our recent EQUIP outcome evaluation (Leeman et al., 1993) found no significant moral judgment gains overall for the EQUIP group, individual group members who gained in moral judgment were less likely to have recidivated later, 12 months following release from the institution.

Other behavioral outcome findings have been less impressive, however. Niles (1986), in a similar study, found moral judgment gain but no conduct gain. Also, our follow-up of a previous study (Gibbs et al., 1984) found no conduct gains associated with the moral judgment gains. Finally, reports of conduct gain in connection with Just Community macrointervention programs (e.g., Power et al., 1989) are anecdotal and do not entail comparisons with a control group.

Although moral-cognitive interventions generally seem to stimulate more mature moral judgment, then, the reduction of antisocial behavior does not necessarily follow. In theoretical terms, this finding suggests that cognitive-structural theory falls short of being comprehensive. For example, cognitive-structural interventions have attended to moral judgment delays but not explicitly to egocentric bias or to primary and secondary cognitive distortions. We suspect that, although some interventions have facilitated gains in moral judgment, the subjects' self-centered orientation (in terms of both egocentric bias and primary cognitive distortion) and associated secondary cognitive distortions have remained more or less in place. It may be possible for individuals to evidence Stage 3 moral judgment and simultaneously to engage in seriously antisocial behavior if egocentric bias and associated distortions preempt consideration of the legitimate expectations and feelings of others in actual social situations. As noted earlier, some delinquents show Stage 3 competence in certain areas but evidence Stage 2 moral judgments when unvalued others (mere acquaintances, strangers) are involved. Schnell's (1986) finding of pronounced antisocial attitudes among delinquents as compared to nondelinquents implied that distortions prominently characterize even Stage 3 juvenile offenders. Interestingly, Schnell also found higher levels of anxiety and guilt among the Stage 3 delinquents; this finding suggests that these subjects' consciences are too developed to be entirely neutralized by defensive attitudes and other distortions.

It is noteworthy that Kohlberg himself encountered evidence of cognitive distortion in his macrointervention work. Kohlberg and Higgins (1987) found that students in a Just Community program in a Bronx, New York, high school

> were morally immobilized by what we call *counter-norms*, peer norms or expectations that violate not only conventional moral norms but the capacity to empathize with each other or take each other's viewpoint. . . . [One counter-norm was] "Look at me the wrong way and you're in for a fight." One of us accidentally brushed against a student in the hall and he angrily yelled and continued threatening even after an explanation and an apology. As far as the norm of trust [is concerned] . . . there was the counter-norm . . . "It's your fault if something is stolen—you were careless and tempting me." (p. 110)

Partly because of the discovery of these "counter-norms" or external-izing distortions, Kohlberg and Higgins suggest taking a multifaceted approach—that is, adding a "critical role" for "teacher structuring and teacher advocacy" to "Piaget's emphasis on non-interference with the spontaneous process of peer interaction as the center of develop-mental moral education" (p. 125). In other words, teachers are encouraged to participate in peer discussions and to assert mature moral arguments.

One can find evidence for a movement toward multifaceted treatment not only in Kohlberg and Higgins' (1987) structuring/advocacy suggestion but also in Arbuthnot and Gordon's (1986) rela-tively successful microintervention, described earlier. Their treatment study incorporated 2 preintervention weeks devoted to exercises designed to promote group cohesiveness, openness, and rapport—precisely the aim of EQUIP's mutual help techniques. In addition, Arbuthnot and Gordon spent "two sessions . . . on active listening and communication ('I' messages) skills, an unplanned diversion from the dilemma discussions necessitated by the participants' gen-eral lack in these skills, a lack which appeared to impede effective discussions" (p. 210). Arbuthnot and Gordon concluded that a com-prehensive program should encompass not only moral discussion but also therapeutic techniques to promote group cohesion and mutual caring and to develop "social skills (for translation of new reasoning into action)" (p. 215). Insofar as Arbuthnot and Gordon's own intervention included such techniques, their singular results in terms of conduct gain may be partly attributable to social skills training. On the other hand, social skills training used exclusively has not been found to produce durable behavioral effects (Hollin, 1990; Long & Sherer, 1985; but cf. Kazdin, Bass, Siegel, & Thomas, 1989). A rationale for social skills training in the context of cognitive-structural theory is suggested in chapter 5.

EQUIPMENT FOR SOCIAL DECISION MAKING

The nature and purpose of equipment meetings, and their role within the EQUIP program, were discussed in chapters 1 and 2. Our focus here is on the component of the EQUIP curriculum that addresses delays in the development of moral judgment. Although this component is essentially moral education, with the youths we use the term *social decision making*. The term *moral education* may have certain misleading connotations. After all, our aim is not to interfere with private "morals" or to dictate morality but instead to facilitate moral-cognitive development along the lines that it would naturally take so that young people will make more mature decisions in social situations. This facilitation is needed because sociomoral developmental delay is one common limitation of antisocial youths.

This limitation is generally not absolute: We have seen very few antisocial adolescents exhibit pure Stage 2 moral judgment (with no use of Stage 3) and egocentric bias so total that no one else's needs or feelings are *ever* considered. In recent studies (Basinger et al., in press; Gregg et al., 1994), we have found that, in contrast to mainstream adolescents' Stage 3 moral judgment, antisocial adolescents showed an average developmental level mainly of Stage 2 with substantial secondary usage of Stage 3, designated as 2(3). In other words, antisocial youths are not strangers to mature moral judgment, at least in terms of questionnaire responses (our clinical impression is that their spontaneous moral judgment is somewhat lower). Remediation does not typically require stimulating the youths to construct third-stage (or even fourth-stage) moral judgment de novo; rather, it means fostering greater use of such moral judgment. Thus, although we are remediating a limitation of antisocial youths, more properly we are actualizing a potential that has already been demonstrated to some extent.

In equipment meetings, the group strives to develop the incipient capability to make mature decisions concerning specified problem situations. In the EQUIP program, we depart from the common practice of using moral dilemmas, which can be genuinely problematic and may not have "right" answers. In contrast, our problem situations generally do have right or responsible answers—for instance, deciding to try to persuade a friend against taking a joy ride in a stolen car (Alonzo's Problem Situation). The "problem" is that the right answer may not be immediately apparent (e.g., resisting the joy ride may not be favored if participation in the ride is mislabeled or misconstrued as "doing fun things with a friend"). Similarly, problem situations in which the right answer is to tell on a friend (e.g., if the friend is dealing in drugs) may be experienced as dilemmas because the peer norm against "ratting" or "narking" is so strong.

When EQUIP youths are asked their impressions of the equipment meeting curriculum, the discussions about social decision making problem situations often prove to be the most popular. Group members sometimes even request such a session or ask when the next one will be. Why is this component of the curriculum so popular? Among the possible reasons, one may involve the fact that group majority positions and reasoning on the problem situation questions tend to be positive, responsible, and mature, especially as they are cultivated by the group leader (in this case, the equipper). In the course of these sessions, then, many group members discover that mature morality is the majority position, that a positive potential exists in themselves and others. Perhaps they find their self-esteem enhanced as they contribute to a group that is "clean" or at least striving for dedication to more mature moral considerations and ideals.

Although the social decision making sessions are popular, they are not necessarily comfortable. The problem situations are designed to create opportunities for participants to take the perspectives of others; on a question that is controversial, this opportunity can involve active challenges from peers (or, if necessary, from the group leader). A group member who makes a negative decision and argues pragmatically for it may lose to a more mature challenge and experience the discomfort of having to acquiesce to the majority. Even group members who join in a positive decision may be made uncomfortable by seeing their arguments (if they are pragmatic) bypassed in favor of a mature consideration as the "best reason" for the decision. In theoretical terms, "discomfort" in this context means the upsetting of equilibrium, or disequilibration. Disequilibration may be crucial if a participant with a predominantly pragmatic equilibrium (e.g., Stage 2) is to transcend that morality and achieve more mature moral judgment.

Preparing for a Social Decision Making Meeting

The equipment meetings that focus on social decision making (i.e., moral education) are based on the problem situations presented in the last part of this chapter. Ideally, the equipper will be able to have each youth independently read each problem situation and respond to the questions about it before joining the group. Obtaining independent prior responses and then presenting the differences for discussion constitutes the "revealed differences technique" (Strodtbeck, 1955), an established methodology in the study of social conflict and decision making.

Based on the responses, the equipper prepares a table that will be used at the meeting. For example, consider Jerry's Problem Situation (pp. 71–73), which juxtaposes a positive decision (loyalty to an old friend, Bob) and a temptation (to have fun with more exciting new friends, Jerry's high school basketball teammates). The positive (responsible, fair, altruistic) decision is to go to Bob's party. Table 3.2 displays a representative set of responses for Jerry's Problem Situation. Note that not all responses are positive ("Bob's party"); some are "can't decide," and some are "go with team." Diversity fosters lively discussion and creates the developmentally stimulating disequilibration that delayed group members need.

At the bottom of the table, the tentative group decisions—those favored by the greatest number of group members—should be indicated with question marks (see Table 3.2). These decisions are good candidates for becoming official group decisions—that is, positions endorsed by the entire group. If the decision for a particular question is already unanimous, it should be circled. (There were no such unanimous decisions in the example, so no decisions are initially circled in Table 3.2.)

After preparing the table, the equipper should analyze the responses. Is the majority position positive? If so, on which questions? Is any positive decision already unanimous? Do individual group members show distinctive response patterns? The tabulated responses to Jerry's Problem Situation show that a number of group members consistently advocate going to Bob's party, while one member, Andy, consistently advocates going with the team. The majority may need to refute Andy's probable pragmatic reasoning if the group's decisions are to become unanimous. Tommy is a waffler (with two "team" responses, two "party" responses, and two "can't decide" responses); he may advocate pragmatic reasons, too, but his flip-flop pattern suggests that he is less likely than Andy to dig in his heels and declare strong objections against a positive group decision. Before dissident group members are even asked for their reasons, however, the majority's mainly mature reasons should be elicited and highlighted (see the next section). In the present example, this would mean starting the discussion with most attention paid to the group members with overwhelmingly positive decisions (Robert, Earl, Jonathan, Brian).

TABLE 3.2

Responses to Jerry's Problem Situation

Name	QUESTION NUMBER						
	1	2	3	4	5	6	7
Dante	party	team	party	party	team	close friend	team
David	team	team	team	party	team	close friend	team
Tommy	can't decide	party	team	party	team	close friend	can't decide
Robert	party	party	party	party	can't decide	close friend	team
Andy	team	team	team	team	team	can't decide	team
Daniel	party	party	party	party	team	close friend	team
Earl	party	party	party	party	party	close friend	party
Jonathan	party	party	party	party	party	close friend	team
Brian	party	party	party	party	party	close friend	party
Group decision	Bob's party?	Bob's party?	Bob's party?	Bob's party?	go with team?	close friend?	go with team?

POSSIBLE GROUP DECISION OUTCOMES

Group decision	Bob's party	Bob's party	Bob's party	Bob's party	go with team?	close friend	go with team?

If responses to the problem situation have not been obtained in advance, group members can be asked to respond at the beginning of the meeting. Then the equipper must create the table on the spot. This option is less desirable for two reasons. First, group members tend to notice other group members' responses and conform, a result that compromises the diversity and genuineness of the responses. Second, the equipper then obviously has less time to analyze the response patterns. Nonetheless, our experience is that valuable social decision making sessions are possible even without use of the revealed differences technique.

Facilitating a Social Decision Making Meeting

The goal of the social decision making meeting is to equip the group with more mature moral judgment so that members can better help one another with problems attributable to moral developmental delay. First, the group leader should display some simple rules for the problem situation discussions:

> Listen to what others have to say.
>
> If you criticize another group member, give that person a chance to answer.
>
> Never put down or threaten anyone.
>
> Stay on the subject when you disagree.
>
> Never talk to anyone outside the group about what is said in the group.

These rules are similar to those for regular guided peer meetings, with which the group should already be familiar. For a helpful reminder, the leader may wish to have a group member read the rules aloud at the beginning of each session and even to have participants sign an agreement to abide by the rules at the outset of the equipment meetings.

The leader next provides guidance in four phases: (1) introducing the problem situation, (2) cultivating mature morality, (3) remediating moral developmental delay, and (4) consolidating mature morality. Our discussion of each phase includes pertinent questions for the leader to ask, the content of which is based on Jerry's Problem Situation. At the close of each session, the group leader should conduct a self-evaluation using a checklist (see Figure 3.1) that corresponds to the four phases.

FIGURE 3.1
Checklist for Group Leader Review/Self-Evaluation

Date _____ Group _____

Problem situation discussed _____

In the various phases, did you ask questions to:

PHASE 1: INTRODUCE THE PROBLEM SITUATION

_____ 1. Remind the group of the ground rules for discussion?

_____ 2. Make sure the group understood the problem situation (e.g., "Who can tell the group just what Jerry's problem is? Why is that a problem?")?

_____ 3. Relate the problem situation to group members' everyday lives (e.g., "Do problems like this happen? Who has been in a situation like this? Tell the group about it.")?

PHASE 2: CULTIVATE MATURE MORALITY

_____ 4. Establish mature morality as the tone for the rest of the meeting (e.g., eliciting, reconstructing, and listing on flip pad or chalkboard mature reasons for each positive majority decision)?

PHASE 3: REMEDIATE MORAL DEVELOPMENTAL DELAY

_____ 5. Use more mature group members and the list of reasons (phase 2) to challenge the hedonistic or pragmatic arguments of some group members?

_____ 6. Create role-taking opportunities in other ways as well (e.g., "What would the world be like if everybody did that?" "How would you feel if you were Bob?")?

PHASE 4: CONSOLIDATE MATURE MORALITY

_____ 7. Make positive decisions and mature reasons unanimous for the group (e.g., "Any strong objections if I circle that decision as the group decision/underline that reason as the group's number one reason?")?

59

Figure 3.1 (continued)

_____ 8. Praise the group for its positive decisions and mature reasons (e.g., "I'm really pleased that the group was able to make so many good, strong decisions and back them up with good, strong reasons." "Would the group like to tape this sheet onto the wall?")?

In general:

_____ 9. Were all group members interested and involved?

_____ 10. Was some constructive value found in every serious group member comment?

_____ 11. Was the *should* supported and relabeled as strong (e.g., "Yes, it does take guts to do the right thing . . .")?

Phase 1: Introducing the Problem Situation

To have an effective social decision making meeting, all group members must understand clearly what the problem situation is and how it relates to their lives. If members have read the problem situation and answered the related questions before the meeting begins, the leader should bring copies of their responses and ask a group member to hand them back. (If group members have answered the questions at the beginning of the meeting, they simply hold their own papers.) The leader then asks another group member to read the problem situation to refresh everyone's memory, then raises questions to stimulate discussion. This phase should not consume more than 10 to 15 minutes in a 1- to 1½-hour meeting.

Possible questions

Who can tell the group just what Jerry's problem is?

Why is that a problem?

Do problems like this happen?

Who has been in a situation like this? Tell the group about it.

Phase 2: Cultivating Mature Morality

Once the group understands the problem situation, the equipping work can begin. If all antisocial adolescents were totally lacking in mature moral judgment, this work would be very difficult indeed. The group leader can propose mature reasons, but antisocial adolescents do not readily adopt reasoning provided by adults. As noted earlier, however, many antisocial adolescents do show some potential to make positive decisions or evaluations on the basis of mature moral reasons. In responding to Jerry's Problem Situation, many group members tend to indicate positive decisions—for example, "going to Bob's party" for questions 1 through 4 and "one close friend" for question 6. Furthermore, the reasons for these decisions tend to be mature (see the leader notes for Jerry's Problem Situation). This potential for mature morality must be exploited.

The purpose of this phase is to cultivate a group atmosphere of mature morality characterized by both positive decisions and mature moral reasoning. The makings of a mature moral climate are typically available from the youths themselves (at least from the majority). The group leader's job is to cultivate the resources available in the group in order to render mature morality prominent and to set the tone for the remainder of the meeting. The leader highlights mature morality by asking group members who indicated positive decisions about their reasons for those decisions and then writing those reasons on the flip pad or chalkboard for the group to consider. (The leader should write down reasons offered for a negative decision separately—after the reasons for the positive choice have been listed.)

For Jerry's Problem Situation, then, the leader would elicit the reasons for the majority "Bob's party" decision for questions 1 through 4 and the "close friend" decision for question 6. Although some of these reasons will be pragmatic, many of them are typically mature, showing Stage 3 or even Transition Stage 3/4 reasoning. Granted, it is often necessary to suggest to group members more mature reconstructions of their thoughts; for example, a rejoinder to "Jerry might still want to have Bob around" might be "So you're saying Jerry might still want keep up his friendship with Bob?"

Possible questions

Those who chose "Bob's party" for questions 1 through 4, like Earl and Brian, were the majority. Brian, why did you decide that Jerry should go to Bob's party? What were the reasons for your decision?

Those who chose "close friend" for question 6, like Dante and Tommy, were the majority. Dante, why did you decide it was more important to have one close friend? Tommy?

Phase 3: Remediating Moral Developmental Delay

If a mature moral atmosphere has been cultivated in the group, the leader has accomplished crucial preparation for the next phase, which addresses the reality that—despite majority tendencies toward mature reasoning—many group members are at least moderately developmentally delayed and in need of moral judgment remediation. These group members can seriously deteriorate the group culture and will do so if allowed. The mature moral atmosphere established at the outset is a crucial defense against the onslaughts of these group members as they are brought into the discussion and challenged.

In theoretical terms, remediating moral developmental delay means creating social perspective taking opportunities or challenging individuals to consider other—especially other more mature—viewpoints. Such opportunities can reduce egocentric bias by engendering disequilibrium and stimulating more mature moral judgment. Exposure to mature moral reasons for positive decisions will already have provided delayed group members an opportunity or a challenge to grow. But mere exposure is not sufficient. The group leader should (1) invite the negative group members to explain their views, (2) publically record on a flip pad or chalkboard their explanations or reasons for their decisions, and (3) invite members of the majority to respond.

Possible questions

David, you're one of the group members who put "go with team" instead of "Bob's party." What were your reasons for that decision? After hearing these reasons [point to flip pad or chalkboard], is that still your decision? Why? How would you answer these arguments made by the group majority?

[To the group] Does David's reason persuade the group to change to "team"? Why or why not?

Particular types of probe questions are especially helpful in creating perspective-taking opportunities. Self-centered reasoners should be challenged to generalize ("What would the world be like if everybody did that?") or to consider the point of view or feelings of another party in the problem situation ("What should Jerry do from Bob's point of view?" "How would you feel if you were Bob?"). Group members with puzzling or contradictory response patterns should be asked to clarify: "Dante, your decision was 'go to Bob's party' on question 1, but 'go with the team' on question 2. How come?" Quiet members should be brought out, and members with "can't decide" responses should be probed for both sides of their thinking: "Tommy, you've been kind of quiet today. Are you still undecided? Why do you partly think Jerry should go to Bob's party?

[List the reason(s) on the flip pad or chalkboard.] Why do you partly think he should go with the team? *[List the reason(s).]*"

The most effective tactic of pragmatic group members is to argue that their reasons are more realistic and hence more compelling. For example, a hedonistic reason ("Jerry would have more fun") for a negative decision ("Jerry should go with the team") is superior because, after all, we know that this is precisely what Jerry is most likely to do. The strategy for handling this line of attack is twofold: First, clarify the distinction between *would* and *should* ("Are you saying this is what Jerry would be likely to do, or that this is what he *should* do? If it's true he'd be likely to go with the team, does that mean he *should* go with the team?"). Second, relabel—specifically, counterattack the positive labeling of the *would* as "only realistic" or "true" with a positive characterization of the *should*: "That's true, it would take real guts for Jerry not to give in to what he feels like doing and instead do what a lot of people might not be strong enough to do—the right thing."

Phase 4: Consolidating Mature Morality

Once mature morality has been cultivated and challenged, it needs to be consolidated. The group's mature morality is consolidated—and the group's culture becomes more positive and cohesive—as the leader seeks consensus for positive decisions and mature reasons. Simultaneously, group members with initially pragmatic moral positions feel pressure to defer to and perhaps even embrace mature morality—in effect a continued phase 3 stimulation. In the discussion of the problem situation, the goal is to convert as many of the positive majority positions as possible into unanimous group decisions. If the phase 3 discussion moves toward the majority position, the group leader should ask whether any members object strongly to declaring the majority decision to be the group's official decision on a given question. Similarly, the leader should ask whether there are any strong objections to the group's official decision. If none is stated, the leader deletes the question mark and circles the decision on the bottom row of the chart (see Table 3.2). If objections are voiced, the decision remains merely a majority position. (This outcome is almost as valuable because the frustration from a deadlock also stimulates group members developmentally.) In either event, the group should be praised or encouraged at the conclusion of the social decision making meeting.

Possible questions

Is the group ready to all agree that Jerry should go to Bob's party? Any strong objections?

It sounds like one of the most positive reasons we have on the board for why Jerry should go to Bob's party is that it would be a chance to renew the friendship. Any strong objections if I underline that reason as the group's number one reason? *[Alternative selections are not problematic unless a pragmatic reason is selected.]*

[If there are objections and the discussion deadlocks] Well, I guess we just won't be able to come up with a group decision/number one reason on this question.

[Encouragement at the end of a successful meeting] I'm really pleased that the group was able to make so many good, strong decisions and back them up with good, strong reasons. This group has shown again what it can do.

[If not so successful] Is the group satisfied with what was accomplished today? I know the group can do better next time, because it did before. *[Recollect positive example, if available.]* What plans will the group make right now before leaving so that more good decisions are accomplished at the next social decision making equipment meeting?

[To build positive group identity] Would the group like to put the sheet(s) showing its decisions/reasons on the wall? Here's some masking tape.

The Problem Situations

The remainder of this chapter consists of 13 problem situations for use in social decision making sessions. The settings for the problems vary from the home to the school or correctional facility to the workplace. Each situation depicts an adolescent with a problem, typically one created by someone else with a problem (an effective way to induce a nondefensive and more objective discussion of the problems).

These problem situations and the associated discussion questions, adapted with the kind permission of the sources noted on the credits page of this book, are intended to be reproduced and distributed to group members in the course of implementing the group. In addition, each problem situation is accompanied by leader's notes designed to help in processing the material.

Group members should be encouraged to characterize the problem situations using the pertinent Positive Peer Culture terms, as listed in Table 1.1—for example, Low Self-Image, Inconsiderate of Self, Inconsiderate of Others, Misleads Others, Alcohol or Drug Problem, Stealing, Lying. In cognitive distortion terms (listed in Table 1.2), Self-Centered is the basic problem in these situations. Other cognitive distortions (Minimizing/Mislabeling, Assuming the Worst, Blaming Others) are embedded in the questions accompanying the problem situations. The questions tend to bring out the implications of the situations in terms of moral values as found in the Sociomoral Reflection Measure–Short Form (Gibbs et al., 1992; see Appendix A): keeping a promise or telling the truth, helping others, saving a life/ living even when you don't want to, not stealing, obeying the law, sending lawbreakers to jail.

For the most nondefensive and objective discussion, the problems should be introduced to the group in the order in which they are given here. For example, situations involving group and relationship building should be discussed before those involving stealing, drugs, and violent crime. A problem situation involving classroom cheating is presented last because, in our experience, groups that discuss that situation sooner have not achieved enough moral development to understand the seriousness of the problem.

The problem situations should be adapted for groups that consist mainly or totally of female adolescents. In our work with such groups, we have adapted the problem situations as follows: The problem situations concerning the Martian's Adviser, Sarah, and Dave are left untouched. In Mark's Problem Situation, the names are simply reversed. Alonzo, George, and Antonio are given female names. Girls' names should be used for both characters in the problem situations concerning Leon, Juan, and Sam; similarly, "Reggie" and "his father" might be changed to "Regina" and "her mother." Finally, Jerry's Problem Situation requires a change not only of names but of situation. Following Guidance Associates (1976), we have used the title "Charlene's Problem Situation" with the following content:

> Charlene and Joanne have been good friends for some time. Now they are in high school. A new girl in school, Tina, comes over to Joanne and Charlene and asks to join them for a snack. Joanne notices that Charlene and Tina are doing most of the talking and that they're getting along well together.
>
> After Tina leaves, Joanne asks Charlene to come over to her house on Saturday afternoon. She has something important she wants to talk over. Charlene says she'll try to come. Later that day, however, Charlene gets a call from Tina asking her to go to a popular movie with her on Saturday afternoon. It's the last chance to see the movie.

The probe questions are then modified according to this alternative content.

EQUIP Problem Situations

The Martian's Adviser's Problem Situation

Jerry's Problem Situation

Mark's Problem Situation

Jim's Problem Situation

Alonzo's Problem Situation

Sarah's Problem Situation

George's Problem Situation

Leon's Problem Situation

Dave's Problem Situation

Juan's Problem Situation

Sam's Problem Situation

Reggie's Problem Situation

Antonio's Problem Situation

The Martian's Adviser's Problem Situation

A man from Mars has decided to move to another planet. He has narrowed his search down to two planets, Planet A and Planet B. Planet A is a violent and dangerous place to live. People just care about themselves and don't care when they hurt others. Planet B is a safer, more peaceful place. People on Planet B do care about others. They still have fun, but they feel bad if they hurt someone. Planet B people try to make the planet a better place.

You're the Martian's adviser. Which planet should you advise him to move to?

Planet A / Planet B / can't decide *(circle one)*

LEADER NOTES

The Martian's Adviser's Problem Situation is designed to set the tone for the problem situations that follow. Whereas the subsequent situations stimulate the development of moral judgment, this situation is designed mainly to facilitate the discovery of common values and to foster a cohesive, prosocial group spirit.

Some reasons group members give for choosing Planet B come straight from the problem situation content: For example, there is not as much violence, it's more peaceful, people get along without fighting, people want to help one another, people have fun without hurting others, and people work to make things better. Other reasons include "You can live longer," "There's less crime," "There's better listening or communication," "People are more trustworthy," "They try to control their anger," "People apologize," and "Parents spend more time with their kids." A few group members may choose Planet A, however, because "There'd be lots of drugs and booze and sex" and "Nobody'd be sticking their nose in your business."

It is important to emphasize that every group member would like, not only for the Martian but for him- or herself, a world that is positive (safer, more caring, more prosocial, and so on). If some members have chosen and argued for the negative planet, the group should be challenged to refute them. The group, then, is united in the endorsement of these positive and strong values. But the world is what people make it, and the responsibility to *act* positively and not just *talk* positively starts with each individual. The same is true for the group. The group should be challenged to make the group a Planet B: "It's up to you."

68

The following specific probe questions are helpful:

[If the group has adequately learned the thinking errors] What is the basic thinking error, the basic problem, on Planet A? *[The answer, Self-Centered, should be fairly easy to elicit.]*

[To those favoring Planet A because no one bothers you; use if the group is faltering and needs assistance] What if someone you did care about—say a parent or brother or sister or close friend—was going to commit suicide? Would you let the person do it and not "bother" him or her? That's what Planet A would be like. *[Prompt the group to consider such a world. Typically, Planet A respondents will acquiesce so that the Planet B choice becomes unanimous.]*

[Use relabeling to make sure that caring is not stigmatized as weak.] Where are the truly strong people? On Planet A or on Planet B?

[Application from the "planet" to the group] What kind of group do you want this group to be—Planet A or Planet B, negative or positive? If Planet B is what you want for this group, have you been living up to it? Planet B won't happen unless everyone practices what he or she preaches to make it happen. *[Relabeling again]* But it's not easy. It takes courage; it takes strength.

Sometimes the Martian's Adviser's Problem Situation can even stimulate soul-searching. Ask who has had a friend or acquaintance die a violent death. (Usually at least a few group members will raise their hands or speak up.) "What do people say about him or her—what kind of difference did he or she make? What kind of difference will people say you made? It's not too early to start thinking about your life—how you're living it, what kind of difference you want to make. Some of your friends may have said they value a Planet B, but their behavior made things more like Planet A. What about you?"

After this session, "Planet A" and "Planet B" become part of the group vocabulary. The terms provide handles for contrasting group atmospheres: a collection of individual self-centered and selfish attitudes characterized by mistrust and disruption (Planet A) or a climate of mutual caring and trust characterized by well-equipped help for group members (Planet B). Such handles make it easier for youths who are otherwise concrete thinkers to bring to mind hypothetical group weaknesses and ideals.

The new vocabulary can be used at the outset and from time to time in subsequent sessions: Instead of simply asking how things have been going, you may ask whether the group has slipped back toward Planet A or continued to progress toward Planet B. If the group feels that it has regressed and that things are hopeless, they'll need a pep talk: "What thinking error is the group making? [*Assuming the Worst should be easy to elicit.*] I know this group doesn't have to be negative because I've seen what a great group this can be. I know the group has what it takes to get back on track."

In connection with this pep talk, we recommend a version of the "sandwich" technique, already described in chapter 2: (1) give examples of occasions when the group has been "great"—that is, exhibited responsible and effective helping behavior; (2) cite problems that the group has encountered; and then (3) return to an emphasis on the group's strengths for overcoming these problems.

Jerry's Problem Situation

Jerry had just moved to a new school and was feeling pretty lonely until one day a guy named Bob came up and introduced himself. "Hi, Jerry. My name is Bob. I heard one of the teachers say you're new here. If you're not doing anything after school today, how about coming over to shoot some baskets?" Pretty soon Jerry and Bob were good friends.

One day when Jerry was shooting baskets by himself, the basketball coach saw him and invited him to try out for the team. Jerry made the team, and every day after school he would practice with the rest of the team. After practice, Jerry and his teammates would always go out together to get something to eat and sit around and talk about stuff. On weekends they would sometimes take trips together.

As Jerry spends more time with the team, he sees less and less of Bob, his old friend. One day, Jerry gets a call from Bob. "Say, I was wondering," says Bob, "If you're not too busy on Thursday, my family is having a little birthday party for me. Maybe you could come over for dinner that night." Jerry tells Bob he'll try to come to the party. But during practice on Thursday, everyone tells Jerry about the great place they're all going to after practice.

What should Jerry say or do?

1. Should Jerry go with the team?

   go with team / go to Bob's party / can't decide (*circle one*)

2. What if Jerry calls Bob from school and says he's sorry, but something has come up and he can't come over after all? Then would it be all right for Jerry to go with the team?

   go with team / go to Bob's party / can't decide (*circle one*)

3. What if Jerry considers that his teammates may be upset if Jerry doesn't come—that they may start to think Jerry's not such a good friend? Then would it be all right for Jerry to go with the team?

   go with team / go to Bob's party / can't decide (*circle one*)

4. What if Jerry thinks that, after all, Bob came along and helped Jerry when Jerry was lonely. Then should Jerry go with the team?

   go with team / go to Bob's party / can't decide (*circle one*)

5. Let's change the situation a bit. Let's say that before Bob asks Jerry to come over, the teammates ask if Jerry will be coming along on Thursday. Jerry says he thinks so. Then Bob asks Jerry. Then what should Jerry do?

   go with team / go to Bob's party / can't decide *(circle one)*

6. Which is more important: to have one close friend or to have a group of regular friends?

   one close friend / group of regular friends / can't decide *(circle one)*

7. Let's change the situation a different way. What if Jerry and Bob are not good friends but instead are just acquaintances? Then should Jerry go with the team?

   go with team / go to Bob's party / can't decide *(circle one)*

LEADER NOTES

Discussion of Jerry's Problem Situation typically promotes a more profound or mature understanding of friendship. Some group members (those who reason at a level no higher than Stage 2) may actually become stimulated to construct Stage 3 moral judgment. For others who already understand and use Stage 3 to some extent, mature reasoning may become more prominent. In either event, at least with respect to the value of friendship or affiliation, this problem situation should facilitate moral judgment development.

   Also important is the contribution such discussions make to the group itself. Discussion of the value of close friendships seems to promote such friendships in the group and hence contributes to the group's social cohesion. In this way, Jerry's Problem Situation continues the cultivation of the group that began with the discussion of the Martian's Adviser's Problem Situation.

   In our experience, most group members advocate going to Bob's party in response to most questions. The main consideration is that of friendship: Group members point out that Jerry and Bob used to be good friends, and here would be a chance to renew that friendship. An additional consideration is the importance of Jerry's keeping the commitment made to Bob so as to be honest and not let Bob down. After all, in fairness, "Bob was there first when Jerry was lonely, before there was any team for Jerry." Mindful of the friendship, commitment, and/or fairness considerations, group members may suggest that Jerry will feel bad if he goes with the team.

   Group members may also make pragmatic points to support going to Bob's party: "Jerry does lots of things with the team, but birthday parties only come once a year" or "Maybe Jerry would like a break from doing things with the team all the time." Pragmatic group members may also suggest that Jerry avoid the problem by attending Bob's party for a while, then catching up with the team. Especially with group leader prompting, pro-Bob group members will counter that leaving early solves nothing: "That's as bad a dump on Bob as not going at all," as one EQUIP member once put it.

Group discussion typically reaches the heart of the matter with question 6; often the choice of "one close friend" is unanimous. Reasons are as follows: "You can tell a close friend anything"; "You need someone you can talk to, who will listen to you"; "You can go to that person with problems"; "Close friends are really friends"; and "A close friend can be trusted not to take advantage of you."

Once a positive peer atmosphere is cultivated through listing and discussion of the reasons for the majority position, attention can turn to the dissenting group members. The few members advocating that Jerry go with the team tend to be unabashed hedonists ("Jerry would have more fun with the team"). They may also try to minimize the harm done to Bob ("Bob won't even notice Jerry didn't come"). These members typically do not care strongly about their positions, however, and will not argue long against majority objections (e.g., that Bob will of course notice). Hence, the choice for going to Bob's party can be made a unanimous group decision on most questions.

The main question on which the majority typically chooses "go with the team" is question 7, which demotes the relationship between Jerry and Bob from friendship to acquaintance. Hence, question 7 makes clear the relevance of question 6 to the original problem situation, in which Jerry and Bob are friends: Jerry should go to Bob's party because a group of regular buddies just isn't the same as a close friend—and here is a chance to restore such a friendship.

To a lesser extent, the majority may also choose "go with the team" for question 5, which has Jerry making the first commitment (of sorts) to the team rather than to Bob. Those group members for whom the prior commitment to Bob was the important factor will tend to switch to the "team" response on question 5.

Mark's Problem Situation

Mark has been going steady with a girl named Maria for about 2 months. It used to be a lot of fun to be with her, but lately it's been sort of a drag. There are some other girls Mark would like to go out with now. Mark sees Maria coming down the school hallway.

What should Mark say or do?

1. Should Mark avoid the subject with Maria so Maria's feelings aren't hurt?

   should avoid subject / should bring it up / can't decide *(circle one)*

2. Should Mark make up an excuse, like being too busy to see Maria, as a way of breaking up?

   excuse / no excuse / can't decide *(circle one)*

3. Should Mark simply start going out with other girls so that Maria will get the message?

   yes / no / can't decide *(circle one)*

4. How should Mark respond to Maria's feelings?

   _____

   _____

   _____

5. Let's change the situation a bit. What if Mark and Maria have been living together for several years and have two small children? Then should Mark still break up with Maria?

   should break up / no, shouldn't break up / can't decide *(circle one)*

6. Let's go back to the original situation. This is what happens: Mark does break up with Maria—he lets her know how he feels and starts dating another girl. Maria feels hurt and jealous and thinks about getting even somehow. Should Maria get even?

   yes, should get even / no, shouldn't get even / can't decide *(circle one)*

7. What if the tables were turned, and Maria did that to Mark?

   yes, should get even / no, shouldn't get even / can't decide *(circle one)*

LEADER NOTES

Mark's Problem Situation continues the theme of mature, caring relationships but focuses on the problem of ending a dating relationship that is going nowhere. The main value of this problem situation for moral judgment development arrives with discussion of the last question, which concerns vengeance.

As with most of the problem situations, many group members do choose positive responses. The majority position tends to be that Mark should discuss breaking up (question 1) rather than making up an excuse (question 2) or simply starting to date other girls (question 3). Accordingly, most of the open-ended suggestions (in response to question 4) are positive: "Just tell her you'd like to date other girls"; "Be considerate and remember she's human, too"; "Explain how you feel, that you don't want to settle down"; "Listen to what she has to say about it." Of the responses we have heard, our favorite is "I think we should see other people. What do you think?" The group member who gave this response also indicated that he would first try to "work things out" before breaking up with Maria. As to the reasons for bringing the subject up (question 1), one group member pointed out that Mark "should be man enough to tell her"; if he doesn't, another suggested, "Maria might lose a chance to get another boyfriend" and "would be hurt more in the long run" than by just being told. Speaking more pragmatically (against the idea of simply starting to date other girls), another group member suggested that then those girls could find out how Mark treated Maria and dump him for being a two-timer.

Of course, not all of the responses are positive. On the open-ended question, one group member wrote, "Do things to try to make Maria drop him." Another wrote that he would say, "I'm dumping you, bag!" These group members may also advocate avoiding Maria or making up an excuse. After discussion, however, they are often willing to acquiesce to the majority position and thereby make a positive group decision possible.

An abrupt turnabout occurs on question 5, in which Mark and Maria are live-in partners with two small children. Then the majority favors not breaking up, on the grounds that Mark has a responsibility to the children (e.g., "The kids should have both a dad and a mom"). If he left "it would hurt the kids, because they would feel it was their fault." One group member suggested, "He loved her once. Why should one argument make him not love her again?" A pragmatic group member pointed out that he might have to pay child support if he leaves.

The majority position continues to be positive on the vengeance questions, 6 and 7. The majority is against either Maria's getting even if Mark breaks up (question 6) or Mark's getting even if the tables are turned (question 7). Suggestions are that "Mark should just tell himself that it's her loss"; that "it's no big deal, there are other fish in the sea"; or that Mark or Maria should "let bygones be bygones." Mark "wouldn't want her to get even with him [so he shouldn't do that to her; Stage 3]," and if one of them retaliated "there would just be more trouble." One group member suggested, somewhat ominously, that Mark shouldn't get even because he "might do something really bad and wind up in here."

Count on several group members advocating retaliation, however—especially by Mark against Maria. Reasons included "Give her a taste of her own medicine" and "He would feel better after he showed her how she hurt him." One group member suggested that Mark should get even because "he'd be mad" and, as further justification, disclosed that he himself had gotten mad and beaten up several girls who had left him for other guys. He remained silent when a peer asked, "Does that make it right?" and asked why he nonetheless thought it was wrong if *Maria* got even with *Mark*. Nor would he acquiesce to a group decision against getting even. At least he felt peer group opposition and perhaps for this reason was more accommodating to positive majority positions on subsequent occasions.

It is sometimes helpful to ask the group exactly what is meant by "getting even." Responses range from "showing off [to Maria] with a new girlfriend" to "telling him [the new boyfriend] that she was a good lay for you" to "slashing their tires"—or faces! These responses, once stated for group consideration, will often be branded as immature or destructive by the majority. Nonetheless, many group members will comment that although Mark or Maria—or they—shouldn't get even, they probably would. If the group is still developing, the group leader may need to model relabeling—that is, comment on how much strength and courage it takes not to "give in to childish desires to get even."

The degree of positive content may be surprising and should be encouraged. The group leader should comment on the great potential the group has shown for becoming a positive or "Planet B" group. Using relabeling, the leader should emphasize that a strong group is one where members care about another's feelings (whether Bob's feelings in the preceding problem situation or Maria's feelings in this one). Bear in mind, however, that the group members expressing more negative sentiments may be speaking more candidly; their words may be consistent with the actual behavior of the majority. After all, consider how common "payback" or vengeance is in the daily life of the troubled school or correctional facility! Similarly, in social skills exercises, the initial absence of caring about another's feelings is striking. Clearly, the group challenge is to accomplish the translation of responsible words into responsible actions.

Jim's Problem Situation

Jim and Derek are high school friends. Jim, whose birthday is coming up, has mentioned to Derek how great it would be to have a tape deck to listen to music while he goes about his job driving a van. Derek steals a tape deck from a car in the school parking lot and gives it to Jim for his birthday. Jim is appreciative, not realizing the present is stolen.

The next day Jim sees Scott, another friend. Jim knows Scott has a tape deck and is good at electronics. Jim mentions that he got a tape deck for a birthday present and asks Scott to come over to help install it. "Sure," Scott says with a sigh.

"You look down, Scott. What's wrong?" Jim asks.

"Oh, I was ripped off," Scott says.

"Oh, boy. What did they get?" Jim asks.

"My tape deck," Scott says. Scott starts describing the stolen tape deck.

Later, Jim starts thinking about how odd it is that Scott's tape deck was stolen just at the time Derek gave him one. Jim gets suspicious and calls Derek. Sure enough, Derek confesses that he stole it, and the car he stole it from turns out to be Scott's car!

It's time for Scott to arrive to help Jim install the tape deck. Scott will probably recognize the tape deck as his. Scott is at the door, ringing the doorbell.

What should Jim—the one who got the stolen birthday present from Derek—say or do?

1. Should Jim tell Scott that Derek took Scott's tape deck?

   should tell / shouldn't tell / can't decide *(circle one)*

2. How good a friend is Derek? Would Jim be able to trust Derek not to steal from him?

   yes, could trust / no, couldn't trust / can't decide *(circle one)*

3. Derek stole the tape deck for a good cause (Jim's birthday). Does that make it all right for Derek to steal the tape deck?

   yes, all right / no, not all right / can't decide *(circle one)*

4. What if Derek didn't steal the tape deck from Scott's car? What if instead Derek stole the tape deck from a stranger's car? Then would it be all right for Derek to steal the tape deck for Jim's birthday?

   yes, all right / no, not all right / can't decide *(circle one)*

LEADER NOTES

Jim's Problem Situation continues the theme of positive caring and friendship embodied in the Martian's Adviser's, Jerry's, and Mark's situations, but it focuses on the importance of trust in a friendship: How trustworthy is a friend who has a stealing problem? Should you tell on a friend who has stolen in order to give you a gift? Or is stealing all right if it's for a friend? Insofar as this problem situation addresses the value not only of affiliation but also of property, it serves as an excellent transition to many of the problem situations that follow.

The majority positions tend to be that Jim should tell Scott that the tape deck is his (question 1), that Jim would not be able to trust Derek not to steal from him (question 2), and that it was not all right for Derek to steal the tape deck even though it was for Jim's birthday (question 3) or even if the tape deck belonged to a stranger instead of another friend of Jim's (question 4). The majority positions tend to be supported by fairly mature reasoning: Jim should tell Scott about the theft because otherwise Jim is letting Derek get away with hurting Scott, because it's the honest thing to do, because Jim would want to be told if he were Scott, and because it would be the way to keep Scott's trust and friendship. Stealing is wrong even if the victim is a stranger because it's against the law and because the stranger is still a person who should be respected instead of hurt. Jim should not consider Derek a good friend because Derek steals things and is untrustworthy: Derek will steal from Jim "the first time Derek thinks he can get away with it." Group members may also suggest that Jim should tell to avoid getting in trouble with Scott.

More pragmatic group members who advocate not telling Scott about the theft may point out that "you'll be out a birthday present" if you tell and that Derek will be angry if he finds out. These group members may also claim that you can trust a friend who steals not to steal from you (question 2) and, by way of support, claim to have such friends. Because they may be adamant, don't count on achieving a unanimous group decision on question 2.

The most controversial question, however, is whether Jim should tell on Derek (question 1). Our groups have often been evenly divided on this question. Group members who favor telling emphasize that Derek took a risk and now has to face up to what he did; if Jim doesn't tell he becomes involved in Derek's stealing, and Derek learns nothing. Those who favor not telling emphasize that Derek is also a friend (after all, he stole because he wanted to do something nice for Jim), and you should never rat on a friend. They acknowledge the importance of disciplining Derek but caution against getting Scott involved—they will offer lurid descriptions, in fact, of what Scott would do to Derek. Don't expect to persuade the group to reach a unanimous decision on question 1.

Occasionally, a group member will argue that it would have been all right for Derek to steal a tape deck for Jim's birthday if only the car hadn't belonged to one of Jim's friends. As noted previously, it is not uncommon for antisocial adolescents to show immature moral judgment, particularly when the persons hurt are strangers. One participant, Joe, explained that if the victim was a stranger, then the theft was "on him"—somehow his fault. Other group members pointed out to Joe that he was making a Blaming Others mistake in his thinking, and Joe acquiesced to a unanimous "no, not all right" group decision on question 4.

Alonzo's Problem Situation

Alonzo is walking along a side street with his friend Rodney. Rodney stops in front of a beautiful new sports car. Rodney looks inside and then says excitedly, "Look! The keys are still in this thing! Let's see what it can do! Come on, let's go!"

What should Alonzo say or do?

1. Should Alonzo try to persuade Rodney not to steal the car?

   should persuade / should let steal / can't decide *(circle one)*

2. What if Rodney says to Alonzo that the keys were left in the car, that anyone that careless deserves to get ripped off? Then should Alonzo try to persuade Rodney not to steal the car?

   should persuade / should let steal / can't decide *(circle one)*

3. What if Rodney says to Alonzo that the car's owner can probably get insurance money to cover most of the loss? Then should Alonzo try to persuade Rodney not to steal the car?

   should persuade / should let steal / can't decide *(circle one)*

4. What if Rodney tells Alonzo that stealing a car is no big deal, that plenty of his friends do it all the time? Then what should Alonzo do?

   should persuade / should let steal / can't decide *(circle one)*

5. What if Alonzo knows that Rodney has a wife and child who will suffer if Rodney gets caught, loses his job, and goes to jail? Then should Alonzo try to persuade Rodney not to steal the car?

   should persuade / should let steal / can't decide *(circle one)*

6. Let's say the car is *your* car. Alonzo is Rodney's friend, but Alonzo is also your friend. Alonzo knows it's your car. Then should Alonzo try to persuade Rodney not to steal the car?

   should persuade / should let steal / can't decide *(circle one)*

7. In general, how important is it for people not to take things that belong to others?

   very important / important / not important *(circle one)*

8. Let's say that Alonzo does try to persuade Rodney not to take the car, but Rodney goes ahead and takes it anyway. Alonzo knows Rodney's in bad shape from being high—he could have a serious accident and someone could get killed. Then what should Alonzo do?

   contact the police / not contact the police / can't decide *(circle one)*

LEADER NOTES

Like Jim in the preceding problem situation, Alonzo must contend with a friend who has a stealing problem. The majority position is that Alonzo should try to persuade Rodney not to steal the car (questions 1 through 6) and that it is very important not to steal (question 7). Mature reasons appeal to the danger and harm to innocent people, including the car owner; to the way one would feel if it were one's own car (a consideration often inspired by question 6); to the guilt one would feel if one did join Rodney; to the fact that prices have to go up to cover crime; and to the loss of order that would result if everyone stole. At least one group member typically spots the Blaming Others error in laying blame on the victim (question 2)—for example, "Everyone's careless at one time or another. That doesn't mean you deserve to get your car stolen." There is concern for what will happen to Rodney's family in question 5. Pragmatic reasons for not stealing or joining Rodney are also prominent, however: "Alonzo could go to jail, so it's not worth the risk"; "There'd be nothing to do in jail"; "Alonzo could get shot or killed"; "The car owner could get even"; "You wouldn't be able to stop Rodney anyway"; "You'd be drunk and wouldn't care what Rodney did"; "This could even be a set-up against Alonzo"; and "Rodney's a fool and deserves whatever happens to him."

One hears both mature and pragmatic reasons, then, in support of the majority positions. For the opposing positions ("Let Rodney steal it"; "It's not important for people not to steal"), however, pragmatic considerations constitute practically the sum total of reasons—for example, "You'd be a big shot"; "You could have lots of fun"; "It's exciting to steal and get away with it"; "You could get money and booze and girls and do whatever you want"; "If you needed to go somewhere, now you could drive" (Self-Centered). Pragmatic group members acknowledge that you could get caught for stealing, but they suggest that that's why it's important for you to "know what you're doing" and "act confident"—so you won't get caught. Thinking errors are plentiful in the pragmatic reasoning: for example, "Everyone steals anyway"; "You'd teach the car owner a good lesson, not to be so careless"; and "The car owner is a dummy, fool, or jerk [for leaving the keys]" (Minimizing/Mislabeling). If group members don't catch and correct these thinking errors, the group leader should intervene to do so.

Question 8 suggests that Rodney goes ahead and—in an intoxicated state—steals the car. Should Alonzo contact the police? Many group members who have persistently advocated trying to persuade Rodney not to steal the car will nonetheless choose against contacting the police because it would mean ratting on a friend and getting him in trouble. They will urge getting Rodney home so he can sleep off his high (alert peers will point out that it's too late for that—Rodney has already stolen the car). Group members who advocate calling the police tend to emphasize the dangers of drunk driving and Rodney's irresponsibility to his family, and they argue that a true friend would contact the police.

Alonzo's Problem Situation is an especially good situation for discussing the gap between moral judgment and moral action. Many group members who proffer superbly mature and compelling reasons for trying to persuade Alonzo against stealing the car will disclose at some point in the discussion that they would probably join Rodney: "I know I *shouldn't*, but I probably *would*." The group leader should listen actively but also relabel: "That's right, this is a tough situation to keep your head in. It does take a lot of guts to say no and do the right thing." The group leader can also remind the group of the skill Dealing Constructively with Negative Peer Pressure, which they learned for coping with such situations (see chapter 5). The group leader should preview that skill if the group has not learned it yet.

Sarah's Problem Situation

Sarah works as a clerk in a small grocery store. The store isn't too busy. Orlando, a friend of Sarah's at school, comes over to her cash register and says, "Hey, I've only got a dollar with me. Ring up these cigarettes and six-pack for a dollar, won't you? The manager's in the back of the store—he'll never know." Sarah likes Orlando, and Orlando has done some favors for her. But Sarah also feels trusted by the manager.

What should Sarah say or do?

1. Should Sarah refuse Orlando, or should Sarah say yes to Orlando's suggestion?

   should refuse / should say yes / can't decide *(circle one)*

2. Was it right for Orlando to put Sarah on the spot with his request?

   yes, right / no, not right / can't decide *(circle one)*

3. What if Sarah feels that other employees at the store do this for their friends? Then what should Sarah do?

   should refuse / should say yes / can't decide *(circle one)*

4. What if Sarah feels that the store is making a profit and wouldn't miss a little money? Then what should Sarah do?

   should refuse / should say yes / can't decide *(circle one)*

5. What if you are the owner of the grocery store where Sarah is working? Then what should Sarah do?

   should refuse / should say yes / can't decide *(circle one)*

6. What if the store owner has been sending Sarah home early, when business is slow, and Sarah's paycheck has been cut in half? Then what should Sarah do?

   should refuse / should say yes / can't decide *(circle one)*

7. How important is it to be honest at a store where you work?

   very important / important / not important *(circle one)*

8. Let's say that Sarah says no. Orlando then just walks out of the store with the cigarettes and six-pack. Should Sarah tell the manager?

   yes, tell manager / no, keep quiet / can't decide *(circle one)*

LEADER NOTES

Like Jim and Alonzo before her, Sarah must deal with an awkward situation created by a friend with a stealing problem. And, like Jim and Alonzo, Sarah may get into serious difficulties if she does not make the right decision. Sarah's Problem Situation is especially similar to Alonzo's: In each situation, the protagonist is experiencing pressure from a "friend" to join in something dishonest—stealing a car in Alonzo's case; stealing from a store in Sarah's.

The majority positions tend to be positive—that Sarah should refuse Orlando's suggestion (question 1, questions 3 through 5), that it was not right for Orlando to put her on the spot in that way (question 2), that it is very important to be honest at a store where one works (question 7), and that Sarah should tell the manager if Orlando just walks out of the store with the cigarettes and six-pack (question 8). The reasons one may hear first are pragmatic: "If she's caught, she loses her paycheck, job, and future chances" and "If Orlando has the nerve to walk out, she should make sure he gets his [just deserts] by telling" (question 8).

With further discussion and some prompting, however, one also hears mature reasons: Sarah "should stay trustworthy and not betray the manager's trust"; "She shouldn't blow this chance to show she's honest"; "She has a responsibility to be honest"; "It's not her money to give away"; "She shouldn't be Easily Misled and pass the buck by Blaming Others" (either Orlando or other employees; prompted by question 3); "If Sarah owned the store, she wouldn't want to lose money" (prompted by question 5); "When some people don't pay, the price goes up and the store could go out of business"; "If she gives in, Orlando will be back, expecting more and more"; and "It will be with you in your mind [that you helped someone cheat the store]." Sarah should be honest because "being honest makes you a better person" and because "you feel good about yourself when you know other people can trust you."

This situation provokes a vigorous discussion, however. Many group members may argue for saying yes to Orlando, suggesting that Sarah can get away with it, that maybe she likes Orlando (and may want to go out with him), that he's a friend who has done favors for her, that she needs to pay him back, that she needs to get him off her back, that maybe then he'll help her out sometime, that he'll get even with her if she doesn't help him. These group members may suggest that Sarah could pay out of her own pocket to make up the difference so that the store isn't hurt. In the ideal group discussion, peers will effectively rebut these assertions without intervention from the group leader—for example, "What kind of a 'friend' would put you on the spot like that?"; "Will this really be the end of it, or will Orlando only try this again, tell his friends, and get more and more demanding?"

George's Problem Situation

One day George's older brother, Jake, tells him a secret: Jake is selling drugs. George and Jake both know that the kind of drug Jake is selling is highly addictive and causes lung and brain damage. It can even kill people. George asks his brother to stop selling. But the family is poor, and Jake says he is only doing it to help out with the family's money problems. Jake asks his younger brother not to tell anyone.

What should George say or do?

1. Should George promise to keep quiet and not tell on his brother?

    should keep quiet / should tell / can't decide *(circle one)*

2. What if Jake tells George that selling drugs is no big deal, that plenty of Jake's friends do it all the time? Then what should George do?

    keep quiet / tell / can't decide *(circle one)*

3. What if George finds out that Jake is selling the drug to 10-year-olds outside a school? Then what should George do?

    keep quiet / tell / can't decide *(circle one)*

4. What if Jake himself won't be harmed by the drug—he tells George he knows how addictive and harmful the stuff is and never touches it? Then what should George do?

    keep quiet / tell / can't decide *(circle one)*

5. What if George finds out that Jake isn't using any of the money at all to "help out the family" but instead is spending it on booze and other things for himself? Then what should George do?

    keep quiet / tell / can't decide *(circle one)*

6. Is it ever right to tell on someone?

    sometimes right / never right/ can't decide *(circle one)*

7. Who's to blame in this situation?

    George (younger brother) / Jake (drug dealer) / other / can't decide *(circle one)*

8. How important is it for judges to send drug dealers to jail?

    very important / important / not important *(circle one)*

LEADER NOTES

With George's Problem Situation, the stakes are raised with respect to the issue of dealing with an irresponsible friend. Instead of a tape deck (Jim's Problem Situation), a car (Alonzo's Problem Situation), or some beer and cigarettes (Sarah's Problem Situation), the lives of those who buy drugs from George's brother are at stake.

The majority positions tend to be responsible: George should tell on his brother (questions 1 through 5), it is sometimes right to tell on someone (question 6), Jake is to blame in this situation (question 7), and it is very important for judges to send drug dealers to jail (question 8).

The reasons for the majority positions tend to be mature. Many of the pro-telling reasons focus on Jake: George would care about Jake; Jake may start taking the drug and die or get messed up himself; Jake could get caught and sent to jail; or Jake could get beaten up or killed in the drug world. Furthermore, Jake is endangering his family because the drug world may get at Jake by killing a member of his family. There is also a concern that Jake is selling a drug that kills, and a particular objection is that he is selling such a drug to kids (question 3). After reading that Jake actually isn't even helping out the family with his profits (question 5), some group members may offer the general reason that Jake is Self-Centered. It is sometimes right to tell on someone (question 6) when human lives are at stake, as they are with Jake's drug dealing. Jake is the one to blame in this situation (question 7) because, as the older brother, he should be more responsible and because by selling drugs he has caused the situation (the "Jake" response to question 7 is often unanimous).

The momentum of responsible reasoning that can be generated through discussion of the earlier questions can be maintained for discussion of the final question (question 8), concerning the reasons it is "very important" for judges to send drug dealers to jail. Some of the reasoning concerns rehabilitation: "So the dealers will learn a lesson and change"; "So the junkies can get their lives together"; "If they can't find a fix, maybe they'll recover and start using their money to pay their rent." The preponderance of reasoning, however, concerns safety to society: "To make things less violent"; "So people won't die"; "To keep druggies off the streets, protect your family"; "So there won't be so many break-ins"; "To set an example for, send a message to, other drug dealers"; and "To save some kids from being pressured into becoming users and pushers."

George's Problem Situation is controversial, however. After all, many antisocial youths are themselves drug traffickers and identify with Jake. Group members who advocate not telling assert that what

Jake does is none of George's business, that George should let Jake learn a lesson, that Jake could be making a lot of money and not be in danger at all, that somebody else will sell the stuff and make money if Jake doesn't, that Jake isn't forcing anybody to buy anything, and that George could get killed if he tells on Jake. Alert majority-position group members can rebut these points: It is George's business if the family is endangered, the "lesson" is too expensive if it's a brother's death, Jake is forcing the drug on 10-year-olds (question 3) because "they don't know what they're doing," and "Jake is kidding himself if he thinks he's not in any danger—you can't sell drugs and not be in danger." Positive group members may also point out the hypocrisy involved in Jake's not taking the drug himself (question 4): "He won't hurt himself, but he'll make money off hurting others, dealing death to others."

Some controversy will probably also arise concerning the importance of sending drug dealers to jail (question 8). Some group members may argue for merely "important" or even "not important" on the grounds that sending drug dealers to jail is "useless" or "hopeless" because you can't send enough of them to make a dent in the problem. Again, alert majority-position group members may invoke the thinking error vocabulary to brand this an Assuming the Worst mistake. They may argue that this is exactly how the drug world wants you to think and that avoiding this mistake means doing what you can rather than doing nothing.

Leon's Problem Situation

Just after Leon arrived at an institution for boys, he tried to escape. As a result, he was given extra time. It took Leon nearly 4 months to earn the trust of the staff again. He now thinks it is stupid to try to go AWOL. However, Bob, a friend of Leon's, tells Leon he is planning to escape that night. "I've got it all figured out," Bob says. "I'll hit the youth leader on the head with a pipe and take his keys." Bob asks Leon to come along. Leon tries to talk Bob out of it, but Bob won't listen.

What should Leon say or do?

1. Should Leon tell the staff about Bob's plan to go AWOL?

   tell / keep quiet / can't decide *(circle one)*

2. What if Bob is a pretty violent type of guy and Leon thinks that Bob might seriously injure, maybe even kill, the youth leader? Then what should Leon do?

   tell / keep quiet / can't decide *(circle one)*

3. What if the youth leader is mean and everyone hates him? Then what should Leon do?

   tell / keep quiet / can't decide *(circle one)*

4. Is it any of Leon's business what Bob does?

   can be Leon's business / is none of Leon's business / can't decide *(circle one)*

5. Is it ever right to nark on somebody?

   yes, sometimes right / no, never right / can't decide *(circle one)*

6. Let's change the situation a bit. Let's say the youth leader is Leon's uncle. Then what should Leon do?

   tell / keep quiet / can't decide *(circle one)*

7. Let's change the situation a different way. Let's say Bob is Leon's brother. Then what should Leon do?

   tell / keep quiet / can't decide *(circle one)*

8. Which is the most important?

   not telling on your friend / not letting other people get hurt/ minding your own business *(circle one)*

LEADER NOTES

Again, the group faces the problem of dealing with a troublesome friend. Like George, Leon must deal with a friend whose actions may be life threatening. Although Leon's friend is not dealing in deadly drugs, he is planning a crime (going AWOL from the institution) in which someone could get killed.

The majority positions with respect to Leon's Problem Situation tend to be responsible. Leon should tell about Bob's plan (questions 1 through 3, questions 6 and 7), it is Leon's business what Bob does (question 4), it is sometimes right to nark on somebody (as when a life is at stake; question 5), and what is most important is not letting other people get hurt (question 8). The majorities are especially strong when the youth leader is Leon's uncle (question 6) and when Bob is Leon's brother (question 7).

Although part of the supportive reasoning for the majority position is pragmatic ("Leon would just get caught and have extra time added"), much of the reasoning is mature: "Leon could prevent someone getting hurt," "It's not worth killing somebody to get out of an institution," "Human life is precious," and "The entire youth group could suffer if Bob goes AWOL."

A few group members may argue that what Bob does is none of Leon's business and so Leon shouldn't get involved. After all, Bob would be knocking off somebody everyone hates (question 3). Alert majority-group members may counter that Bob has made it Leon's business by telling Leon of his plans, and the youth leader doesn't deserve to get killed.

Dave's Problem Situation

Dave's friend Matt does some dealing on the street. Once in a while, Matt even gives Dave some smoke for free. Now Matt says to Dave, "Listen, man, I've got to deliver some stuff on the south side, but I can't do it myself. How 'bout it—will you take the stuff down there for me in your car? I'll give you some new stuff to try plus $50 besides for just a half-hour's drive. Will you help me out?"

What should Dave say or do?

1. Should Dave agree to deliver the stuff for Matt?

   yes, should deliver / no, shouldn't deliver / can't decide
   (circle one)

2. What if Dave knows that the stuff Matt wants him to deliver is laced with poison? Should he agree to deliver it?

   yes, should deliver / no, shouldn't deliver / can't decide
   (circle one)

3. What if Dave knows that his sister, who lives on the south side, might take some of the laced stuff? Then should he agree to deliver it?

   yes, should deliver / no, shouldn't deliver / can't decide *(circle one)*

4. Should Dave be taking the free stuff from Matt?

   yes, should take it / no, shouldn't take it / can't decide *(circle one)*

5. What if Matt says that doing drugs is no big deal, that plenty of his friends use drugs all the time? Then should Dave be taking the free drugs?

   yes / no / can't decide *(circle one)*

6. Let's say that Dave does make the drug delivery. Since Dave is just helping out Matt, he doesn't feel he's doing anything wrong. Should Dave feel he's doing something wrong?

   yes, wrong / no, not wrong / can't decide *(circle one)*

7. How important is it to stay away from drugs?

   very important / important / not important *(circle one)*

LEADER NOTES

Like the protagonists in previous problem situations, Dave finds himself placed in an awkward position by an irresponsible friend. Once again, a protagonist must cope with negative peer pressure: Should Dave help out his drug-trafficking friend by making a drug delivery?

The majority positions tend to be responsible: Dave should not deliver the stuff (questions 1 through 3) and should not be taking the free stuff (questions 4 and 5). It is very important to stay away from drugs (question 7). The first reasons one hears are typically pragmatic: Dave will get caught, have his license revoked and go to jail, or get his car confiscated; Dave is playing with the possibility of ruining his life and should think ahead to the potential consequences. There is also some resentment at the way Matt is manipulating Dave to take the risk: "That's unfair—you'll get stuck and he won't"; "Matt couldn't be much of a friend [to treat you like that]." Questions 2 and 3 are especially helpful in prompting group members to consider also that drugs are harmful, even lethal: "You could wind up killing your own sister!"

With reference to question 3, the "personalizing" technique of positing a prospective victim to be a family member was used by Agee (1979) in a role-reversal procedure:

> The [value] clarification may have to be personalized and blunt for them to understand it. . . . Using their own family members as examples is a frequently used procedure, for example, "If it's okay for you to do that to someone's sister, is it okay for them to do it to your sister?" One hard core sociopath who frequently discussed killing people was led through an elaborate fantasy where he received a phone call that his brother had been murdered. He responded with an equally elaborate fantasy where he painstakingly tracked the killer down and killed him slowly. The therapist then replied that she hoped that the families of whoever he killed would do that to him. The response from the youth was shock and a small beginning of some insight into the value of human life. (pp. 113–114)

Despite the usually responsible position of the majority, Dave's Problem Situation is often controversial. A few group members— and sometimes even a majority—will argue that Dave should make the drug delivery. Their reasoning is purely pragmatic: "Dave's been doing drugs anyway"; "Matt's offering a good deal, you can make some money"; "This could lead to bigger opportunities"; "If you don't do it, somebody else will anyway"; "Nobody's forcing anybody to take anything"; "It's their fault if they get hurt"; and "You've got to take care of yourself before you worry about anybody else."

Don't expect to arrive at many unanimous group decisions in this problem situation. In fact, like Alonzo's Problem Situation, this exercise can be discouraging: Majority group members arguing for the responsible position report that they would probably make the irresponsible decision in the actual situation. "Who really thinks in these situations?" they may say. "Most guys would just take the money and not think about whether they or somebody else is going to get hurt."

The group leader may very well have to intervene to correct these errors. If a group member cannot identify the Minimizing/Mislabeling and Assuming the Worst errors, then the leader must assert that in fact most people do think ahead and think of others; most people won't sell people things that will kill them just so they can make money off them—that's why most people don't do crimes and aren't locked up! Relabeling will help: "It's certainly possible to think before you act and make the responsible choice—although nobody said it was easy; it does take a lot of personal strength." Encouragement is also in order: "I've seen you guys in action—I know what you can do when you try. I know this can be a Planet B group, and with the group's help each of you can become strong enough to think before you hurt people again. The bottom line is what kind of life each of you is going to decide to live, what kind of difference you want to make in your life: one for the better, or one for the worse." Discussions of Dave's Problem Situation sometimes arrive at a point where an "existential/spiritual" discussion can be helpful (see chapter 6). As with Alonzo's Problem Situation, it may also be helpful to apply the social skill Dealing Constructively with Negative Peer Pressure (see chapter 5). In this connection, the group leader should emphasize that Dave *does* have a choice: "We do not choose to contract [an infectious disease] from a friend, but we do choose to use heroin offered by a friend" (Wilson, 1983, p. 202).

Juan's Problem Situation

Juan and Phil are roommates at a juvenile institution. They get along well and have become good friends. Phil has confided that he has been getting pretty depressed lately and has managed to get hold of some razor blades. Juan sees where Phil hides the blades. The youth leader, having learned of the razor blades, searches their room but doesn't find them. So the youth leader asks Juan where the razor blades are hidden.

What should Juan say or do?

1. Should Juan cover for Phil, saying he doesn't know anything about any razor blades?

   cover for Phil / tell the leader / can't decide *(circle one)*

2. What if Phil has told Juan that he plans to cut his wrists with the razor blades that night? Then what should Juan do?

   cover for Phil / tell the leader / can't decide *(circle one)*

3. Would Phil feel that Juan cared about him if Juan told?

   yes, would feel Juan cared / no, would not feel Juan cared / can't decide *(circle one)*

4. What if Juan and Phil actually don't get along well and are not friends? What if Phil has been a real pest? Then what should Juan do?

   cover for Phil / tell the leader / can't decide *(circle one)*

5. What if Juan isn't Phil's roommate but does know about the razor blades and where they are? The youth leader suspects Juan knows something and asks him about the razor blades. Then what should Juan do?

   cover for Phil / tell the leader / can't decide *(circle one)*

6. How important is it for a juvenile institution to have rules against contraband?

   very important / important / not important *(circle one)*

7. How important is it to live even when you don't want to?

   very important / important / not important *(circle one)*

8. Who might be affected (in addition to Phil himself) if Phil were to commit suicide?

_____

_____

_____

LEADER NOTES

How to deal with an irresponsible friend is again the problem. With Juan's Problem Situation, however, the life threatened by the friend's activity is not someone else's (as with George's Problem Situation) but instead the friend's own life.

The majority positions tend to be positive: that Juan should tell the youth leader (questions 1, 2, 4, and 5), that rules against contraband are very important (question 6), and that it is very important to live even when you don't want to (question 7). Pragmatic reasons for telling are that you can get in trouble if you don't tell and that you might get hurt—Phil might cut *you* with a razor blade. Following are some mature reasons we have heard: Juan should care about Phil; telling might enable Phil to get some help before he hurts himself; any life is precious and worth saving; Phil's family and friends will be hurt if Phil kills himself; you wouldn't want to watch someone kill himself; you'd feel guilty if you knew you could have done something and didn't. Living even when you don't want to is very important because things get better and there's a lot to live for; there's a reason you're here; there are things to do and see; committing suicide is selfish—you're thinking only about yourself (group members may even identify a Self-Centered thinking error); think how your family would feel; consider that you may change your mind. Family—especially parents—are mentioned prominently in response to question 8, "Who might be affected (in addition to Phil himself) if Phil were to commit suicide?" The majority of the group members may also rate rules against contraband "very important" because some things are dangerous to both oneself and others.

A few group members may advocate covering for Phil on the grounds that Juan should mind his own business and not get involved. One is especially likely to see "cover" responses in connection with question 4 ("What if Phil has been a real pest?"): Then "you couldn't care less what happens to him." These group members may also assert that living even when you don't want to (question 7) is not important because "it's your life—you can do whatever you want with it." One group member asserted that rules against contraband are not important because "I want to smoke and stuff" (another group member correctly critiqued that reason as a Self-Centered error).

Because it concerns life and death, Juan's Problem Situation often invites consideration of existential/spiritual concerns. This is where supplements to EQUIP such as Bible studies or referral to the institutional chaplain can play a helpful role. We have found it helpful to mention the near-death experience because most adolescents have heard of it, because it is a matter of research (e.g., Greyson, 1993; Ring, 1993; Sabom, 1982) rather than specific religious teaching, and because the implications of the research support the basic values of the EQUIP program. With reference to research on the near-death experiences of suicide attempt survivors, one can mention their universal impression that suicide is wrong because it is destroying God's gift of life. This message provides a spiritual grounding for the majority position that life is precious and that choosing to live or die is not simply a matter of personal preference.

Sam's Problem Situation

Sam and his friend John are shopping in a music store. Sam has driven them to the store. John picks up a CD he really likes and slips it into his backpack. With a little sign for Sam to follow, John then walks out of the store. But Sam doesn't see John. Moments later, the security officer and the store owner come up to Sam. The store owner says to the officer, "That's one of the boys who were stealing CDs!" The security officer checks Sam's backpack but doesn't find a CD. "Okay, you're off the hook, but what's the name of the guy who was with you?" the officer asks Sam. "I'm almost broke because of shoplifting," the owner says. "I can't let him get away with it."

What should Sam say or do?

1. Should Sam keep quiet and refuse to tell the security officer John's name?

   keep quiet / tell / can't decide *(circle one)*

2. From the store owner's point of view, what should Sam do?

   keep quiet / tell / can't decide *(circle one)*

3. What if the store owner is a nice guy who sometimes lets kids buy tapes or CDs even if they don't have quite enough money? Then what should Sam do?

   keep quiet / tell / can't decide *(circle one)*

4. What if the store owner is Sam's father? Then what should Sam do?

   keep quiet / tell / can't decide *(circle one)*

5. Is it ever right to tell on someone?

   yes, sometimes / no, never / can't decide *(circle one)*

6. Who's to blame in this situation?

   Sam / John / the store owner / other / can't decide *(circle one)*

7. How important is it not to shoplift?

   very important / important / not important *(circle one)*

8. How important is it for store owners to prosecute shoplifters?

   very important / important / not important *(circle one)*

LEADER NOTES

With Sam's Problem Situation, the "telling on an irresponsible friend" issue reverts from life (e.g., Juan's Problem Situation) to property (e.g., Sarah's Problem Situation).

The majority positions tend to be responsible: Sam should give the security officer John's name (questions 1 through 4), it is sometimes right to tell on someone (question 5), John's to blame in this situation (question 6), it's very important not to shoplift (question 7), and it's very important for store owners to prosecute shoplifters (question 8). The main pragmatic reason in support of telling is that Sam thus protects himself from possible prosecution. Most of the supportive reasons are mature: John was unfair to Sam in getting him into this spot, John's stealing problem will continue until he's stopped and made to think about the consequences, shoplifting makes the prices for everyone go up, the store owner is losing money and will become a popular target if John gets away with it and tells others, the store owner will stop being so nice to kids (question 3), and John is harming Sam's dad (question 4). Reasons for the importance of not shoplifting sometimes even reach into Stage 4: "for the sake of order in society" and "because it harms the trust that's needed for society."

Dissenters argue against "ratting on your friend" and suggest that Sam can best stay out of trouble by keeping quiet: "They can't get him—he doesn't have to say anything." These group members may also attribute blame to the store owner (question 6) on the grounds that the owner should have had customers check things like backpacks before they came in. Alert group members will point out the Blaming Others error in such an attribution.

Reggie's Problem Situation

"Your father is late again," Reggie's mother tells Reggie one night as he sits down to dinner. Reggie knows why. He passed his father's car on the way home from school. It was parked outside the Midtown Bar and Grill. Reggie's mother and father had argued many times about his father's stopping off at the bar on his way home from work. After their last argument, his father had promised he would never do it again. "I wonder why your father is late," Reggie's mother says. "Do you think I should trust what he said about not drinking any more? Do you think he stopped off at the bar again?" Reggie's mother asks him.

What should Reggie say or do?

1. Should Reggie cover for his father by lying to his mother?

   yes, should cover / no, should tell the truth / can't decide *(circle one)*

2. Was it right for Reggie's mother to put Reggie on the spot by asking him a question about his father?

   yes, right / no, wrong / can't decide *(circle one)*

3. What if Reggie's father drinks a lot when he stops at the bar and then comes home and often beats up on Reggie's mother— sometimes even on Reggie? Then what should Reggie do?

   cover for him / tell the truth / can't decide *(circle one)*

4. Which is most important for Reggie's decision?

   what's best for himself / what's best for his mom / what's best for his dad / what's best for the family *(circle one)*

5. In general, how important is it to tell the truth?

   very important / important / not important *(circle one)*

LEADER NOTES

Unique among the problem situations, Reggie's Problem Situation concerns parental rather than peer pressure. Furthermore, whereas in peer situations the peer has a negative or irresponsible aim, in Reggie's Problem Situation the mother is at least well intentioned in her questions about the father.

This situation is problematic for groups until question 3 ("What if Reggie's father drinks a lot when he stops at the bar and then comes home and often beats up on Reggie's mother—sometimes even on Reggie?"); then the majority position tends to be that Reggie should tell his mother what he knows. The majority tend also to choose "what's best for the family" as most important for Reggie's decision (question 4) and "important" for telling the truth (question 5). Reasons for telling the truth include the following: By covering, Reggie would be helping his dad become an even worse alcoholic; Reggie should help stop his father's deception and harm to the family; Reggie wouldn't want his mother or himself beaten up (question 3); the truth will come out sooner or later anyway; someone could get killed by the father's drunk driving. Reasons for the importance of telling the truth are typically mature: You wouldn't want someone to lie to you (otherwise your word would mean nothing), and society is based on truth and trust (an especially mature [Stage 4] reason).

Dissenters emphatically suggest that it was wrong for Reggie's mother to put Reggie on the spot (question 2) and that getting Reggie involved is too heavy a burden to place on a child—Reggie could feel guilty if his disclosure resulted in a divorce. They may suggest that Reggie could help in a limited way by having a private talk with his dad. Pragmatically, however, if Reggie tells his mother (question 1), his dad may beat him up. In response to one group member's minimizing comment ("She shouldn't hassle him just because he had a beer on the way home"), other group members countered that it's rarely just one beer, that they know from their personal experience how often it happens that dad is drunk and violent (question 3) by the time he gets home.

Antonio's Problem Situation

Antonio is in school taking a math test. Suddenly, the teacher says, "I'm going to leave the room for a few minutes. You are on your honor not to cheat." After the teacher has gone, Ed, Antonio's friend, whispers to him, "Let me see your answers, Antonio."

What should Antonio say or do?

1. Should Antonio let Ed copy his answers?

   yes, let cheat / no, don't let cheat / can't decide *(circle one)*

2. What if Ed whispers that cheating is no big deal, that he knows plenty of guys who cheat all the time? Then should Antonio let Ed cheat?

   yes, let cheat / no, don't let cheat / can't decide *(circle one)*

3. What if Antonio knows that Ed is flunking because he doesn't study? Then should Antonio let Ed cheat?

   yes, let cheat / no, don't let cheat / can't decide *(circle one)*

4. What if you were the teacher? Would you want Antonio to let Ed cheat?

   yes, let cheat / no, don't let cheat / can't decide *(circle one)*

5. Is it possible to have a really close, trusting friendship with someone who has a cheating or lying problem?

   yes, possible / no, not possible / can't decide *(circle one)*

6. Let's change the situation a little. What if Antonio hardly knows Ed? Then should Antonio let Ed cheat?

   yes, let cheat / no, don't let cheat / can't decide *(circle one)*

7. In general, how important is it not to cheat?

   very important / important / not important *(circle one)*

8. Is it right for teachers to punish cheaters?

   yes, right / no, not right / can't decide *(circle one)*

LEADER NOTES

Antonio's Problem Situation returns to the theme of negative peer pressure, in this case from a friend who wants to cheat on a test.

Majority positions tend to be that Antonio should not let Ed cheat (questions 1 through 3, question 6), that the respondent in the position of the teacher would not want Ed to cheat (question 4; this position may be unanimous from the outset), that a close relationship with someone who cheats is not possible (question 5), that it's very important not to cheat (question 7), and that it is right for teachers to punish cheaters (question 8). Pragmatic reasons are that the teacher might come back unexpectedly and catch both of you and that if Ed isn't caught he might wind up with a grade higher than yours. Mature reasons are that it's unfair for Ed to get the benefit of Antonio's work, that letting Ed cheat will encourage his attitude that he can let other people do his work for him (alert group members will identify such an attitude as a Self-Centered thinking error), that Ed deserves to flunk and needs to learn a lesson, that Ed is hurting himself in the long run by cheating instead of learning, that Ed is also hurting his parents, and that the teacher has placed trust in Ed and you and you are on your honor not to cheat. One cannot have a close relationship with a person who cheats (question 5) because "you never know when they might be planning to cheat you." Teachers need to punish cheaters (question 8) because otherwise "there would be no order in the classroom."

Again, alert group members will likely identify the thinking errors in the arguments of dissenters: "There's nothing wrong with giving a little help to a friend" (Minimizing/Mislabeling); "It's the teacher's fault for leaving the room" (Blaming Others). Many group members who advocate cheating will acknowledge on question 4 that they as teacher would not want Antonio to let Ed cheat; they should be challenged to say whether the teacher has a right to expect honesty. If so, then isn't their "cheating is okay" attitude Self-Centered and wrong?

CHAPTER 4

Equipping with Skills to Manage Anger and Correct Thinking Errors

Gary is in the kitchen of his apartment. Gary's girlfriend, Cecilia, is angry at him for something he did to hurt her. She yells at him. She pushes his shoulder. Gary becomes furious. He swears at her. A sharp kitchen knife is nearby. Gary picks up the knife and stabs Cecilia, seriously wounding her.

As already noted, antisocial youths—the Garys of this world—have certain limitations that contribute to their angry and violent behavior. Chapter 3 was devoted to the issue of moral developmental delay. Certainly, we can imagine that Gary has a pronounced ego-centric bias (attending to his own feelings more than anyone else's) as well as immaturity of moral judgment (perhaps a combination of Stage 1 power-and-punishment morality with Stage 2 payback morality). We can imagine that he would benefit from participating in the sort of group discussions described in the previous chapter. We would hope the discussions would stimulate him to consider others' viewpoints and to develop a more mature moral understanding of interpersonal relationships as based on mutual caring (Stage 3 reasoning).

Delay in the development of moral judgment is but one limitation, however. Even if Gary gained moral judgment maturity, we might still fear for Cecilia's safety in the kitchen confrontation. Mature moral judgment will not reduce aggressive or antisocial behavior in actual social situations unless certain other problems are also addressed in treatment. Other important limitations described in chapter 1 were social skill and cognitive deficiencies (Gary did not adequately think before he acted) and cognitive distortions (what Gary did think—perhaps, "How dare she touch me!"—was wrong and served to fuel rather than inhibit his violent impulses). These deficiencies and distortions (as well as social skill deficiencies, which will be addressed in chapter 5) must also be corrected if antisocial

103

adolescents are to be effective in changing and in helping one another to change. EQUIP is a multicomponent program for this reason.

DEFICIENCIES IN SELF-CONTROL

Anger is a normal reaction to a painful stimulus or a blocked goal (Izard, Hembree, & Huebner, 1987; Stenberg, Campos, & Emde, 1983). Angry emotions can be adaptive insofar as they mobilize energy needed for self-defense, for appropriate assertion, or for overcoming of obstacles. Anger is not adaptive or healthy, however, when it characteristically leads to intentional, unjustifiable harm to others—that is, to aggressive or violent behavior. If anger is to lead to constructive or responsible rather than aggressive behavior it must be controlled, managed, or regulated. Yet this is precisely what Gary and so many antisocial youths fail to do.

Although anger management in EQUIP is an acquired skill or practiced ability, it also tends to develop naturally—at least among "normal" (i.e., not chronically aggressive) youths—as a special case of self-control or the general ability to guide one's behavior symbolically. *Self-control* is not a term normally associated with early childhood. Young children tend to be impulsive; they often act without thinking and respond to here-and-now phenomena without remembering past warnings, thinking about what they are doing, or considering likely consequences. As Kopp (1982) observed, "One has only to spend a short time observing young children to appreciate the very real limitations of their self-control. Given a strong stimulus, for example, a desired ball rolling in the street . . . they become heedless of safety, rules, or exhortations" (p. 208). Maccoby (1980) noted the tendency of toddlers to cry or throw tantrums when required to wait or to delay attainment of goals.

Older children who have not achieved self-control also throw tantrums and immediately become aggressive when goals are blocked or gratification is delayed. This behavior is illustrated in the following episode, recounted by Fritz Redl and David Wineman (1951), directors of Pioneer House, a 1940s residential treatment center for "out-of-control" preadolescent boys:

> The kids burst out of the station wagon . . . and barged
> madly up the steps into the house. Luckily, this time the
> door was open so the usual pounding, kicking of door, etc.,
> wasn't necessary. I was in my office tied up in a phone call
> and the door was closed. Mike yelled for me, shouting

something about his jack knife which I was keeping in the drawer for him. I put my hand over the receiver and said, "O.K., come in." But the lock had slipped on the door and he couldn't open it. Before I even had a chance to excuse myself from my phone conversation, and say, "Just a minute, I'll be back" he was pounding on the door, kicking it, calling me a "sonofabitch" repetitively. I opened the door and gave him his knife. Even this failed to quiet his furor, and when I commented on the obvious fact that I hadn't even meant to make him wait, that the lock had slipped, all I got was a snarling, contemptuous "shit." (p. 92)

The ability to inhibit aggressive or antisocial impulses normally originates in early childhood. Although toddlers may throw tantrums or otherwise resist adult directives, they also begin to be able to comply voluntarily with simple requests and commands. Lytton (Lytton, 1977, 1980; Lytton & Zwirner, 1975) found that toddlers who complied with parental demands or prohibitions were also likely spontaneously to self-correct deviance even in the apparent absence of parents—for instance, to stop jumping on a sofa or reaching for a forbidden item. Especially intriguing has been the phenomenon of overt speech, as when a child alone says out loud, "No, don't" when getting off the sofa or retracting an outstretched hand (Sears, Maccoby, & Levin, 1957).

The directive function of speech in compliance and subsequently in self-guided activity was first studied experimentally by the Russian psychologists Vygotsky and Luria. Luria (1961) studied age trends in children's responses to adults' commands—for example, to pick up a nearby object and give it to the adult or to start and stop an activity such as squeezing a rubber bulb. Luria noted that the younger children would often spontaneously verbalize—for instance, saying, "Go, go" when pressing the bulb. Vygotsky (1987/1934) noted similar self-directed utterances by children as they engaged in complex activity such as drawing or sketching ("Where's the pencil? I need a blue pencil. Never mind, I'll draw with the red one and wet it with water; it will become dark and look like blue," p. 70). These utterances, at first clearly audible, later became increasingly replaced by soft whispers, mutterings, or silent lip movements (cf. Bivens & Berk, 1990). Finally, such "private speech" disappeared altogether, perhaps because it had become completely internalized as verbal thought—"the verbal dialogues we carry on with ourselves while thinking and acting in everyday situations" (Berk, 1994, p. 255).

The role of private speech or verbal thought in self-control was studied by Mischel (1974). He investigated the cognitive strategies children used to resist temptation during delay-of-gratification tasks. In 1983 Mischel found that a child's ability to wait for a highly attractive reward (e.g., marshmallows) was predicted more by "what is in the child's head" than by "what is in the situation" (p. 201). Children who thought of the marshmallows in terms of nonarousing images (e.g., as white, puffy clouds or cotton balls or as round, white moons) were able to delay gratification much longer than children who thought of the marshmallows' chewy, sweet, tasty qualities. Also able to wait longer were children who used self-statements to reduce their arousal states. One self-controlled 11-year-old reported that he would tell himself, " 'I hate marshmallows, I can't stand them.' But when the grown-up gets back, I'll tell myself 'I love marshmallows' and eat it" (Mischel & Mischel, 1983, p. 609). Mischel also found that the self-controlled children thought of diversions or distractions from the desired objects—for example, covering their eyes, singing songs, inventing games, or even going to sleep. In other words, these children accomplished self-control or impulse inhibition by engaging in arousal-reducing self-talk and incompatible activities.

Other investigators have also found that self-statements can shape emotions or modify arousal levels. Rimm and Litvak (1969) found that affectively loaded self-statements increased both rate and depth of respiration. Other researchers found corresponding effects on heart rate (e.g., Kenardy, Evans, & Oei, 1989), skin conductance (May & Johnson, 1973; Russell & Brandsma, 1974), and body sensations (e.g., Warren, Zgourides, & Englert, 1990).

The role of verbal thoughts in mediating actions and making constructive social behavior possible was also studied by Spivack and Shure (1974, 1989). They found that children rated high in social adjustment by teachers were better at describing strategies for resolving social conflict situations—in other words, they evidenced greater problem-solving skills. Among the most important skill indicators were the number and variety of conflict solutions the child could generate, whether the child could anticipate and describe the possible consequences of a completed action for him- or herself and others, and whether the child could describe the steps by which an interpersonal problem could be solved (Dubow & Tisak, 1989; Rubin & Krasnor, 1985). Similar results have been found for adolescents (Slaby & Guerra, 1988). The failure of undercontrolled children and adolescents to anticipate the consequences of their actions for others—that is, to perspective take—exacerbates their egocentric bias and thereby links their cognitive deficiencies to their delays in moral development.

Overall, then, children use their developing language ability to control and guide their behavior. In a pertinent research review, Little and

Kendall (1979) concluded, "There is considerable evidence to support the belief that self-control develops largely as a function of a child's development of [internal] language mechanisms" (p. 104). Helpful language mechanisms include not only self-statements or self-talk but also knowledge about self-talk strategies, commonly called metacognition. Children with better metacognition regarding strategies helpful for self-control can in fact wait longer in delay-of-gratification situations (Mischel & Mischel, 1983; Rodriguez, Mischel, & Shoda, 1989).

The research on the role of verbal thought in self-control has led to interventions with children evidencing self-control problems and other behavioral disorders. Meichenbaum (1977) asked, "Could we systematically train hyperactive, impulsive youngsters to alter their problem-solving styles, to think before they act, in short, to talk to themselves?" (p. 249). Accordingly, Meichenbaum and associates innovated an intervention program called "self-instructional training." Self-instructional training and related programs have been applied not only to hyperactivity or impulsivity problems but also to problematic classroom behaviors (Monahan & O'Leary, 1971; Robin, Armel, & O'Leary, 1975), difficulty in resisting temptation (Hartig & Kanfer, 1973), anxiety (Barlow & Cerny, 1988; Meichenbaum, Gilmore, & Fedoravicius, 1971), and anger (Lochman, Burch, Curry, & Lampron, 1984; Lochman, Nelson, & Sims, 1981; Lochman, White, & Wayland, 1991).

In 1975, Novaco sought to apply the self-instructional training approach to chronically angry adolescents. Novaco defined anger as "a combination of physiological arousal and cognitive labeling of that arousal. . . . Anger arousal results from particular appraisals of aversive events. External circumstances provoke anger only as mediated by their meaning to the individual" (pp. 252–253). In other words, "anger is fomented, maintained, and influenced by the self-statements that are made in provocation situations" (p. 252). Hence, Novaco's intervention program consisted partly of training aggressive subjects to use anger-inhibiting self-statements or self-talk, such as "I'm not going to let him get to me"; "My muscles are starting to feel tight. Time to relax and slow things down"; and "He'd probably like me to get really angry. Well, I'm going to disappoint him." Studies of anger management training generally find that such programs do reduce anger, aggression, or both (Coats, 1979; Green & Murray, 1973; Kaufman & Feshbach, 1963; Mallick & McCandless, 1966; McCullough, Huntsinger, & Nay, 1977; Moon & Eisler, 1983; Schlichter & Horan, 1981; Snyder & White, 1979; Stein & Davis, 1982). Subsequent researchers have expanded upon and refined Novaco's techniques (Feindler, 1991; Feindler & Ecton, 1986; Goldstein & Glick, 1987; the present authors in this chapter).

COGNITIVE DISTORTIONS AND
AGGRESSIVE BEHAVIOR

Gary's violent behavior reflects not only deficiencies, or cognitive errors of omission, but also distortions—that is, cognitive errors of commission. Deficiencies and distortions often co-occur in aggressive behavior. For example, in the episode at Pioneer House, Mike's battering of the counselor's inadvertently locked door probably reflected both kinds of errors: Not only did Mike fail to apply arousal-reducing self-talk, he also inaccurately attributed a hostile intention to the counselor, repeatedly calling him a "sonofabitch." Similarly, Mike's snarling and saying "shit" even as the counselor attempted to explain reflected both a deficiency (inadequate attending and perspective taking) and a distortion (continuing to misattribute blame).

Impulsivity and other cognitive deficiency–related problems may not lead to consistently antisocial behavior unless cognitive distortions are also present. Cognitive distortions are inaccurate or rationalizing attitudes, thoughts, or beliefs concerning one's own or others' social behavior (Beck, 1976; Ellis, 1977; Gibbs, 1993; Yochelson & Samenow, 1976, 1977). According to Gibbs, antisocial youths typically exhibit cognitive distortions or "thinking errors" (Yochelson & Samenow, 1976, 1977). Four categories of thinking errors—Self-Centered, Assuming the Worst, Blaming Others, and Minimizing/Mislabeling (described by Gibbs & Potter, 1992)—are important in the context of EQUIP.

Self-Centered

Self-Centered thinking errors stem from egocentric bias and represent primary cognitive distortion. We have defined self-centered thinking as "according status to one's own views, expectations, needs, rights, immediate feelings, and desires to such an extent that the legitimate views, etc., of others (or even one's own long-term best interest) are scarcely considered or are disregarded altogether" (Table 1.2). Insofar as the Self-Centered thinking error entails an error of omission (failing to take the perspective of others), it entails a deficiency or egocentric bias. However, self-centeredness also entails distortive attitudes—for example, "Because I want to do it, that means I am entitled to" or "Because I want it, that makes it mine" (Yochelson & Samenow, 1976, 1977). Gary's putative "Nobody touches *me*!" attitude was self-centered insofar as his own person was accorded a special, uniquely privileged status. Similar was the attitude expressed by a 14-year-old delinquent: "I was born with the idea that I'd do what I wanted. I always felt that rules and regulations were not for me" (Samenow, 1984, p. 160). Redl and Wineman (1957) described Self-Centered thinking errors as fundamentally

> the attitude of "the world owes me this," with the implication that all other considerations, including value issues, are secondary. . . . All the ego now has to do is to classify a specific gratification that the individual's impulse is after as "basic, something he has coming to him," and from then on no holds are barred. . . . During the initial phase of treatment at Pioneer House, Sam stole the Director's cigarette lighter. In an interview with him we tried to get at some of his motivation for the theft. His only defense seemed to be, "Well, I wanted a lighter." When further challenged, "Yes, you wanted a lighter but how about going to such lengths as to steal it from someone?" he grew quite irritated. "How the hell do you expect me to get one if I don't swipe it? Do I have enough money to buy one?" There was no question that, having narrowed down his chances of getting a lighter to stealing it, the act itself was quite justifiable to him on a "closed issue" basis: "I want it, there is no other way, so I swipe it—just because I want it." (pp. 154–155)

Such attitudes or beliefs wrongly attribute subject status only to oneself; all others—other human subjects—are accorded status only as objects that should serve the unique subject (i.e., oneself) or at least should not interfere. Gibbs (1994) asserted that "there is something faulty or erroneous about such thinking. After all, it does not follow logically from the fact that I desire something that I am entitled to it" (p. 15). Nonetheless, self-centered youths' sense of entitlement can be so strong that any resistance to their doing what they want is experienced as outrageously unfair. In the widely publicized gang rape and near-murder of a New York City Central Park jogger, several of the gang youths recollected group indignation and outrage at the woman's attempted resistance to their assault (Stone, 1989).

Egocentric bias and primary cognitive distortion may encourage impulsive, antisocial behavior so blatantly harmful to others that certain psychological stresses may result. These stresses derive from the existence in virtually all individuals—including undercontrolled youths—of (1) some degree of empathic predisposition (Agee, 1979, pp. 91, 97; Henggeler, 1989; Hoffman, 1978, 1981) and (2) a motivation to maintain self-consistency or avoid "cognitive dissonance" or inconsistency between behavior and self-concept (e.g., Blasi & Oresick, 1986; Kelman & Baron, 1968; cf. Steele, 1988). Particularly where harm to others is obvious and difficult to ignore, a youth engaging in antisocial behavior may encounter the psychological stresses of (1) incipient guilt from empathy aroused by salient victim distress cues (Miller & Eisenberg, 1988) and (2) cognitive dissonance between behavior that unjustifiably harms to others and a concept of the self as one who does not unjustifiably harm others.

Anticipation of such empathy-based guilt and threats to self-concept normally inhibits at least obviously harmful behavior—unless secondary cognitive distortions are in place to neutralize these inhibitions. Secondary cognitive distortions have been characterized in psychodynamic terms as "special machinery these children's ego has developed in order to secure their [impulse-gratifying] behavior against . . . guilt" (Redl & Wineman, 1957, p. 146). In Bandura's (1991) cognitive social learning theory, distortions or rationalizations permit one to disengage one's objectionable conduct from moral self-evaluation. Whereas a less-aggressive adolescent in a delay-of-gratification situation may use self-statements to strengthen inhibitions, a highly aggressive adolescent may use distortive self-statements to weaken or neutralize inhibitions such as empathy-based guilt or dissonance with self-concept. Looking back on his burglaries and victims, one delinquent reflected, "If I started feeling bad, I'd say to myself, 'tough rocks for him. He should have had his house locked better and the alarm on' " (Samenow, 1984, p. 115). Redl and Wineman (1957) suggested that we find encouragement in delinquents' use of such neutralizing distortions; after all, a youth truly without empathy, values, and conscience would not need any neutralizations because there would be nothing to neutralize!

Distortive self-statements or secondary cognitive distortions, then, permit the delinquent to continue engaging in antisocial behavior with few or no pangs of conscience. Gibbs and Potter's (1992) thinking error categories for such secondary cognitive distortions are Assuming the Worst, Blaming Others, and Minimizing/ Mislabeling.

Assuming the Worst

Assuming the Worst has been defined as "gratuitously attributing hostile intentions to others, considering a worst-case scenario for a social situation as if it were inevitable, or assuming that improvement is impossible in one's own or others' behavior" (see Table 1.2). Misattribution of intentions was investigated experimentally by Dodge and associates (Dodge, 1980; Dodge, Price, Bachorowski, & Newman, 1990) in their studies of aggressive boys' reasons for engaging in unprovoked aggressive acts. Dodge found that, before committing aggressive acts toward other boys, the subjects apparently engaged in distorted thinking. Although the other boys' intentions were in fact presented as ambiguous, the aggressive boys (unlike the otherwise comparable control subjects) interpreted the other boys' actions as hostile, gratuitously attributing aggressive intentions. Consistent with this experimental finding, Dodge, Price et al. (1990) found higher levels of hostile attribution among severely aggressive juvenile offenders. A recent longitudinal study found hostile attributional bias and other distortions already present in 4-year-olds who had been physically abused. After entering kindergarten 6 months later, these children displayed high rates of aggressive behavior (Dodge, Bates, & Pettit, 1990).

In Dodge and associates' experimental studies, the aggressive boys assumed the worst about the other boys' intentions—just as Mike at Pioneer House assumed the worst about the counselor's intentions. Assuming the Worst provided ostensible justification for any aggression that followed: "That guy is against me, so whatever I do to him is okay" (cf. Lochman, Wayland, & White, 1993). Highly aggressive adolescents, both male and female, are also more likely to assume the worst regarding consequences to their reputations of refraining from aggression—that is, they more frequently endorse belief statements such as "If you back down from a fight, everyone will think you're a coward" (Slaby & Guerra, 1988). Assuming the Worst is also evident in overgeneralizing rationalizations such as "Everyone steals—you might as well get your share" (Barriga & Gibbs, 1995; Gibbs, Barriga, & Potter, 1995).

When a young person assumes the worst about him- or herself (his or her own capabilities, future, etc.), the result is behavior typically more destructive to the young person than to others. A self-directed Assuming the Worst thinking error is often linked to a Low Self-Image behavior problem and to internalizing disorders (cf. Quay's, 1987, "anxiety-withdrawal-dysphoric" psychological subtype).

Blaming Others

Closely related to Assuming the Worst is Blaming Others, defined as "misattributing blame for one's harmful actions to outside sources, especially to another person, a group, or a momentary aberration (one was drunk, high, in a bad mood, etc.), or misattributing blame for one's victimization or other misfortune to innocent others" (Table 1.2). The burglarizing youth who neutralized his conscience by blaming his victims (they were negligent in protecting their homes and so deserved whatever happened to them) was engaging in Blaming Others. Similarly, we can imagine Gary blaming his girlfriend for being so careless as to leave available a sharp knife in the kitchen; if she were a better housekeeper, she never would have gotten hurt. The comments of the juveniles who attacked the Central Park jogger showed them blaming the victim: By being foolish enough to be in Central Park at night, she "committed suicide" (Kunen, 1989; Stone, 1989).

Blaming Others may extend to considering a victim somehow blameworthy and hence a legitimate target because of one's own prior victimization. Redl and Wineman (1957) describe an incident in which one of their Pioneer House children "really tried to prove that his stealing was all right because 'somebody swiped my own wallet two weeks ago'" (p. 150). "Taking it out on the rest of the world" is a common theme that emerges from the life stories told by group members during mutual help meetings.

In our EQUIP work, we first discovered the problem of Blaming Others during a discussion of one of the shoplifting problem situations (Sam's Problem Situation; chapter 3). During the discussion, Gibbs was prompted to ask—rhetorically, he thought—"Who's to blame in this situation?" Gibbs thought it was obvious that the primary person to blame was the shoplifter. To his surprise, several of the boys in the group quite seriously answered that the store owner was at fault. Their reasoning was that if the store owner wasn't alert enough to spot and catch a shoplifter, he deserved to be robbed. "It's on him," as one group member put it.

Once we realized that our supposedly rhetorical question was not necessarily so rhetorical for this population, we started asking it in other problem situation discussions as well. In the car theft situation (Alonzo's Problem Situation), we learned that the theft was the car owner's fault because, after all, the owner had left the keys in the car. That made the owner a fool; anyone that careless or stupid deserved to get ripped off. Similarly, we learned that a teacher who says that she trusts a class taking a test and leaves the room for a few minutes is to blame for whatever cheating takes place (Antonio's Problem Situation). The teacher, for being such a trusting fool, has it coming if the students cheat.

Sykes and Matza (1957) pointed out that externalizing rationalizations offer an obvious advantage to the offender: "By attacking others, the wrongfulness of his own behavior is more easily repressed or lost to view" (p. 668). Indeed, the delinquent tends to perceive him- or herself not as a victimizer but as a victim (Samenow, 1984; cf. Coie, Dodge, Terry, & Wright, 1991; Redl & Wineman, 1957, pp. 179–180): "Why is everyone always picking on me?" The roles in the victimization process are reversed as the delinquent "moves himself into the position of an avenger and the victim is transformed into a wrongdoer" (Sykes & Matza, 1957, p. 668). Offenders may see their crimes as righting injustices inflicted upon them (Wilson & Herrnstein, 1985)—for example, real or imagined slights to their self-esteem. Groth and Birnsbaum (1979) cite the distorted thinking reported by a sadistic rapist, who attributed his "excitement" to "the prospect of having a young, pure, upperclass girl and bring her down to my level—a feeling like 'Well there's one fine, fancy bitch who [has been humiliated]. . . . Bet she don't feel so uppity now' " (pp. 45–46). Similarly, Kahn and Chambers (1991) found higher sexual recidivism rates among juvenile sex offenders who blamed their victims for the offenses; an example is "a youth who raped a woman in front of her children: 'That broad was lucky to get a cool dude like me—she wanted me or she would have fought harder' " (Agee, 1979, p. 96).

Minimizing/Mislabeling

Minimizing/Mislabeling thinking errors have been defined as "depicting antisocial behavior as causing no real harm or as being acceptable or even admirable, or referring to others with belittling or dehumanizing labels" (Table 1.2). Like Blaming Others, Minimizing/Mislabeling has been quite evident in our group work. For example, a group member who had grabbed a purse dangling from a supermarket cart recalled thinking that the theft taught the purse's owner a good lesson, to be more careful in the future. We could imagine our hypothetical group member, Gary, suggesting that the stabbing was good for his girlfriend, to teach her her "place" and to be a better housekeeper (i.e., not to leave dangerous items lying around). In discussing the situation involving drug delivery (Dave's Problem Situation), several group members argued that making the delivery would be "helping out a friend" despite a clear indication in the problem situation that the drug was illegal and quite harmful to those who would receive it. Also, group members often minimize the severity of their actions—for example, by attempting to characterize an assault as "just screwing around" or vandalism as "mischief" or a "prank" (Sykes & Matza, 1957). The brutal gang rape of the Central Park jogger was minimized and mislabeled through the juveniles' use of a novel term, "wilding," which apparently meant just having spontaneous, uninhibited fun (Kunen, 1989).

Implicit in such mislabeling is a minimizing of the harm to others resulting from one's actions. Slaby and Guerra (1988) found that highly aggressive adolescents were more likely to endorse statements such as "People who get beat up badly probably don't suffer a lot." Barriga and Gibbs (1995) found similar results with incarcerated offenders responding to questionnaire items such as "People need to be roughed up once in a while."

Mislabeling can be used to provide a pseudolegitimation for egocentric bias and self-centered attitudes (primary cognitive distortion). In a television interview, an incarcerated offender who had murdered a sales clerk justified his lack of remorse, explaining that the woman had refused to "cooperate" and "follow the rules" (i.e., resisted giving him the merchandise and money he demanded). In addition to blaming the victim, he was also mislabeling or misrepresenting the event: *Cooperation*, a socially decentered word that means "working together toward a common end," was euphemistically misapplied to represent "giving me what I unfairly want." Similarly, *my desires* was mislabeled and rendered more presentable as "the rules."

Like the other secondary cognitive distortions, then, Minimizing/ Mislabeling serves the Self-Centered error by weakening inhibitions or neutralizing the pangs of conscience. The just-quoted murderer would probably have found it more difficult to kill if his frame of mind or implicit self-talk had accurately represented his act: "I chose to murder her for trying to keep me from stealing the store's money and jewelry for my own gratification." Instead, his attitudinal frame of mind provided a pseudolegitimation for it: "How dare she! She has left me no choice, the fool. Now she's gonna get it for not cooperating and breaking the rules."

A common practice during combat training of soldiers—or, for that matter, of gang members who are to fight another gang—is to use derogatory and dehumanizing labels for the class of human beings who are to be the enemy, so that killing them will be easier. Most government torturers, to be able to continue, must constantly be reminded that their victims are "vermin" (Timerman, 1981). Similarly, Conquest (1986) quoted the troubled recollection of a communist activist who aided in the forced starvation of 14 million Ukrainian peasants and had to see and hear "the children's crying and the women's wails":

> It was excruciating to see and hear all this. And even worse
> to take part in it. . . . I persuaded myself, explained to
> myself I mustn't give in to debilitating pity. We were realizing
> historical necessity. We were performing our revolutionary
> duty. We were obtaining grain for the socialist fatherland.
> For the Five Year Plan. (p. 233)

The activist further mislabeled by persuading himself that the peasants were in fact "enemies" of the plan (Baumeister, 1991).

Most of the intervention initiatives inspired by cognitive distortion theory have addressed problems such as anxiety or depression (e.g., Beck, 1976; Ellis, 1977), the so-called internalizing disorders.

A growing body of literature, however, has applied cognitive therapy techniques to people with externalizing disorders—that is, impulsivity/hyperactivity, aggression, or other antisocial behaviors. The internalizing-externalizing distinction, introduced by Achenbach and Edelbrock (1978), was graphically illustrated in terms of attributional style by Kendall (1991; cf. Dodge, 1993):

> Consider the experience of stepping in something a dog left on the lawn. The first reaction ("Oh, sh—") is probably a self-statement that reflects dismay. Individuals then proceed to process the experience. . . . The manner of processing the event contributes to the behavioral and emotional consequences. After the unwanted experience (i.e., stepping in it), conclusions are reached regarding the causes of the misstep. . . . Some may attribute the misstep to their inability to do anything right; such a global, internal, and stable attribution often characterizes depression (Abramson, Seligman, & Teasdale, 1978). An angry individual, in contrast, might see the experience as the result of someone else's provocation ("Whose dog left this here—I bet the guy knew someone would step in it!"); attributing the mess to someone else's intentional provocation [Assuming the Worst] is linked to aggressive retaliatory behavior. (p. 9)

Kazdin (1994) observed that "the [internalizing-externalizing] distinction is easily remembered by noting that internalizing symptoms tend to be troubling or disturbing to oneself; externalizing symptoms tend to be troublesome or disturbing to others" (p. 298). Kazdin also notes, however, the secondary other-disturbing consequences of internalizing symptoms (e.g., effects on loved ones of a suicide attempt), as well as the secondary self-disturbing consequences of externalizing symptoms (e.g., injury or incarceration following an aggravated assault). Pointing out such consequences can be helpful in therapy with either type of client. Inducing awareness of the self-defeating nature of antisocial behavior (e.g., "Is what you are doing helping you?") is a standard feature of reality therapy for delinquents (Glasser, 1965) and is emphasized in Week 1 of our anger management/thinking error correction course, presented later in this chapter.

Beck and associates (Beck & Freeman, 1990) have recently adapted their cognitive therapeutic techniques for treatment of externalizing disorders (see chapter 8); the one-on-one emphasis of their interventions, however, reduces the applicability of their work to group programs such as EQUIP. Fortunately, much of the literature is group-oriented (e.g., Guerra & Slaby, 1990; Kahn & Lafond,

1988; Vorrath & Brendtro, 1985; Yochelson & Samenow, 1976, 1977). The confronting, reversing, and relabeling techniques of Positive Peer Culture (see chapter 2) address respectively the Self-Centered, Blaming Others, and Minimizing/Mislabeling thinking errors of externalizing adolescents; in EQUIP, these techniques are adapted and used both in guided mutual help meetings and in equipment meetings.

Although self-instructional programs have focused mainly on the remediation of deficiencies, they have addressed distortions as well. Among the self-statements taught in Novaco's (1975) anger management program, for example, were several that could reduce Self-Centered thinking errors by inducing perspective taking (e.g., "I can't expect people to act the way I want them to"; "For someone to be that irritable, he must be awfully unhappy"; and "Let's take a cooperative approach. Maybe we're both right"; pp. 95–96). Other self-statements in Novaco's program could reduce Assuming the Worst misattributions (e.g., "Look for the positives. Don't assume the worst or jump to conclusions"; pp. 95–96). Feindler and Ecton (1986) encountered many aggressive adolescents with dysfunctional attitudes and beliefs who attributed all causes of behavior to external sources and would "not take responsibility for their own behavior and/or behavior change" (p. 119; i.e., Blaming Others). Furthermore, they noted that "some adolescents have an all-or-none attitude about their behavior and environment. If they try an anger control technique once and it does not work 100%, they will quickly abandon it" (p. 120; Assuming the Worst, in this case that improvement is impossible). Feindler and Ecton suggested addressing these deficiencies through pretraining or an extra step in the training process; this suggestion is consistent with our innovation in the EQUIP mutual help meeting (namely, sensitizing youths to their cognitive distortions as part of problem reporting), which sets a context for the equipment meetings. The all-or-none thinking problem embodied in Assuming the Worst is combated both in Feindler and Ecton's program and in EQUIP as youths are taught to make full use of a graduated self-report anger scale included in their daily logs (see Week 3, later in this chapter).

EQUIPMENT FOR MANAGING ANGER AND CORRECTING THINKING ERRORS

Gary and the violent youths he represents must learn before acting to *think*—both adequately and accurately. In EQUIP, antisocial youths acquire skills for managing their anger and gaining self-control by remedying errors of both omission (deficiencies) and commission (distortions) in their thinking, as well as by learning social skills, behaviors incompatible with anger and aggression (presented in chapter 5). Skills for remediating cognitive deficiencies should reduce arousal and buy the time that is needed if constructive social skills are to be used. Skills for monitoring and remediating cognitive distortions should tap the positive potential of antisocial adolescents: Once adolescents are equipped to expose and deal with thinking errors in themselves and others, egocentric bias should decline, empathy and conscience should gain inhibitory power, and these youths should become less angry and more caring.

The remainder of this chapter is devoted to anger management dealing with deficiencies and distortions. Like the other two equipment components, the anger management program comprises 10 sessions. The sessions are designed to remediate deficiencies and distortions in both reactive and proactive aggression (Dodge, 1991; Dodge & Coie, 1987): Sessions 1 through 7 address anger and aggression in response to provocation from others (reactive aggression), and sessions 8 through 10 address anger and aggression initiated against others (proactive aggression). Each session after the first begins with a review of the key points or skills learned in the previous session. For many of the sessions, the group leader (in this case, the equipper) will need a felt marker and a flip pad on an easel. Masking tape is helpful as well; as a sheet is filled, the leader can request that a group member remove the sheet and tape it on the wall for future reference.

Following is a week-by-week description of the anger management/ thinking error correction component of the EQUIP curriculum. The indented portions of text are suggested language for the group leader (equipper) to use. Comments or instructions for the leader are bracketed and italicized.

The Anger Management/ Thinking Error Correction Course Component

Week 1—Evaluating and Relabeling Anger/Aggression

Week 2—Key Role of Mind in Anger

    —Monitoring Mind and Body

    —Reducing Anger

Week 3—Monitoring and Correcting Thinking Errors

Week 4—More Techniques for Reducing Anger: Relaxation

Week 5—Powerful Self-Talk Techniques for Reducing Anger: Thinking Ahead to Consequences and TOP (Think of the Other Person)

Week 6—Constructive Consequences

Week 7—Self-Evaluation

Week 8—Reversing

Week 9—More Consequences for Others

    —Correcting Distorted Self-Views

Week 10—More Correction of Distorted Self-Views

    —Grand Review

Week 1—Evaluating and Relabeling Anger/Aggression

OVERVIEW OF ACTIVITIES

1. Discussion of anger and aggression, benefits of controlling anger

2. Relabeling of anger/aggression (as weak, immature, counterproductive, etc.) and nonviolence (as putting youths in a stronger position by giving them options besides fighting)

3. Expression of a qualifier, important for "selling" the program: The goal of this equipment meeting is anger management, not anger elimination or any claim that fighting is always wrong

PROCEDURE AND LEADER NOTES

Like a number of anger control programs, EQUIP anger management begins with a discussion of anger or aggression that lets youths "step back" from anger and see its disadvantages. During the discussion, the group leader must be alert for opportunities to relabel—that is, to counteract the tendency of aggressive adolescents to see anger and aggression in a positive light and nonviolence as weak. The group leader should point out that, in fact, it is uncontrolled anger that is weak. The leader's thesis that anger management is part of the equipment the group needs should be strengthened by the fact that the group will already know Easily Angered as a problem reported in the mutual help meetings.

As Goldstein (1988) suggests, the leader can point out as potential role models people who must have excellent self-control to be successful—for example, prominent personalities in professional boxing or the martial arts. The leader can thus underscore the idea that having self-control does not mean being a "wimp." On the contrary, self-control is a source of power: "Trainees are *more powerful* when they are in control of their reactions to others despite the attempts of others to provoke them. By being aggressive, they allow others to control them" (Goldstein, 1988, pp. 261–263).

On the other hand, the leader should support the valid elements of group sentiment—for example, by pointing out that there is nothing wrong with anger itself if it is managed and used to motivate constructive behavior. Also, aggression and fighting may sometimes be the right option (as in some situations of self-defense). However, aggression should not be the only option available. Again, group members should become motivated to learn anger management as the leader helps them realize that having more options means becoming a more powerful person.

We like to use the words of the Texas Youth Commission (1987) in their aggression control skills module: "If you get angry pretty often, it must have some advantages for you. You also may have noticed some disadvantages of letting your anger get out of control." As the youths discuss the advantages and disadvantages of anger, the group leader lists them in separate columns on the flip pad. In our discussion, we have heard three main themes as aggressive youths discuss the advantages of anger: (1) self-defense ("to protect myself"; "so no one will step on me"; "so others won't take advantage of me"); (2) power ("makes me feel big, powerful, superior"; "then I'm free to get things, do what I want"); and (3) vengeance ("to get even"; "to not let others get away with putting me down or pushing me around"). The leader should watch for opportunities to point out the thinking errors in these themes. First, although anger may be linked to legitimate self-defense, illegitimate aggression is often Mislabeled and Minimized as mere self-defense. Second, to hurt others so that you can "do what you want" irrespective of others' rights is Self-Centered. Finally, hurting others to "get even" reflects a low-level eye-for-eye, tooth-for-tooth morality that should be beneath the mature level of an EQUIP group. Besides, such an appeal could amount to Blaming Others— that is, claiming some concocted offense to rationalize aggression against one's victim.

As EQUIP youths have "stepped back" on anger in reflective discussion, they have also described disadvantages, often emerging from continued discussion of the seeming advantages. First, instead of preventing others from "stepping on you," often aggression only "causes more problems, more fights, makes things worse." Second, instead of feeling big or powerful, you may feel "stupid," "embarrassed," or "sorry" (the group leader should probe "sorry" to see if it entails feeling bad for having harmed others). Countering a "rush" or feeling of power from pushing people around are the points that "you lose friends" because they "can't trust you" and that other people fear you but "don't respect you, don't want to be around you." Finally, after you get even, "the other person would get angry, could try to get back at you." As a particularly verbal EQUIP group member put it, "The cycle of revenge never stops." This point is helpful against occasional claims in the "advantage" column that angry aggression "is fun," "relieves tension," and "reduces stress." To the contrary, more often angry aggression increases stress and tension and therefore winds up being self-defeating—anything but fun. As much as possible, these points should emerge from the group itself with no more input than is necessary from the leader.

The group leader will need to do some teaching, however, to accomplish the relabeling of anger/aggression. For example, the leader should draw on illustrations from athletics concerning the necessity for self-control and self-discipline (the point is all the more compelling when one points out how quickly famous athletes fall in the standings when they lose their self-discipline). To relabel fighting as foolish, Feindler and Ecton (1986) use what we have adapted as the Clown— or Clowns?—in the Ring diagrams (see Figure 4.1). The group leader's teaching takes the following tack:

> The clown in the ring *[indicate Figure 4.1a]* is the guy who's trying to start a fight. He's a clown and a fool because he's not thinking of all the disadvantages of anger and violence. His goal is to make you a fool, too, to draw you into the circus ring with him. He wants to attach his strings to you. *[Draw strings as in Figure 4.1b.]* Then he can pull on the strings and draw you into the ring with him. If you let him attach the strings and pull you in, then who's in control? And he wins if you start fighting. How many clowns are there in the ring now *[point to Figure 4.1c]*?

The leader can conclude the discussion by inviting the group to list the benefits of managing anger. The benefits are usually expressed in terms of the way others treat you (e.g., "Staff will feel more like helping you achieve your goals"; "Other people will trust you and be your friend"); the way you treat others (e.g., "You won't hurt anybody"); and the way you feel about yourself (e.g., "You'll feel more relaxed"; "You'll feel better about yourself because you'll know you can control yourself") and your future (e.g., "You'll know you can have a positive future").

FIGURE 4.1
The Clown—or Clowns?—in the Ring

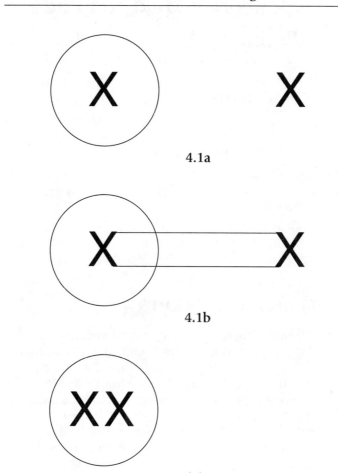

4.1a

4.1b

4.1c

Week 2—Key Role of Mind in Anger
—Monitoring Mind and Body
—Reducing Anger

OVERVIEW OF ACTIVITIES

1. Review of Week 1 session

2. Introduction to the anatomy of anger (AMBC)

3. Instruction in the basic thesis of the program: It's your mind (attitude, belief, what you tell yourself) that makes you angry, not the event "out there"

4. Attention to the early warning signs of anger (B)

5. Self-talk reducers (M) that help a person buy time

PROCEDURE AND LEADER NOTES

After reviewing the opening session's conclusions regarding the benefits of controlling anger and the strength that comes from having options besides fighting, the leader should again enable the group members to "step back" from anger, this time to examine its working parts and attain some key insights. Week 2 entails teaching the functional anatomy of anger, mainly to convey the key role of the mind—not the outer event—in either making the individual angry or keeping the individual calm. Either way, the mind is the key to the emotions. Taking advantage of this principle, the group learns to monitor anger-generating thoughts or attitudes and to displace them with responsible self-talk that reduces anger and buys time for more controlled, constructive behavior to take over. Group members also learn to recognize and monitor bodily signs that anger is building and must be reduced.

The acronym used to teach the anatomy of anger is AMBC: A for activating event, M for mind activity, B for body reaction, and C for consequences. (The term *acronym* is easy to communicate and illustrate through example: TV, NFL, etc.) We prefer to teach A, B, and C before we teach M. It is helpful for the leader to use the flip pad to show the components of the acronym as the discussion proceeds.

As directed to group members, our teaching goes as follows:

> The activating event, or the A, is the thing that can get you
> angry, that leads up to your anger. These events are also
> called "hot spots." What are some of your hot spots?

In our experience, the most frequent category of examples mentioned is physical intimidation (someone "bullies you"; "glares at you"; "hits, pushes, or punches you"; "puts their hand in your face or makes you flinch"), followed by verbal insults or threats ("putting you down," "writing your gang's name upside down on the wall," "calling your mother a name," "teasing you," "cussing you out," "bragging they can beat you," etc.), an unfair demand or accusation (staff "pick on you" or accuse you of something you didn't do), the discovery that someone has lied about you (a peer "starts a rumor about you"), and the discovery that someone has stolen something of yours.

Skipping M for the moment, we go straight to the B:

> What do you usually see happening after the activating
> event, after someone has been punched or put down?
> What do you think the B stands for?

Our experience is that someone soon will suggest the word *body*, which can be accepted and responded to as "body reaction." The group usually generates a substantial list: fast, shallow, or hard breathing; cold, clammy, or sweaty hands; tense neck, shoulders, stomach; clenched fists; gritted or clenched teeth; louder or lower voice; squinted eyes; jittery or light-headed feeling.

> These have been called the early warning signs of anger, and
> you need to be alert and notice when they're happening. The
> last letter of anger is C. What do you think C stands for? What's
> a general word for the results of an activating event like a
> put-down, followed by, let's say, those body reactions?

Our EQUIP youths have mentioned threats, fights, making enemies, disciplinary write-ups, getting hurt, and so on. Occasionally, a group member will even guess that the C stands for consequences, but more often the group leader provides the generic label for these events.

> So that's the ABC of anger and aggression. But there's
> something crucial missing, something we haven't covered
> yet, something that happens between the A and the B. What
> does that M stand for, do you think? [*A group member may say*

"mind," which can be accepted and responded to as "mind activity."] If you think back to when someone put you down or threatened you, you can usually remember thoughts you had or maybe attitudes or beliefs, "talk" to yourself that went through your mind and made you angry. We call this "self-talk." You may not even realize you're doing this self-talk until you think about it. What were some of the thoughts you can remember having when you were in a hot spot?

EQUIP groups have suggested "I'm not taking this any more!" "I'm going to get my respect back," "I'll get him back," "I'll teach him!" "I'm getting my way," and "Kill!"

So now we have the AMBC of anger and aggression. We put the M between the A and the B for a reason. We said B stands for "body reaction." What is the body reacting to? Is it reacting to whatever event "out there" happened? Or is it reacting to the meaning you attach to the event, to your thoughts about what the person said or did?

In EQUIP, this "M" idea has usually caused some discussion. Valuable points emerging from discussion may be how often one is unaware of one's mind activity, how quickly the mind activity or an angry attitude can "kick in" to cause the body reaction, and how important it is to become more aware of the thoughts running through one's head so that one can do something about them. The group leader should point out the importance of noticing the early warning signs of anger as signals that one needs to do something about the thoughts that are causing those bodily reactions.

When thoughts in your mind are making you sweat, and clench your teeth and your fists, and so on, you're not in control. The other guy is the one who's in control because you're letting him pull your strings. He's probably having fun watching you! Remember the clown in the ring? He's the clown, he's the fool or the one with the problem, and he'll keep pulling until there are two fools in the ring, you and him. So if you don't want to be a fool, you've got to change your mind activity from thoughts that make you start to lose control to thoughts that help you keep your head. What are some calming thoughts you could tell yourself?

EQUIP youths have suggested "Chill out," "I'm not going to let him get to me," "He never even met my mother," and "As long as I keep my cool, I'm in control." The leader can add examples from the literature, as mentioned before, such as "For someone to be that irritable, he must be awfully unhappy" and "Look for the positives." A list of other possible self-statements is provided in Table 4.1.

> From now on when you get into a hot spot, use the anger-reducing self-talk to stay in control, especially if you notice early warning signs. Next week I'll ask you how it went.

As a hook into the next session, the leader may conclude with the suggestion that mind activity causing anger usually involves thinking errors and that, therefore, the anger-reducing self-talk needs to include corrections of those errors. The leader can mention that correcting thinking errors will be covered in the coming week's meeting.

TABLE 4.1
Examples of Self-Talk Anger Reducers

ANTICIPATION OF AN ACTIVATING EVENT

"This could be a bad situation, but I believe in myself."

"Try not to take this too seriously."

POSITIVE MIND ACTIVITY IN RESPONSE TO AN ACTIVATING EVENT

"I'm going to keep my cool and let this guy get in trouble."

"If he wants to make a fool of himself he can, but he's not gonna make a fool out of me."

"Time for a few deep breaths."

"It's really a shame he has to act like that."

"He's the one with the problem."

"He can be okay when he's not showing his Aggravates Others problem."

"I don't have to even look at him. I'll just walk away and not let it get to me."

"Don't Assume the Worst—maybe it's just an accident, or I took it the wrong way."

Table 4.1 (continued)

"I'll try to stay calm and listen—maybe there's something I should hear in what he's saying."

"Chill out. I ain't gonna get all riled up."

"You don't need to prove yourself."

"My muscles are starting to feel tight. Time to relax and slow things down."

"I'm not going to get pushed around, but I'm not going haywire either."

"He'd probably like me to get really angry. Well, I'm going to disappoint him."

"I can't expect people to act the way I want them to."

"Think ahead—don't lose *your* head."

SELF-EVALUATION

When the Conflict Is Unresolved

"These are tough situations, and they take time to straighten out."

"I'll get better at this as I get more practice."

"It could have been a lot worse."

When the Conflict Is Resolved or Coping Has Been Successful

"I handled that one pretty well. It worked!"

"I actually got through that without getting angry."

"That wasn't as hard as I thought."

"I'm doing better at this all the time."

"I thought ahead. It worked."

Week 3 —Monitoring and Correcting Thinking Errors

OVERVIEW OF ACTIVITIES

1. Review of Week 2 session

2. Learning and correcting the thinking errors

3. Monitoring the thinking errors in everyday behavior: introducing the self-help daily logs (problems and thinking errors, positive behaviors)

PROCEDURE AND LEADER NOTES

The third week focuses on mind activity, especially thinking errors. Following a review of AMBC, the group leader uses the Gary's Thinking Errors exercise (Figure 4.2) to bring home the connection between distorted thinking and violence and the resulting importance of correcting thinking errors before it is too late. For new EQUIP groups, the self-help daily logs are introduced during this session (Figures 4.3, 4.4, and 4.5).

The leader can conduct the opening review by asking the group what each letter of AMBC stands for. (If the list generated during the previous meeting is still displayed on the flip pad or wall, it should be removed temporarily before the meeting begins.) The leader again asks what the body reaction (shown in the early warning signs of anger) is a reaction *to*. Because anger is caused by the meaning attached to the activating event and not the event itself, the M or mind activity clearly deserves special attention in anger management (although techniques like deep breathing are valuable and will be learned as well).

The leader next reminds group members about anger-reducing self-talk and asks for further examples, then inquires about group members' experiences using these self-statements to reduce anger and help avoid losing control in hot spots.

To introduce the notion that anger-arousing mind activity often involves distortions or errors, we ask:

> Who has felt angry in discovering you have to wait in a long line for something you need to do or want to buy? *[Typically, several group members will recall being angry in such a situation.]*

FIGURE 4.2
Gary's Thinking Errors

Gary is in the kitchen of his apartment. Gary's girlfriend, Cecilia, is angry at him for something he did to hurt her. She yells at him. She pushes his shoulder. Thoughts run through Gary's head. Gary does nothing to correct the errors in his thoughts. Gary becomes furious. He swears at Cecilia. A sharp kitchen knife is nearby. Gary picks up the knife and stabs Cecilia, seriously wounding her.

1. What thoughts ran through Gary's head, do you think, both during the situation and afterward? Suggest some sample thoughts.

2. What are the errors in these thoughts? Cecilia was mad at Gary because he had done something to hurt her. What do you think that might have been?

3. What might Gary have told himself in this situation? In other words, how might Gary have "talked back" to his thinking errors? Suggest some things Gary could have said to himself to correct each type of thinking error.

4. If Gary had corrected his thinking errors, would he still have stabbed Cecilia?

FIGURE 4.3
Self-Help Daily Log: Problems and Thinking Errors

Name_____

Date _____ Morning ____ Afternoon ____ Evening ____

Where were you?

Class   ____   Cottage ____   Dining ____   Hall ____

Group meeting ____   Program ____   Gym ____   Other____

*What kind of **problem(s)** did you have?*

Low Self-Image   ____   Misleads Others   ____

Inconsiderate of Self   ____   Easily Misled   ____

Inconsiderate of Others ____   Alcohol or Drug Problem ____

Authority Problem   ____   Stealing   ____

Easily Angered   ____   Lying   ____

Aggravates Others   ____   Fronting   ____

*You had this/these **problem(s)** because of what kind of **thinking error?***

Self-Centered ____   Blaming Others (or Blaming Bad Mood) ____

Assuming the Worst ____   Minimizing/Mislabeling ____

Describe the problem(s)_____

_____

What were you thinking (describe the thinking error)? _____

_____

How angry were you?

1-Burning mad	2-Really angry	3-Moderately angry	4-Mildly angry	5-Not angry at all

How did you handle yourself?

1-Poorly	2-Not so well	3-Okay	4-Well	5-Great

I won't have this/these problem(s) in the future if I _____

_____

_____

FIGURE 4.4

Self-Help Daily Log: Positive Behaviors (Structured Version)

Name _____

Date _____ Morning ____ Afternoon ____ Evening ____

I maintained myself (took shower, took care of clothes,   ____
brushed teeth, etc.).

I did my assigned chores.   ____

I followed the institution's safety rules.   ____

I went to classes without being reminded.   ____

I worked hard in classes.   ____

I did the assigned work in class.   ____

I accepted a constructive criticism.   ____

I stood up for my rights in a positive way.   ____

I went to programs I was assigned to.   ____

I participated in programs I attended.   ____

I accepted responsibility for my actions and   ____
did not make an excuse.

I talked somebody out of fighting.   ____

I complimented someone for something they did.   ____

I showed consideration for another.   ____

I _____

_____

_____

_____

FIGURE 4.5

Self-Help Daily Log: Positive Behaviors (Open-Ended Version)

Name_____ Date_____

What did you do to help yourself today?

I _____

_____

_____

What did you do to help someone else today?

I _____

_____

_____

You probably thought, "This is unfair, I shouldn't have to wait in this line." But that's an error. Why? *[Invite group discussion.]* Because it is fair. What's the thinking error here?

In our experience, EQUIP group participants can, with a little prompting, get the point that others are also having to wait, that they are no exception, and that the attitude expressed exemplifies a Self-Centered thinking error.

Next, the leader should ask the group to consider how some of the self-statements learned from the previous meeting help to reduce anger by correcting various errors in mind activity. For example, "I can't expect people to act the way I want them to" corrects the Self-Centered error, as do self-statements that invite perspective taking (e.g., "For someone to be that irritable, he must be awfully unhappy").

To learn more about thinking errors typically involved in anger and violence, the group then discusses the Gary's Thinking Errors exercise (Figure 4.2). The leader should distribute the handout and ask a group member to read the narrative paragraph. The discussion then follows the first three questions. As the discussion proceeds, the leader lists group members' suggested thoughts (question 1) and corrective self-talk (question 3) on the flip pad. (In response to the second part of question 2, regarding what Gary might have done initially to hurt Cecilia, EQUIP group members often suggest that Gary probably "came home drunk," "beat her," "busted the furniture in a rage," "ran around with other women," and/or "blew his [or her] whole paycheck.")

If the leader knows the four thinking error categories well, he or she can organize the group members' contributions into those categories while writing them down, as shown in Table 4.2. This list represents the collective results of EQUIP group discussions we have held concerning Gary's Thinking Errors (the leader may suggest some of these self-statements to help prompt and guide the discussion). The left-hand column represents the web of self-centered rationalizations and other distortions that lead to violence; the right-hand column represents truthful self-talk that reduces anger by correcting those distortions.

TABLE 4.2
Analysis of Gary's Thinking Errors

WHAT GARY THOUGHT	WHAT GARY SHOULD HAVE THOUGHT
Self-Centered	**Talking Back to Self-Centered**
"How *dare* she touch me!"	"I'd be mad, too, if I were her.
"Who does she think she is?"	She has a right to expect better."
Minimizing/Mislabeling	**Talking Back to Minimizing/Mislabeling**
"I'll teach *her*!"	"You don't teach anybody by stabbing and maybe killing them."
"She's got to learn her place!"	
"I have to defend myself!"	"I won't die from a push in the shoulder."
Assuming the Worst	**Talking Back to Assuming the Worst**
"She hates me; it's hopeless; she's going to leave me." (May lead to: "And if I can't have her, nobody will" [Self-Centered].)	"She's mad now, but she still loves me. This isn't the end of the world. If I start treating her better, our relationship will improve."
Blaming Others	**Talking Back to Blaming Others**
"She was asking for it."	"I started it by treating her unfairly."
"If she'd bothered to clean up around here, she wouldn't have gotten hurt with that knife."	"Nobody's forcing me to grab that knife—it's my fault if I do."

The leader concludes the discussion of Gary's Thinking Errors by raising question 4: "If Gary had corrected his thinking errors, would he still have stabbed Cecilia?" We have seen this question provide the "clincher" that gives this exercise considerable impact: The youths realize the connection between lies and violence or the importance of catching lies and thinking the truth to avoid acting violently. One group became very quiet as they pondered the question of whether Gary would have stabbed his girlfriend if he had corrected his thinking errors. A group member finally said "no" in a soft and earnest voice, while others nodded silently. They had gotten the point.

Gary's Thinking Errors can move the group to be receptive when the leader concludes the session by introducing or examining the self-help daily logs (Figures 4.3, 4.4, and 4.5), structured devices for helping the youths to monitor their behavior, thoughts, and feelings. The logs will have to be introduced only for a totally new EQUIP group; groups that include members who have already been through an equipment cycle will already be using them, inexperienced members having learned the procedure from veterans.

The primary self-help daily log is Problems and Thinking Errors (see Figure 4.3), which promotes users' ability to monitor anger/ aggression; to gain awareness or metacognition concerning which settings are high risk and which kinds of problems and thinking errors they are most likely to have; to practice evaluating the degree of their anger (counteracting tendencies to think that anger is always hopelessly intense), as well as assessing how well they handled themselves in anger situations; and to consider how they might better cope with such situations in the future. This daily log provides an excellent reminder of problem incidents that can be reported in the regular guided group meetings (although group members are free to report problems other than those recorded on the logs). If a youth is using the sheet to report more than one incident, he or she should answer the open-ended questions for the additional incidents by using the back of the sheet.

Once a youth is sufficiently advanced in the change process (specifically, is self-critical in a sincere, humble way), that youth may begin completing not only the Problems and Thinking Errors log, but also the Positive Behaviors log (structured or open-ended version, as appropriate; see Figures 4.4 and 4.5). Just as the first log helps the youth recognize and monitor thinking errors, the latter two logs help the youth recognize and monitor growth in responsible, caring behavior.

Following is an overview of the typical use of the Problems and Thinking Errors log in EQUIP groups. Our experience is that, for residential facilities, the place where most reported problems occur is the cottage or dorm area, followed by the classroom, the dining room, the hallway, and "outside" (on the grounds). The most commonly cited behavior problem category is Easily Angered, although other categories are used as well. Typical self-report statements are listed in Table 4.3. Self-Centered is the most frequently used thinking error category, followed by Assuming the Worst. Minimizing/Mislabeling is only rarely identified by itself, correctly or incorrectly (although it is sometimes checked in conjunction with Self-Centered or Assuming the Worst errors). Even the popular categories can be misapplied. Apparently taking Assuming the Worst to mean "made things worse," one youth checked Assuming the Worst and explained, "People on group were messing up and I got upset and was yelling at them and made it worst [sic]." Blaming Others (or Blaming Bad Mood) is used less frequently and sometimes incorrectly: Youths sometimes interpret "bad mood" to mean feelings following an incident, rather than a rationalization (e.g., "I was in a bad mood both times when they told me I did not do something I did"; "Today is my mom's birthday, and I'm down cause I can't be with her").

A common misuse of the Problems and Thinking Errors log across all categories is as a vehicle for complaints—for instance, "Miss Carter is always putting me down for any little thing and I don't feel that's right." As a Self-Centered problem, one youth reported, "Two people got in trouble and our whole group had to suffer." He wrote that he wouldn't have this problem in the future if he didn't "worry about what other people do and look out for myself"—quite the opposite of the way to correct a self-centered attitude! Our approach to such misuse is balanced. On the one hand, we acknowledge that unfair treatment is a problem and mention that learning how to deal constructively with unfair situations is one of the skills that will be covered in the equipment meetings. On the other hand, we emphasize that there are also plenty of problems—including some "unfair" treatment problems—that are at least partly attributable to the youths' thinking errors and that it is these problems that we wish them to focus on in completing the daily logs.

To provide a hook into the next anger management session, the group leader can mention that sometimes, in hot spots, anger can build so quickly that by the time one starts to correct one's thinking errors, it's too late—one is already engaged in some foolish violence. The leader then suggests that some techniques for coping with this problem will be covered next time.

TABLE 4.3

Examples of Problems and Thinking Errors Log Entries by Type of Thinking Error

SELF-CENTERED

Cottage: Stealing

"Broke into someone's room and stole their belongings. . . . [I was thinking] that it don't really matter cause I need it more than they do. . . . [I won't have this problem in the future if I] learn to work for the stuff I want and need."

Hall: Authority Problem

"I was at MedLine and the staff told me not to talk and I talked. . . . I was Self-Centered because I was thinking of myself at the time."

Outside: Authority Problem

"I was told to stop throwing the ball and didn't cause I was playing with the staff [Minimizing/Mislabeling]. . . . [I won't have this problem in the future if I] take things more serious and not play with someone when they don't want to play."

Outside: Easily Angered

"We was playing softball and the rec staff made a call that I thought was not right. . . . [I won't have this problem in the future if I] think about the other point of view."

Cottage: Easily Angered

"I was playing the Nintendo and David . . . was messing with me and I told him I was going to beat him up. . . . I was thinking of myself."

ASSUMING THE WORST

Outside: Easily Angered

"I seen some girls outside and got Easily Angered because I thought I wasn't [ever] going to leave."

Cottage: Inconsiderate of Self

"I Assumed the Worst [about my release date] because my girl-friend told me there wasn't any date on the letter they got from my judge."

Table 4.3 (continued)

Cottage: Easily Angered, Low Self-Image

"[I was] thinking about going home and someone said they seen a sheet up front that I had extra time . . . [I won't have this problem again if I] don't believe everything I hear."

Cottage: Easily Angered

"Another youth lied about me and tried to make me look bad . . . I thought staff was mad and was going to start picking with me."

Cottage: Authority Problem

"Staff asked me to dust mop and I started to argue about it . . . I Assumed the Worst because I thought he was just picking on me. . . . [I won't have the problem again if I] do what some one asks if it can't hurt me."

Cottage: Easily Angered

"I almost got into a fight with Burns. . . . I thought he was gonna soak me."

Cottage: Easily Angered, Low Self-Image

"My dad almost didn't come [but] he did come. . . . I was thinking that my grandma was sick again."

MINIMIZING/MISLABELING

Cottage: Easily Angered

"I was horseplaying with a youth and it got a little too rough and he got mad. . . . [I won't have this problem in the future if I] stop [calling the assault] horseplaying."

BLAMING OTHERS

Cottage: Easily Angered

"I blamed the whole group [and got really angry at them] because someone stole something from me."

Week 4—More Techniques for Reducing Anger: Relaxation

OVERVIEW OF ACTIVITIES

1. Review of Week 3 session

2. Instruction and practice in deep breathing, counting backward, pleasant or peaceful imagery

3. Reinforcement of the importance of using self-talk reducers to buy time

PROCEDURE AND LEADER NOTES

A key technique in anger management is engaging in activities incompatible with anger. Calming self-statements are one example. Other activities, covered in this fourth session, are breathing deeply, counting backward, and invoking peaceful imagery. These activities are important because they are simpler and therefore more readily used than self-statements: "Once a child is well trained in the relaxation response, even thinking the word, *relax,* at moments of high stress seems to provide the pause necessary to prevent uncontrolled anger or rage" (Rose & Edleson, 1987, p. 229). As mentioned in the previous anger management session, sometimes, in hot spots, anger can build so rapidly that by the time one starts to correct one's thinking errors, it's too late—one finds oneself already engaged in some foolish violence or aggression. The techniques covered in this session, then, play an important advance role in anger management.

The techniques to be covered are breathing deeply, counting backward, and calling up peaceful imagery. All of these activities have the advantage of being quick and simple; for example, one can prevent anger buildup by starting to take deep breaths even before one begins to deal with thinking errors. Using all of these anger-reducing techniques will enable group members to stay calm long enough to start using constructive social skills such as Expressing a Complaint Constructively (chapter 5). The group leader should emphasize that remembering and practicing these techniques could have life-saving value.

The session should begin with a review of the previous session. If a sheet showing an analysis of Gary's Thinking Errors is still on the flip pad or wall, the leader can point to the thinking error and the "talking back" columns, reminding the group of the previous week's focus on the importance in anger management of recognizing and correcting one's thinking errors. The review should also include group feedback on use of the self-help daily logs.

Breathing Deeply

We have introduced the value of the first technique—slow, deep breathing—by using the example of a basketball player who has just been fouled by an opponent. We say:

> He's angry at being fouled, and he's nervous because the attention's on him and he needs to make this shot for the team. But he knows he won't make it if he stays angry and nervous. He's at the free throw line. What does he do? *[Discuss.]* He probably tries to think calming thoughts, but he also tries to calm down from being fouled by breathing deeply and slowly a few times. You can see him taking those slow, deep breaths. He knows from experience that that's one of the best ways to get back in control of the situation. As soon as you start taking a few slow, deep breaths, your body reactions are going to get less angry and nervous, and you're going to have a better chance of making that shot— or in the situation you're in, doing something responsible rather than destructive.

> Now remember to make sure the breathing is slow and deep. "Slow" means that taking in the breath should take 5 or 6 seconds. Hold the breath for a few seconds. Then slowly breathe out, again taking 5 or 6 seconds. Wait a few seconds, then breathe slowly in and out again. It should be a slow rhythm. "Deep" means that your lungs should be full. You'll know your lungs are full enough if they're putting some pressure down on the top of your stomach. You should be able to feel that downward pressure.

> Okay, let's give it a try. Let's imagine some activating event. What are some things, again, that put you in a hot spot? *[Discuss.]* Imagine that that's happening, whatever it is for you. Now start slow, deep breathing. *[Model deep breathing.]* Could you feel that helping? *[Discuss briefly.]*

Counting Backward

The leader next explains how counting backward can prevent dangerous anger buildup:

There are two more things that can come in handy. The second thing after deep breathing is counting backward. You silently count backward (at an even pace) from 20 to 1 when you feel that anger coming on. With some of these activating events, you may be able to turn away from what's provoking you while counting. You can count backwards while breathing deeply. You should use these techniques together to get as much power as you can for regaining control.

Counting Backward Plus Slow, Deep Breathing

The next approach combines the two techniques taught previously:

So let's try both of these things together. Okay, imagine that worst event. *[Allow 10 to 15 seconds.]* Now get the deep breathing started. *[Model; make sure group is breathing deeply.]* Now we'll count aloud from 20. Now start. *[Model; start counting backward; make sure group is both breathing deeply and counting.]* Could you feel that helping? *[Discuss.]* Of course, when you're using this technique you'll be counting silently. Let's try deep breathing and counting backward silently. *[Lead the group in deep breathing; remind them that they should be counting backward silently.]*

Invoking Pleasant or Peaceful Imagery

In addition to deep breathing and counting backward, pleasant or peaceful imagery will help group members calm down:

The third thing you can do is to imagine pleasant or peaceful scenes. You can calm yourself down from angry mind activity by imagining a pleasant or peaceful scene. This is a lot like calming self-talk, except that we're talking about mental pictures instead of thoughts. What are some happy or peaceful scenes you can imagine? *[Through discussion, make a list.]* It's pretty hard to be saying to yourself how you're going to tear somebody's head off while you're imagining yourself sunbathing on the beach!

For happy or peaceful scenes, our EQUIP groups have suggested making a foul shot and winning the game, lying on the beach (the sun is warm, there is a slight breeze, waves have a calming effect), being out in the woods, being in one's own bed at home, and reading a book.

All Three Techniques Together

Once group members become proficient at these techniques, they can practice using all three at once:

Let's try it—let's see if we can do it. First, think of that
activating event that tends to start off that anger-causing
self-talk. [Allow 10 to 15 seconds.] Now let's start slow, deep
breathing. [Model; make sure group is breathing deeply.]
Now start counting backward from 20, silently. [Allow 10
to 15 seconds.] Now imagine your favorite peaceful scene
while breathing deeply and counting backward. [Allow 10
to 15 seconds.] Could you feel that helping? [Discuss.]

These three techniques—slow, deep breathing; counting
backward; pleasant imagery—will help you reduce those
angry body reactions. If you can, use these three things
together for maximum anger-control power. They will buy
you crucial seconds; they would have bought Gary crucial
seconds, right? Then you can start to think straight. You can
reduce your anger even more with calming self-talk and
with self-talk that corrects the errors in your thinking.

The group leader encourages participants to try these techniques
outside the group, letting them know that they will be asked during
the next session how their practice went. The leader suggests the focus
of the next session: learning two powerful self-talk techniques for
reducing anger.

Week 5—Powerful Self-Talk Techniques for Reducing Anger: Thinking Ahead to Consequences and TOP (Think of the Other Person)

OVERVIEW OF ACTIVITIES

1. Review of Week 4 session

2. Learning if-then thinking or thinking ahead to consequences

3. Learning TOP (think of the other person)

PROCEDURE AND LEADER NOTES

After a review of the previous week's relaxation techniques, the group leader returns to anger-reducing techniques that involve self-statements. One of the two self-talk techniques covered in this session has been called "if-then" thinking or "thinking ahead" (Feindler & Ecton, 1986); its importance is suggested by findings, reviewed earlier, that highly aggressive, poorly adjusted children are poorer at anticipating and describing the possible consequences of a completed action for themselves and others (Spivack & Shure, 1974, 1989). To develop an awareness of consequences, thinking ahead to consequences includes in-depth discussion of the many ramifications of aggressive or antisocial behavior (immediate and long term, practical and emotional, for self and for others). With its emphasis on consequences for others, the discussion naturally leads into a second self-talk technique that has the acronym TOP, for "think of the other person." The TOP strategy is expanded during Week 9 to include the meaning "think of the pain your actions have caused other people." At this point, the perspective taking entailed in TOP is critical for remediating egocentric bias and Self-Centered thinking errors, the primary cognitive distortion of antisocial youths. The prompts "think ahead" and "TOP" should be presented both as self-statements and as cues for young people to use with one another (along with "check yourself").

The group leader should begin by briefly reviewing the relaxation techniques learned in the previous session and asking about the group's experience with those techniques in the past week. Then the leader introduces thinking ahead:

> Today we're going to get back to self-talk techniques for reducing anger. What self-talk techniques have we learned so far? [Discuss calming self-talk and correcting thinking errors.] The self-talk techniques for today are very powerful ones. The first one is called thinking ahead, or if-then thinking. If I do this negative thing, then that negative consequence will follow, so I'd better not do it. You can use thinking ahead before you're even in a hot spot—in fact, to prevent one. For example, let's say you have a car, and it's in the repair shop, and you know you've had problems in the past when picking your car up at the repair shop. So now your car is in the shop again, and you can think ahead. You can think, When I go to pick up my car at the repair shop, it may not be ready. So you're thinking ahead to a consequence right there. And your thinking ahead might result in your thinking of something you can do right now, before you even get to the shop. What's that? [Discuss phoning ahead to make sure the car is in fact ready.] Okay, let's say they said it would be ready, but you realize that when you get to the shop you may find it still isn't. So you can think ahead: What if this happens? How will I feel? [Discuss feelings of frustration and anger.] Okay, but keep thinking ahead. Think of the possible consequences if you lose control because of that anger. Say to yourself, "Think ahead!" Think: If I lose control and blow up and haul off and slug the guy, then they'll call the police. Plus, they'll have my car! So I'd better keep my cool and remember how to express a complaint constructively, to complain in a calm and straightforward way. That's if-then thinking—that's thinking ahead.
>
> Now, in thinking ahead, you have to think of all kinds of likely consequences. For example, there are not only the first things that are likely to happen, there are also the things that are likely to happen later on. So let's say someone is teasing you, and you don't use any skills—you just lose it, and you beat the person up. What's the first thing that's likely to happen? [Discuss the likely immediate consequence—that the person will stop teasing for the moment.] But now let's keep on thinking ahead. What else might happen a little later? [Discuss the likelihood that the other person will try to hit back, will get some of his or her buddies to exact revenge, etc.] So

chances are, it's not going to end there. So in thinking ahead, you've got to think ahead long enough to think of all the consequences because you may not check yourself if you just think of some positive things that might happen first.

So you need to think ahead, both to first-off consequences and to later consequences. So far, we've talked about consequences to yourself, but it's also important to consider consequences for the other person.

At this point, the leader writes headings for two columns on the flip pad: "Consequences for Self (TOP; First and Later)" and "Consequences for Others (First and Later)," as shown in Table 4.4. The leader continues to refer to this chart to help organize the following discussion:

And this thinking ahead isn't just for anger-type situations. Let's take stealing a car. If I steal a car, chances are I'll get caught, go to court, get sent to jail, and so on. Even if I don't get caught, I could get hurt, could get killed in a bad enough accident. Can you think of any other consequences for yourself? Maybe some long-run consequences? What has happened in your life after you've done a crime? How have other people treated you afterward? Have you lost certain of your friends? Have you gotten a certain reputation you didn't really want? Have you lost the respect of some people you care about? *[Discuss.]*

TABLE 4.4

Analysis of Consequences

	Consequences for Self (First and Later)	Consequences for Others (TOP; First and Later)
General Consequences (Other Than Feelings)	*[Discuss first.]*	*[Discuss second.]*
"Feelings" Consequences	*[Discuss fourth.]*	*[Discuss third.]*

Again, it's very important to think ahead not only to consequences for yourself, but also to consequences for the other person, other people. Thinking of the other person is so important, in fact, that we have a special name for it— TOP. Remembering TOP will help you stop. If you just think about consequences for yourself, what kind of thinking error is that? *[Discuss Self-Centered thinking errors.]* TOP means you think about the other person, about the consequences for others of your actions. What hassles will the other person have? If you steal that car, what hassles will the victim have?

As consequences to others, group members might raise job problems (time away from work and having to get to work without a car) and the hassles of talking to police, filling out insurance forms, negotiating with the insurance company if it doesn't cover the loss, and so on. Broader "spill-over" problems for family and for society also exist (e.g., people can't get insurance coverage if the companies go out of business).

It may be necessary to engage in special probing for "feelings" consequences for others:

So how would the other person feel? *[Discuss.]* What about later on—some indirect consequences? When other people who know the victim find out, how will they feel? *[Discuss how the feelings of others are like those group members have had: hurt, angry, confused, panicky, upset, depressed, wanting to get even, etc.]* And when the victim breaks the news to his family, and to close friends, how do you think they feel? *[Discuss.]* What are some more, later consequences? Will the person ever be quite the same again? *[Discuss.]* A little something inside you has been destroyed— it's gone. A little faith in people, a little trust, a little good feeling is gone. You're never quite the same again after you've been victimized. And what about all those people the victim talks to? The people who aren't there at the time but who are affected anyway—his friends, his family? *[Discuss.]* In a tiny way, even that one theft means that part of society isn't the same again. The trust that is required for society to function, one little piece of that trust for some people has been destroyed.

Finally, the leader probes for "feelings" consequences to the perpetrator of the theft:

How will you feel if you steal the car? What about in those moments when you're not making Minimizing/Mislabeling and Blaming Others thinking errors, like saying, "That jerk deserved it"? The person is no more of a jerk than you are, and he did not deserve to have you come along and make him a victim. When you're strong enough to face what you're doing and be honest with yourself, you'll feel you did a rotten thing to someone, you'll feel how you would feel if someone did that to you, you'll feel pretty rotten inside, you'll lose self-respect, you'll feel you deserve nothing but disgust from responsible people. Have you had feelings like that? *[Discuss.]*

When you tell yourself "think ahead," the consequences you're thinking ahead to are all of the kinds we've talked about. It's important to think ahead to consequences for yourself, but it's especially important to think ahead to consequences for others, to think "TOP." We're going to have more to say about TOP in a later session. There's lots of self-talk you can use, not only "think ahead," but "TOP," "check yourself," and "check your thoughts." These self-talk phrases can stop behavior that hurts others or yourself before it starts. Use these phrases not only to help yourself but also to help a fellow group member. And don't wait to use these aids until you're about to commit a harmful act or crime; by then it might be too late. Use them to stop yourself even from dwelling on harmful thoughts. What happens if you choose not to stop those thoughts? *[Discuss.]* That's right—sooner or later you'll probably choose to do the crime.

Week 6 — Constructive Consequences

OVERVIEW OF ACTIVITIES

1. Review of Week 5 session
2. Negative consequences of anger (put-downs and threats)
3. Use of "I" statements instead of "you" statements (put-downs and threats)
4. Use of "I" statements in Expressing a Complaint Constructively

PROCEDURE AND LEADER NOTES

In the AMBC anatomy of anger and aggression, M (or mind activity) has received most of the attention. In this context, group members have learned and practiced several kinds of anger-reducing self-statements: calming, correcting, and if-then thinking or thinking ahead. They have also learned to reduce anger through activities with minimal cognitive involvement, such as deep breathing and counting backward. The A and the B of AMBC have also been discussed, but mainly in terms of the point that the body is reacting not directly to the activating event but instead to the meaning attached to that event by the mind activity. Week 6 moves the anger management curriculum along to the C in the acronym. Group members learn that using the anger-reducing and cognition-correcting techniques enables them to stay calm and think straight and that calm, straightforward thinking enables them to engage in calm, straightforward behavior that leads to constructive rather than destructive consequences. Operationally, group members learn to replace "you" statements (put-downs and threats) with "I" statements. Use of this skill is linked with a constructive social skill, Expressing a Complaint Constructively; this linkage reinforces the connection between the anger management and the social skills component of the EQUIP curriculum, detailed in chapter 5. The session concludes with a discussion of the difference between making a threat and stating a consequence.

Following a review of the anger "anatomy" learned so far, the group leader should relate destructive consequences to "you" statements and explain in contrast how "I" statements typically lead to more positive consequences:

> We've spent most of our time on the M in AMBC. We have also talked about the body reaction and the activating event,

or hot spot. We said that the body that's getting angry is reacting to . . . what? *[Review the point that mind activity is so crucial because the body reacts directly to that, not to the activating event.]* But we have not said anything about the C yet. *[Review the meaning of C in AMBC and stress that an angry mind and body will, if untreated with the techniques learned, lead sooner or later to destructive consequences.]* In other words, if you've allowed yourself to get too upset to think straight, then you're going to start to say some destructive things. There are basically two kinds of destructive things you say when you're angry: put-downs and threats. For example, let's say you loaned somebody your radio, and now you want it back, and the person keeps not returning it, so when you see the person you say, "Hey, jerk, you better give me back my radio if you know what's good for you!" Where was the put-down? Where was the threat? *[Discuss.]*

Put-downs and threats are "you" statements: "*You* jerk. *You'd* better do this or else." They are destructive because they attack the other person and provoke fights. Instead of being destructive we want to be constructive, and we do this by replacing those "you" statements with "I" statements. Telling someone how you feel—like "I'm feeling pretty upset about this"—involves an "I" statement. An "I" statement makes a constructive suggestion: I would like you to do this instead. "I" statements were part of a social skill we learned. Do you remember what social skill that was? *[Discuss the skill Expressing a Complaint Constructively, which participants should remember from Week 1 of social skills equipment; see chapter 5.]*

If you've been using your anger reducers in hot spots, then you should be calm and straightthinking enough to express yourself in a calm, straightforward way. Is your tone of voice threatening when you express a complaint constructively? *[Discuss the calm, constructive tone used in this social skill.]* Now, the first step in Expressing a Complaint Constructively was to state to yourself what the problem was, how you were feeling about it, and whether you were partly responsible for the problem. The second step was to make plans for expressing your complaint, like deciding what person you were going to complain to and what you were going to say. The third step was when you actually role-played Expressing a Complaint Constructively. And there were three things you did as part of that step: You told the person what the problem was, how you felt about it, and what you'd like done about it. For example, if someone has borrowed your radio and still hasn't given it back, you can say, "Joe, you borrowed my radio, and I'm getting upset because it was a while ago. I'd like it back now." What "I" statements do you hear there? [Discuss.] And you say this in what kind of way? [Discuss calm, straightforward delivery.] A final part of the third step said: "If you've contributed to the problem, mention how you may be partly at fault and what you are willing to do." If you told Joe he could borrow the radio for as long as he liked, you would say as part of that step something like: "I know I told you that you could keep it as long as you liked, but it turns out I miss it more than I thought." What's constructive about saying that? [Discuss the value of showing that you understand the other person's point of view for encouraging the other person to listen to your point of view.]

But still, it may not always work. So then what? If the other person continues to violate your rights or ignores legitimate points, the nice thing about starting out low-key is that you still have room to gradually firm up your position—without becoming destructive. You still don't threaten. But you do— in a calm, straightforward way—tell the other person what the consequences will be if the situation is not resolved satisfactorily. If you say it in a menacing tone of voice, trying to use fear to get your way, you are being threatening, and the other person could be provoked into even worse actions. Besides, the person would probably like nothing better than to see you lose control. To be effective, the consequence should be realistic—something you are willing to carry out. That's the difference between stating a consequence and making a threat: It's the difference between staying calm and being angry, between saying something realistic and saying something crazy. Like with the radio, you can gradually escalate. If you keep meeting with resistance after you've tried the calm, straightforward approach, you could say, "I asked you to return my radio." Finally, you could say, "I want my radio now." Calmly and with a matter-of-fact tone of voice, state the consequence: "If you don't give me my radio now, I will tell staff." Is that different from a threat? How? [Discuss.]

Week 7—Self-Evaluation

OVERVIEW OF ACTIVITIES

1. Review of Week 6 session
2. Self-evaluation statements (self-reward, constructive self-criticism)
3. Self-evaluation and correction of thinking errors

PROCEDURE AND LEADER NOTES

Week 7 moves the anger management curriculum beyond the AMBC model to consider the role of self-statements once an AMBC cycle is completed. Whereas calming self-talk (Week 2) was self-instructional, the self-statements covered in Week 7 are self-evaluative. Group members should already be familiar with self-evaluation thanks to the self-help daily logs (see Figures 4.3., 4.4, and 4.5), which entail both anger rating and identification of thinking errors. The self-reflection required for self-evaluation provides an excellent prelude to the more metacognitive or consciousness-raising material encountered in the remaining sessions.

The leader begins with a review of the previous session, which focused on the C of AMBC, then reviews the way to achieve constructive consequences: by replacing "you" statements or put-downs and threats with "I" statements, as in Expressing a Complaint Constructively.

The leader then introduces the main topic of the session:

The anger management skill for today goes beyond consequences—it's something you should do after the consequences, after an incident is over one way or the other. And it's something you've already been doing on your daily logs: self-evaluation. Where have you been rating yourself on the logs? [Discuss the anger and coping behavior evaluations.] On the logs, you did only number evaluations, however. You really should do more than just that. If you gave yourself a 4 or a 5 ("well" or "great") for the way you handled yourself in a situation, then give yourself rewarding self-talk, a kind of mental pat on the back—like "Hey, I really kept cool" or "I handled that one pretty well" or "I'm doing better at this all the time." [See Table 4.1 for additional self-talk *examples.]* If you didn't handle the situation well, give yourself constructive feedback on what you can do to handle a situation better the next time—like "Next time I'll notice my early warning signs sooner, like my tense face or my angry self-talk." You may also need to tell yourself other constructive things, like what thinking errors you were making in the situation and what you need to tell yourself next time to talk back to those thinking errors. *[Discuss how Gary, even after stabbing his girlfriend, could do a constructive self-evaluation and practice telling himself the truth so that he wouldn't hurt someone again.]* Don't mislabel yourself a failure if you don't control your anger perfectly overnight. Instead, stay constructive. What can you do differently and how can you do better next time? Is there any technique you can use from what you've been learning in anger management? Part of your self-evaluation should be something like this: "These are tough situations—they take time to learn how to straighten out" or "I'll be better at this when I get more practice."

Week 8 —Reversing

OVERVIEW OF ACTIVITIES

1. Review of Week 7 session
2. Things one does that make other people angry: realizing how one aggravates others (correcting for a Self-Centered tendency)
3. What to say when a group member makes a Blaming Others error

PROCEDURE AND LEADER NOTES

Much of the material in the remaining three anger management sessions is designed to be metacognitive or consciousness-raising, especially as therapy for Self-Centered attitudes in anger and for Blaming Others tendencies generally. Week 8 shifts the perspective from oneself as the victim of provocations to oneself as a provocateur of others. The focus, then, is on group members' tendencies to ignore their own provocations and to blame others totally when they are in fact partly at fault—that is, to make Self-Centered and Blaming Others errors. Each group member suggests two things he or she does to aggravate or hurt others. (The daily logs shown in Figures 4.3, 4.4, and 4.5 may be helpful in this connection.) Group members discuss how to correct their Self-Centered and Blaming Others thinking errors, and they practice "reversing" techniques for helping group members who inappropriately blame others.

The leader begins with a recap of the previous week's work, then shifts the focus:

> This week in anger management, we're going to take a slightly different angle on things. Up until this week, when we've talked about activating events, we've talked about the things other people do to make you angry, the hot spot you're in because of someone else's Aggravates Others problem. It was always that other person. But someone's got to be that other person; most of us are that other person at least sometimes. So think about when *you're* that other person. In fact, if you're that other person a lot more often than you think, then what kind of thinking error are you making?

This introduction encourages discussion of Self-Centered attitudes in terms of emphasizing others' roles in provocations but ignoring one's own. It is helpful in this regard for the leader to remind the group of Gary and review how Gary ignored what he did to make his girlfriend, Cecilia, angry in the first place.

The leader next brings up the Blaming Others thinking error:

> If you blame the other person when you should be at least partly blaming yourself, what kind of thinking error is that? *[Discuss Blaming Others.]* You see, anger isn't just a problem of what others do to anger us and how we should reduce our anger and express a complaint constructively; it's also a problem because of things we do to make other people angry. We may tend to ignore the times we tease people or threaten them in some way or start rumors about them. That's where the daily logs can be helpful, to give you a chance to slow down, remember such times, and report when you've aggravated or otherwise harmed someone.

> So what do you do that amounts to someone else's activating event, someone else's hot spot? What have you done lately, or what did you do in the past? Look back at your daily log or ask the group. *[Distribute copies of Figure 4.6 or write the information presented there on the flip pad.]*

> As with the self-evaluation that we learned about last week, the aim here is to be constructive. Once you're more aware

FIGURE 4.6
Things You Do That Make Other People Angry

Name_____

Date_____

List two things you do that make other people angry or two things you have done that made someone else feel hurt or angry.

1. _____

_____

2. _____

_____

of how you aggravate others—or how you're partly at fault when others are aggravating you—you're in a position to do something about it. How did we say that Gary should talk back to his Self-Centered thinking error? *[Review Gary's taking his girlfriend's point of view and telling himself the truth: that she has a legitimate right to be upset and expect better treatment.]* And how did we say that Gary should talk back to his Blaming Others thinking error? *[Review Gary's telling himself the truth: that he started the provocations and that grabbing the knife was his choice.]* Now let's say a group member makes a Blaming Others thinking error, not silently but out loud. How would the group "talk back" to the group member to correct that Blaming Others thinking error?

The leader next distributes the Reversing exercise (Figure 4.7) and helps the group process it:

The first three thinking error examples are answered for us. *[Discuss.]* What about the next one? What would you say? *[Read and discuss each subsequent example.]*

FIGURE 4.7
Reversing

1. The group member says: "I don't have any problems. You jerks are the ones with the problem, man. The only problem I have is you dummies keep hassling me, man."

   You say: "You know, it'll be great when you get the courage to face your problems. Then you'll thank people trying to help you instead of putting them down and blaming them."

2. The group member says: "I got in trouble because both my parents are alcoholic and don't care about me."

   You say: "You mean that all people with parents who have problems go out and hurt people?"

3. The group member says: "It's all my mother's fault I'm in here. They never would have caught me if she didn't tell the police I was stealing."

Figure 4.7 (continued)

You say: "Did your mother do the stealing? Did anybody force you to steal? No? So whose fault is it, really, that you're in here?"

4. The group member says: "My friends talked me into it, it's their fault. I just got mixed up with the wrong guys."

   You say:

5. The group member says: "I got in trouble because both my parents did drugs and neglected me."

   You say:

6. The group member says: "I don't feel like playing basketball. They never pass the ball to me."

   You say:

7. The group member says: "He was asking for it. He kept fooling."

   You say:

8. The group member says: "The guy left his car unlocked. A fool like that deserved to get his car stolen."

   You say:

Week 9—More Consequences for Others
—Correcting Distorted Self-Views

OVERVIEW OF ACTIVITIES

1. Review of Week 8 session

2. Empathy for victims and awareness of the self as one who has harmed innocent people

3. Discussion of TOP as "think of the pain your actions have caused other people"

PROCEDURE AND LEADER NOTES

Week 9 continues to raise consciousness. In the previous session, group members became more aware of the ways in which they aggravate others and attempt to escape accountability by blaming others. "Telling themselves the truth" meant admitting to themselves their acts of provocation. The present session broadens the referent for this awareness from acts of provocation to any acts of victimization. Week 9 accomplishes this consciousness raising through use of an empathy-inducing exercise. This material expands upon not only the previous week but also the Week 5 discussion of thinking ahead to consequences for others. Consequences for victims are discussed systematically, and emotional consequences are reemphasized. TOP, or "think of the other person," is discussed again, this time as "think of the pain your actions have caused others." Participants are urged to imagine themselves in the place of their victims (cf. Yochelson & Samenow, 1977, chap. 9). In the discussion of "victimizers" and "victims," the point is made that victimizing others because you were a victim is a Blaming Others thinking error. The discussion concludes with personal applications, as group members come to grips with the extent of their victimization of others (cf. California Department of the Youth Authority, 1994).

The leader begins with a recap of Week 8 and lets the group know that this session will provide more ways to take the perspective of others—specifically, of their victims.

> First of all, what is a victim? [*Discuss "victim" as someone who is unfairly hurt by someone else.*] What is a victimizer? [*Discuss*

"victimizer" as someone who hurts others, especially someone who unfairly hurts another person or people.] We have a good list of victimizing behaviors right in this room. *[Point to the problem list, as shown in Table 1.1.]* Included on that list are some self-victimizing behaviors. Where are they?

In response to this question, EQUIP group members have been able to point to Low Self-Image, Alcohol or Drug Problem, and Inconsiderate of Self.

The group leader next invites group members to consider a concrete situation involving victims and victimizers. The leader distributes the Victims and Victimizers exercise (Figure 4.8) and encourages the group to discuss the questions presented there. Question 4 is especially good for stimulating awareness of the permanent psychological harm that can result from victimization (some group members have explained articulately why getting insurance payments may *not* "make the situation all right" again). Consequences to victims are then discussed systematically in question 5; this discussion should be related to the Week 5 discussion of thinking ahead to consequences for others. EQUIP groups have illustrated the question 5 categories as follows:

In body: Disfigured, bruised, broken bones, bloodied, heart attacks, loss of senses, beaten, raped

In mind: Fear, apprehension, insecurity, loss of control over life, loss of concentration, confusion, thoughts of losing life, trauma, anxiety, irritability, guilt, grief over losing something personally meaningful, embarrassment, positive thoughts changing to negative thoughts, reliving of victimization, lack of trust, emotionally guarded, paranoid or uncontrollable emotions

In money: Loss of job, unpaid bills, loss of money, cost to replace lost or damaged things, court costs, medical costs

In daily living: Loss of sleep, disrupted schedule, can't get to work, loss of appetite, anxiety caused by red tape, increased stress/strain problems, health problems

With their friends: Isolated from others, teased by others, ignored, family stress, family problems

Question 7 provides an opportunity to broaden the discussion:

Remember TOP, from a few weeks ago? Who remembers what TOP stands for? *[Discuss how "think of the other person"*

FIGURE 4.8
Victims and Victimizers

You are attending a family wedding when you are asked to drive your grandparents home. Your grandparents have lived in that home for many years. You arrive home and help your grandparents into the house. When you open the front door you see that the house has been broken into. Many of your grandparents' things have been thrown all around. Their crystal glasses have been smashed. Their family photo album has been destroyed. Some of their things, like a wedding ring that belonged to your great grandmother, have been stolen.

1. What would be the first thing that you would do?

2. How do you think you would be feeling? Have you ever had anything stolen from you? How did you feel? Does that help you understand how your grandparents feel?

3. Would you leave your grandparents in the house alone for the night? Why or why not? Do you think your grandparents would feel afraid or worried? When have you felt afraid or worried? Does that help you understand how your grandparents feel?

4. Do you think your grandparents will get their things back? Do you think insurance (if they have any) can make the situation all right? Why or why not?

5. Who are the victims in this situation? Can you think of any long-run or indirect victims? List some ways that victims suffer (in body, in mind, in money, in daily living, with their friends).

6. Who are the main victimizers in this situation? If a victimizer were to think ahead to the many ways a victim would suffer, would he still go ahead and do the crime?

7. Have you been a victim? From whom? Have you victimized others? Whom have you victimized? Do most people who have been victimized go on to victimize others? Which have you been more of, victim or victimizer?

is informed by the previous list of ways victims suffer.] TOP also stands for something else, something I'll tell you about after we talk about question 7.

> In general, how have you been a victim in your life? From parents? Friends? Teachers? Police? *[Discuss.]* Okay, now how have you been a victimizer? Of your family? Friends? Teachers? Society? *[Discuss. Ask group members whether their victims have suffered in some of the ways previously listed.]* Do you think most people who have been victims become victimizers? *[Discuss the fact that although some do, many don't.]* So can you use the fact that you've been a victim as an excuse for going out and victimizing others?

The group leader underscores the point that group members' own victimization does not mean that they have to victimize others; if that were true, then every victim would become a victimizer. The leader also points out that such an excuse is a Blaming Others thinking error: One is in effect blaming innocent people for what someone else did.

> Which do you think you have been more, a victim or a victimizer? *[Discuss.]*

It is typical for many EQUIP group members to conclude that they have victimized others more than they have been victims—an excellent prelude to the final session.

The group leader continues by expanding the meaning of TOP from "think of the other person" to include "think of the pain your actions have caused other people."

> TOP also stands for "think of the *pain* your actions have caused other people." This is self-evaluation on a big scale— evaluating your life, how you've harmed others, where you want to go from here. In the Alcoholics Anonymous 12-step program, this step is called "taking a searching and fearless moral inventory." Now instead of thinking ahead, you're thinking back. And that's the best way to think ahead to consequences for others—to think *back* to how your past irresponsible behavior has harmed them. Imagine yourself as your victim—the pain, how it feels. Continue to think TOP, to think of the other person *and* the pain you've caused, to stop yourself before you harm yourself or someone else again.

> One man saved his life by using TOP. He had a drinking problem and was about to backslide, to take another drink.

Before he did, he thought about how when he was drinking he beat his wife and kids, and bought booze with the money his family desperately needed. His wife had left him. Now his wife was giving him another chance, trusting him to mean what he said about becoming responsible and helping his family. He was thinking ahead to what could happen if he took that drink. And he was thinking TOP. Do you think he took that drink? *[Discuss.]* That's right, he didn't. *[See Yochelson & Samenow, 1977, pp. 333–334.]*

Week 10—More Correction
of Distorted Self-Views
—Grand Review

OVERVIEW OF ACTIVITIES

1. Review of Week 9 session

2. Awareness of self-centered self-views

3. Grand review

4. Commitment to use the skills learned for managing anger and correcting thinking errors

PROCEDURE AND LEADER NOTES

The final anger management session consummates the personal consciousness raising of the previous two sessions. The concluding focus of Week 9, on group members' victimizations, is maintained and made the main focus of Week 10, which explores the distorted mind that makes possible a life of crime. The aim of the session is to induce empathy-based guilt and a genuine commitment to develop—with the positive peer group's help—the mind and life of a responsible person. Week 10 concludes with a grand review of key points in the anger management program.

The leader begins the final anger management session with a review of the key points of the previous session: the many ways in which acts of victimization harm others, the fact that most victims are not in turn victimizers, the error of thinking that having been a victim entitles one to victimize (a Blaming Others thinking error), and the acknowledgment by many group members that they have been victimizers more than victims. The leader then suggests that the group explore the mind of the victimizer more fully, not in order to feel bad but, more positively, to understand what must change:

> There's a psychologist named Stanton Samenow who has written about victimizers. He calls them criminals. And he claims that there's such a thing as a criminal mind, that it's because of the criminal mind that there's crime. Let's study an excerpt from one of Dr. Samenow's books, *Inside the*

Criminal Mind. Dr. Samenow is describing the minds of
people who make victimizing others into a way of life, so
I've put the word *victimizer* where he had *criminal*.

To process The Mind of a Victimizer exercise (Figure 4.9), the leader
asks a group member to read the initial quotation aloud to the
group. The leader then asks a different group member to read each
question, and the group discusses.

Our EQUIP groups have correctly identified the mind of the victimizer as Self-Centered and have acknowledged that the description
matches the way they think or have thought in the past. In response to
question 2, they have described their attitudes as follows: "If I like it, I
deserve to have it"; "I want it, so I'll take it"; "If I can't buy it, I'll steal it";
"I need it more than they do—they're rich enough to get another one";
"Fuck that person"; "I'm cool, I'm smart, I can get away with it." The
phrase "earthly life" has proved useful as a cue for expanding the intro-
spection into a kind of life review in which one's life is seen for the
first time in its true light. Responses to question 3 have been that the
responsible person may feel anger, may feel sorry for victimizers, and
may feel that victimizers can't be trusted. Question 4 returns to the TOP
theme: Think of the other person and the pain your actions have
caused other people. When question 4 is discussed, it is important
to stress that, although the group can help its members, only they can
really make the change and the change must be in both mind and
behavior. The change process should be appealingly labeled as not for
the wishy-washy, as a tough, long-haul effort, and so on.

The session concludes with a grand review of the key points of
anger management: the benefits of managing one's anger for gaining
control and having behavioral options; the reaction of the body directly
to the mind and only indirectly to the event; the violence stemming
from Gary's thinking errors; the use of anger reducers (using calming
and correcting self-talk, counting backward, breathing deeply, invoking peaceful imagery, thinking ahead, TOP); the use of "I" statements
rather than "you" statements in constructive social skills; the role of
self-evaluation; the myriad ways in which victimizing harms others;
the importance of telling oneself the truth about one's victimizing;
and the need to make a commitment to develop, with the group's
help, the mind and life of a responsible person.

FIGURE 4.9
The Mind of a Victimizer

The [victimizer] believes that he is entitled to whatever he desires. . . . Wherever the [victimizer] is—[walking] down the street, buying groceries at the supermarket, driving in rush hour traffic, riding the elevator to his apartment—he [sees] other people and property as opportunities for conquest. The sports car parked by the curb with the keys in the ignition could be his for the taking. The purse dangling from the supermarket cart is a tempting target. The bank he passes looks like an easy hit. . . . Put a [victimizer] and a responsible person in the gift department of a department store and ask each as he comes out to recount his thoughts while there. The responsible person comments on the attractiveness, quality, and price of the merchandise, and perhaps on the efficiency of the service. In addition, he may describe a pretty salesperson or customer and recount a conversation overheard. The [victimizer] notices little of this. He determines the best means to gain access to the merchandise as well as to customers' purses, wallets, and other personal belongings. He also notices the location of the cash register, the security arrangements, and the location of the nearest exit. In addition, he regards any attractive woman as his for the taking.

—From *Inside the Criminal Mind*, by S. E. Samenow (1984, pp. 96–97)

1. Do these words describe how you think when you are on the outside, as you are walking down the street, driving in a car, shopping in the supermarket or department store? What thinking error do the above words describe? If you think like a victimizer, you will act like a victimizer.

2. In general, what has been your attitude toward other people and their property as you have gone through your earthly life? How have you treated people?

3. Most people try to be responsible, but some people don't care—they victimize others to get what they want. When a responsible person is hurt by a victimizer, how does the responsible person feel about the victimizer? In general, what should society do with victimizers?

4. Think about other people you have victimized, the suffering you caused them—how do you feel? Do you want to change, to develop the mind and life of a responsible person? Can the group help you to change? Who has to make the choice to change, the effort to change?

Chapter 5

Equipping with
Social Skills

Social skills typically mean balanced and constructive behavior in difficult interpersonal situations. An example is the behavior of a youth
who deals constructively with deviant peer pressure by suggesting a
nondeviant alternative or one who calmly and sincerely offers clarification and/or apologizes to an angry accuser. Social skills contribute to a constructive C (for consequences) in the AMBC anatomy
of anger and aggression presented in chapter 4. That chapter dealt with
thinking skills for reducing anger in activating or "hot" situations,
skills that are crucial for the obvious reason that constructive behavior is virtually impossible as long as rage grows instead of declines.
Anger management alone, however, is not sufficient. EQUIP youths
who can think—and even think straight—before acting may still
need to learn the steps of constructive social action if they are to be
effective in helping themselves and fellow group members. The
steps of responsible social behavior are the focus of this chapter.

SOCIAL SKILLS

We begin by describing the role of social skills in the displacement
of aggression and the development of balanced perspective taking.
In this light, social skill deficiencies are conceptualized as "unbalanced" behavior. The prevalence of social skill deficiencies among
antisocial youths underscores the need for providing social skills as
a component of the EQUIP curriculum.

Social Skills Displacing Aggressive Behavior

The key to anger management, as presented in chapter 4, is engage-
ment in activities incompatible with anger. This principle is clearest
in physical terms: The use of slow, deep breathing substitutes for
rapid, shallow breathing and tends to counteract the other early
warning signs (rapid heartbeat, flushed face, clenched fists, etc.) of a

risky bodily reaction to angry mind activity. The same principle is at work elsewhere in anger management: For example, constructive mind activity (calming self-talk, accurate thinking, thinking ahead) tends to displace erroneous anger-generating or criminogenic thinking. Especially relevant to the mastery of social skills is the technique of thinking ahead to consequences; as we will see, thinking ahead is often explicitly incorporated into social skills training as one of the steps of constructive social action. Also relevant to social skills is Week 6 of the EQUIP anger management component, on constructive consequences. In this session the group analyzes a social skill, Expressing a Complaint Constructively, using the incompatibility principle: Group members practice using "I" statements as substitutes for high-risk "you" statements.

The social skills component continues the displacement of out-of-control destructive responses by incompatible constructive ones. However, whereas anger management techniques remain largely cognitive (self-talk), social skills focus mainly on overt behavior or performance. McFall (1982) defined social skills as "specific abilities that enable a person to perform competently at particular social tasks" (p. 23). Carducci (1980) referred to deficiencies in competent social performance in his observation that antisocial adolescents "do not know what specific steps are involved in constructive social problem solving" (p. 158), an observation corroborated by research on this population (Dubow & Tisak, 1989; Rubin & Krasnor, 1985; Spivack & Shure, 1974). For example, Akhtar and Bradley (1991) concluded that "'aggressive' or 'acting out' children are aware of fewer individual steps (means) in problem-solving, mention fewer potential obstacles, and are less cognizant of the importance of the passage of time" (p. 628). Hence, social skills equipment presents constructive social action in terms of step-by-step performance; these steps are modeled by the leader (in this case, the equipper) and then imitated by group members as they role-play realistic "hot spots" or tense social situations.

Like moral education and anger management, social skills training equips the group to help its members more effectively during mutual help meetings. Some social skills, such as Helping Others, Expressing Care and Appreciation, and Caring for Someone Who Is Sad or Upset, contribute to the behaviors needed for the EQUIP group to be a safe, supportive environment for its members. Other skills, such as Dealing Constructively with Negative Peer Pressure, can be helpful as the group tries to help a member solve a reported problem such as Easily Misled. Skills such as Keeping Out of Fights, Dealing Constructively with Someone Angry at You, Dealing Constructively with Someone Accusing You of Something, and Expressing a Complaint

Constructively are valuable tools for addressing Easily Angered and Authority Problems and even for helping the group remain constructive when tensions run high (cf. Prothrow-Stith, 1987).

The 10 social skills in the EQUIP curriculum, adapted from Goldstein and Glick's (1987) Aggression Replacement Training, address the interpersonal skill needs most in evidence among juvenile offenders. Many of those youths could also benefit from remediation in a wide range of skill areas. The 10 EQUIP social skills are included in but far from exhaust an array of 50 social skills available in Goldstein's (1988) Prepare Curriculum (e.g., Starting a Conversation, Asking Permission, and Concentrating on a Task). The 50 Prepare social skills are listed in Table 5.1; those adapted for EQUIP are indicated by boldface type. Groups with sufficient time and interest can supplement their core EQUIP curriculum skill learning by also learning some of the Prepare Curriculum skills.

Social Skills and Social Perspective Taking

Teaching the steps of constructive social action can in part be construed as practical training in taking the perspectives of others in specific social situations (Little & Kendall, 1979). Indeed, Platt and Spivack (1973) found that role taking loaded on the same factor as means-ends thinking in a factor analysis of the components of social problem solving. Platt, Spivack, Altman, Altman, and Peizer (1974) suggested that such a finding was "not surprising since seeing complex relationships among people and events as one develops a course of action is a necessary ingredient to developing a successful plan" (p. 792). In our terms, equipping with social skills means, at least in part, practical or behavior-oriented training to reduce egocentric bias or correct thinking errors such as Self-Centered. While asserting his or her own legitimate expectations, the socially skilled individual also spontaneously considers—and communicates—the other person's viewpoint, feelings, and legitimate expectations in the course of the social interaction episode.

We can illustrate the notion of social skills training as practical social perspective taking training with the steps used to present the first EQUIP social skill, Expressing a Complaint Constructively. The following skill steps operationalize perspective taking in specific interpersonal situations involving the need to express a complaint.

> *Step 1:* Identify the problem. How are you feeling? What
> is the problem? Who is responsible for it? Did you
> contribute—or are you contributing—to the problem
> in any way?

TABLE 5.1

Prepare Curriculum Interpersonal Skills List

GROUP I: BEGINNING SOCIAL SKILLS

1. Listening
2. Starting a Conversation
3. Having a Conversation
4. Asking a Question
5. Saying Thank You
6. Introducing Yourself
7. Introducing Other People
8. Giving a Compliment

GROUP II: ADVANCED SOCIAL SKILLS

9. Asking for Help
10. Joining In
11. Giving Instructions
12. Following Instructions
13. Apologizing
14. Convincing Others

GROUP III: SKILLS FOR DEALING WITH FEELINGS

15. Knowing Your Feelings
16. Expressing Your Feelings
17. **Understanding the Feelings of Others**
18. **Dealing with Someone Else's Anger**
19. **Expressing Affection**
20. Dealing with Fear
21. Rewarding Yourself

GROUP IV: SKILL ALTERNATIVES TO AGGRESSION

22. Asking Permission
23. Sharing Something
24. **Helping Others**
25. Negotiating
26. Using Self-Control
27. Standing Up for Your Rights

Step 2: Plan and think ahead. To whom should you express your complaint? When? Where? What will you say (see step 3)?

Step 3: State your complaint. In a calm, straightforward way, tell the person the problem and how you feel about it. If you've contributed to the problem, mention how you may be partly at fault and what *you* are willing to do.

Step 4: Make a constructive suggestion. Tell the person what you would like done about the problem. Ask the other person if he or she thinks your suggestion is fair. If the *other* person makes a constructive suggestion, say that you appreciate the suggestion or that it sounds fair.

An EQUIP youth named Joe role-played such a situation "between me and my father . . . him always wanting to go to the bar instead of spending time talking to me." Going through the steps, he reported that he was feeling "angry". His father was responsible for the problem, although Joe himself did contribute to the problem in trying to avoid it—for example, by "running off and partying" (step 1). Joe planned to bring the matter up when his dad was "at home when he's in a good mood and just say it in a polite way" (step 2). A very touching role-play followed: After acknowledging his own contribution to the problem, Joe constructively expressed the complaint to his "dad" (a fellow group member):

> Dad, I'd like to talk to you about how you like to go to the bar and not spend time with me. I feel that I'm coming home from school and you're at the bar and I'm upset about something and want to talk to you and you're not there to talk to me.

Joe and his "dad" worked out times when "Dad" agreed to be home and available (step 3). Furthermore, "Dad" agreed that Joe's complaint and suggestion were fair, and Joe said that he appreciated "Dad's" responsiveness (step 4).

Perspective taking played a major role in the execution of the social skill: Joe considered the moment when his "dad" would be approachable, anticipated and accepted his "dad's" likely viewpoint by acknowledging at the outset his own runaway behavior, listened openly to his "dad's" ideas as an understanding was reached, solicited his "dad's" feelings about the agreement, and expressed appreciation for his "dad's" cooperation. Spontaneous perspective taking occurred, then, not just once but repeatedly throughout the episode. Such varied proactive and reactive perspective taking illustrates the important point that a social skill is not a single "snapshot" act but rather an ongoing ability to negotiate an evolving social interaction episode. Indeed, "Equipping with Social *Interaction* Skills" would be a more precise title for this chapter.

Joe's social interaction role-play was followed by discussion. The group told Joe that he had done well on all the steps. The group leader pointed out that Expressing a Complaint Constructively was not always going to work out so well in real life. However, constructive behavior was seen to be superior to the Self-Centered alternatives of either running out or hurling put-downs and threats, which group members agreed were less promising approaches.

Social Skill Deficiencies as "Unbalanced" Behavior: Assessment and Treatment

Research on social skills has generally found deficiencies among antisocial youths relative to control groups. Freedman, Rosenthal, Donahoe, Schlundt, and McFall (1978) found evidence of extensive social skill deficits or deficiencies among male incarcerated juvenile offenders in a study of a then-new measure, the Adolescent Problems Inventory (API). Lower API scores were found not only for the delinquents overall but also for a delinquent subgroup that frequently violated institutional rules. Relations between social skill deficits and antisocial behavior were replicated by Dishion, Loeber, Stouthamer-Loeber, and Patterson (1984) but not by Hunter and Kelly (1986). Simonian, Tarnowski, and Gibbs (1991) corrected for a procedural flaw in the Hunter and Kelly study and used a new measure, the Inventory of Adolescent Problems–Short Form (IAP-SF; see Appendix B). The IAP-SF represented a streamlined and adapted derivative of the API as well as of the Problem Inventory for Adolescent Girls (Gaffney & McFall, 1981). Using the IAP-SF, Simonian et al. found that social skills did correlate inversely with numerous indices of antisocial behavior (most serious offense committed, number of correctional facility placements, self reported alcohol problems, and AWOL attempts and successes).

Although social skills involve taking the perspective of another person, that perspective taking should not exclude one's own perspective. Social skills may be characterized as behavior conducive to achieving a balance between respect for one's own personhood (one's rights, expectations, feelings, etc.) and respect for the personhood of another; hence, socially skilled behavior is "neither aggressive nor obsequious" (Carducci, 1980, p. 161; cf. Jakubowski & Lange, 1978). In Positive Peer Culture (PPC) terms, such behavior means that one has neither an Inconsiderate of Others problem nor an Inconsiderate of Self problem. Correspondingly, Deluty (1979) conceptualized social skills as appropriately assertive responses intermediate between aggression and submission. In the role-play example, Joe's behavior was balanced and appropriately assertive: He expressed his legitimate expectation that his parent be available and responsive, but he also took his parent's perspective and showed respect in various ways.

This view of social skills provides a framework for conceptualizing socially *unskilled* behavior as unbalanced functioning in two subdomains found by Simonian et al. (1991): (1) deviant peer pressure, wherein unskilled behavior is inappropriately submissive or avoidant and tantamount to disrespect for self (cf. Easily Misled or Inconsiderate of Self in the PPC problem list) and (2) anger provocation, wherein socially unskilled behavior is inappropriately aggressive and tantamount to disrespect for the other (cf. Aggravates Others, Inconsiderate of Others in the PPC problem list). Using factor analytic techniques, Simonian et al. confirmed the peer pressure subdomain and labeled it Antisocial Peer Influence ("either peer pressure to engage in serious violation of social norms/legal mandates or adult concern about negative peer influences," p. 24). The anger provocation subdomain differentiated into two factors: Immediate Response Demand ("item loadings on [this] factor required a response to social situations that tended to be anger-arousing and that presented response demands that were immediate," p. 23) and Deferred Response Demand:

> Items loading on [this] factor described situations which were similar to those of the [Immediate Response Demand] factor except that they tended to differ in the time parameter between the stressful situation (e.g., you are late for work) and the time of actual response occurrence (e.g., you know that you will need to respond to your boss's confrontation about your tardiness). In other words, these situations afforded more response planning time. (p. 23)

Simonian et al. (1991) found their male delinquent sample to be deficient in social skills in terms of all three factors. Delinquents severely deficient in social skills related to Antisocial Peer Influence were more likely to have committed serious offenses (e.g., aggravated burglary) and to have attempted, successfully or unsuccessfully, to go AWOL from the institution—consistent with "low behavioral resistance in situations of negative peer influences" (p. 24). Delinquents severely deficient in the Immediate Response Demand factor of anger provocation/aggression were also more likely to have committed serious offenses and to have had greater numbers of prior institutional placements. The Deferred Response Demand factor of anger provocation/aggression was related to alcohol/drug rehabilitation placement, prompting Simonian et al. to suggest that "drug use is potentiated under conditions of pronounced social stress where the individual has deficient social problem solving skills" (p. 24). Simonian et al.'s three factors are included in the IAP-SF as presented in Appendix B.

The IAP-SF (but without separate factor scores) was used to assess social skills gains in the Leeman et al. (1993) EQUIP evaluation study reported in chapter 1. The Freedman et al. (1978) finding was replicated: Social skills correlated with various measures of antisocial behavior (frequency of self-reported preincarceration, institutional misconduct, institutional incident reports, and unexcused school absences; see Table 5.2). Furthermore, social skills gains were greater in the EQUIP group, and social skills gains correlated with gains in self-reported institutional conduct. Finally, there was a tendency for social skills to correlate inversely with recidivism within 12 months after release, $r(53) = -.24$, $p = .084$. More mixed is the evidence for effectiveness where social skills training has been conducted in single-component programs and social skill gains measured using other instruments (Henggeler, 1989; Hollin, 1990). Chandler (1973), however, did find conduct gains attributable to situational role-play and the reduction of egocentric bias. Chalmers and Townsend (1990) found gains in prosocial behavior among delinquent adolescent females who had participated in social perspective taking training.

EQUIPMENT FOR SOCIAL INTERACTION

The EQUIP social skills are derived and adapted from Goldstein, Sprafkin, Gershaw, and Klein's (1980) Skillstreaming approach—in particular, the 10 "structured learning skills" presented in Goldstein and Glick's (1987) *Aggression Replacement Training*. Specifically, the EQUIP curriculum includes the following skills:

1. Expressing a Complaint Constructively

2. Caring for Someone Who Is Sad or Upset

3. Dealing Constructively with Negative Peer Pressure

4. Keeping Out of Fights

5. Helping Others

6. Preparing for a Stressful Conversation

7. Dealing Constructively with Someone Angry at You

8. Expressing Care and Appreciation

9. Dealing Constructively with Someone Accusing
   You of Something

10. Responding Constructively to Failure

The specific steps for these skills are presented at the end of this chapter; each skill is accompanied by a list of suggested situations in which it could be used and specific guidelines for teaching. Before teaching a given skill, the group leader will want to provide each member with a "skill card," a sheet or card on which the skill steps have been reproduced.

TABLE 5.2

Correlations between Social Skills and Conduct†

Major Variables	1	2	3	4	5	6	N	M	SD
PREINCARCERATION MISCONDUCT									
1. Self-reported	1.00 (56)	-.65*** (56)	.54*** (54)	.20 (47)	.27 (50)	.11 (47)	56	49.39	15.68
MEDIATING VARIABLE									
2. Social skills			-.48*** (54)	-.29* (53)	-.33* (53)	-.24 (53)	57	3.60	1.21
INSTITUTIONAL MISCONDUCT									
3. Self-reported				.35* (45)	.44** (48)	.16 (46)	54	16.70	5.23
4. Incident reports					.72*** (52)	.19 (46)	57	0.83	1.20
5. Unexcused school absences						.28 (47)	57	1.54	1.80
POSTRELEASE MISCONDUCT									
6. Recidivism within 12 months							56	0.34	0.48

†Social skills and self-reported institutional misconduct are based on time 1 scores. *p<.05. **p<.01. ***p<.001.

The present section describes the general procedures for equipping antisocial youths with social skills. As with other skills, people typically learn social skills in four phases: acquiring some notion of the skill by observing a model; attempting to perform the skill by imitating or role-playing what was modeled; improving one's performance through feedback concerning one's attempts; and, finally, further refining and generalizing the newfound skill by practicing it in increasingly diverse and challenging contexts. These phases of social skill learning—modeling, rehearsal, performance feedback, and practice—can be characterized to young people as "showing the skill," "trying the skill," "discussing the skill," and "practicing the skill." The procedures to be used for the social skills component of the EQUIP curriculum will be described according to these four phases, which are preceded by a general introduction to social skills learning.

General Introduction to Social Skills Learning

To begin the first session devoted to social skills, the group leader should introduce the idea of learning a skill and explain to the group the importance of practicing that skill, labeling role-play activity in appealing terms. Ideally, before the first session, the group leader will have recruited a colleague or a suitable group member as a partner for the modeling of the first social skill.

We introduce social skills with the following questions and discussion. (Indented portions of text suggested language for the leader to use; instruction or comments for the leader are bracketed and italicized.)

> How do you learn any skill? How did you learn to ride
> a bicycle? Swim? Play basketball, football? *[Discuss and*
> *write on flip pad the four phases in learning a skill: seeing*
> *someone doing the skill (show), trying to do what you saw*
> *(try), finding out what you did right and wrong and how you*
> *can do better (discuss), and then practicing the skill and seeing*
> *improvement (practice).]* Well, social skills are no different.
> Dealing constructively with negative peer pressure or with
> someone angry at you, or even caring for another group
> member, is a skill; it's not something you're born knowing
> how to do.

Either during the introductory discussion or later, if a group member challenges the need for role-playing, we also relabel the role-play in social skills learning as important:

To try to do the skill, you'll be pretending you're in a situation where you need the skill. This is called "rehearsal" or "role-play." In some part of the role-play, you'll even be talking out loud to try out the thinking that you'll do silently later as you practice. This role-play is serious business; it's the only way to learn some skills that could save your life or someone else's. Don't let anybody tell you different. Remember, learning a social skill isn't really any different from learning a skill like, say, boxing. When a boxer is getting ready for a big fight, does he ever say to his sparring partner: "Hey, this is dumb, man. You're not my opponent. This is just pretending, just playacting. This is silly. I'm not going to do this any more. I'll just wait for the real thing"? What would happen if the boxer did that? *[Discuss how the boxer would probably lose the match, just as group members would fail at positive behavior.]*

Group members are responsible for independently practicing each skill and documenting their practice on a copy of the Social Skills Practice Sheet (Figure 5.1). The group should be encouraged to discuss and agree upon ground rules, including consequences for any member who does not complete a practice follow-up and bring the practice sheet to the group meeting. The leader might ask, "What would the group expect to happen if a group member doesn't do a practice and bring in the practice sheet?" The group might then propose logical consequences such as missing a desired time slot like recreation or leisure time in order to make up the assignment. Also, the group should be encouraged to prevent such consequences by helping members to think ahead—to fulfill their responsibility by completing the practice and bringing along the completed practice sheet.

In the first session, the general introduction should take 10 to 15 minutes. In subsequent weeks, that time is used for practice reports. The group leader reviews and discusses the practice follow-ups on the previous session's skill. The leader should solicit group members' self-evaluation ratings from the practice sheets and encourage reporting of successful outcomes. If a group member has neglected to complete the follow-up and/or bring the practice sheet to group, the leader should encourage the group to recommend to staff that their agreed-upon sanction be applied to that member.

Introducing Individual Skills

Each session, the group leader introduces the target social skill by doing as follows:

FIGURE 5.1
  Social Skills Practice Sheet

Name_____ Date_____

Fill in during this meeting

　　1. Practice assignment

　　　a. Skill

　　If applicable:

　　　b. Use with whom

　　　c. Use when

　　　d. Use where

Fill in before next meeting

　　2. Describe what happened when you did the practice assignment. For example, did you skip any steps? What was the other person's reaction?

　　3. Rate yourself on how well you used the skill *(check one)*:

　　　Excellent_____　　Good_____　　Fair_____　　Poor_____

Announcing the skill to be learned during that session

Giving each group member a skill card on which the skill and its steps are listed

Discussing with the group when the skill would have been helpful in past situations, basing the discussion on group members' own experience; reading the list of suggested situations so group members get the idea

Having the group decide which members will give feedback on which skill steps (often two group members share responsibility for a given step)

Having a group member read out loud the steps of the skill while the others read along silently

At this point it is helpful to preview the remaining session activities:

Now *[a group member]* and I are going to *show [refer to flip pad]* how to do this social skill by going through these four steps. Then a group member will think of an example and *try* the skill. Then we'll *discuss* how the group member did, and then, after everyone has finished, we'll make plans to *practice* the social skill during this coming week.

Showing the Skill

Once the group has assigned responsibilities for feedback and read the skill steps, the group leader models the skill with an assistant—a colleague or a group member previously enlisted to prepare the role-play. The leader reminds the group that the first step in learning any skill is usually watching someone else do it. The leader also mentions that feedback on his or her performance of each step will be expected from the designated group members.

The group should be reminded that showing and trying the skill will often involve thinking out loud. The leader could say:

Normally, of course, we would think inside our heads, silently. It's like any other skill. At first it doesn't feel natural, and you have to do some artificial things to get the hang of it, but gradually with practice it becomes part of you and does feel natural. Then you do it automatically, without thinking out loud or thinking much at all about the steps.

In preparation for discussing the skill, the group leader then elicits comments from the group members responsible for the respective steps: "How did I do? Step 1?" and so on. Although having group members evaluate the leader's performance enhances group involvement, it entails some risk: Especially in a still immature group, a youth may misuse the feedback opportunity to put down the group leader—for instance, by rating the performance of a step as "lousy" or "pitiful." The leader's response should model social skills for the group. For example, the leader could say, "I'm sure my role-play could have been better, and I'd like to know specifically what to work on: Was part of a step missed? How in particular could the role-play have been improved?" By remaining constructive, the leader encourages the group member to give up on power games and enter into the enterprise of learning the equipment.

Trying the Skill

After the demonstration of the social skill, each member takes a turn role-playing the skill just observed. We remind group members that the next step after showing the skill is trying the skill, so it's their turn now: First, group members must think of situations in which they might need the skill. Occasionally, a person claims to be unable to think of such a situation (sometimes the claim is a subtle form of resistance to group participation). When this happens, the leader should again read (or ask a peer to read) the list of sample situations provided with each skill and give the group member permission to use one of the sample situations—preferably one relevant to the group member's problems.

For all but the skill Preparing for a Stressful Conversation, a second group member is needed as a coactor. Next, then, each group member must choose another member as a partner for the role-play. Explain that the most helpful role-play is one that is as realistic as possible; if a group member is in some way similar to the person in the actual situation, that group member should be chosen.

Finally, group members who are not participating directly in the role-play are reminded of their feedback assignments. The leader may announce the skill step numbers and ask group members to indicate their assignments by raising hands. If the leader lists the steps on the flip pad, group members can be guided by either the skill cards in their hands or by the list on the flip pad as they observe the performance of the respective steps. Their main attention, of course, should be on the role-play.

Group members take turns volunteering to role-play the social skill. In preparation, the situational context for the role-play is described. For realism, the descriptions should include the physical setting, the events immediately preceding the role-play, and the manner the coactor should display. During each role-play, the leader and the group provide whatever help, coaching, and encouragement the actors need to keep the role-play following the prescribed steps. An actor should "break role" only for prescribed reasons—for instance, to think out loud. If the role-play is clearly diverging from the skill steps, it should be stopped temporarily: The group leader should provide the needed coaching and then encourage the role-play to resume.

The role-play procedure can be even more effective if the group leader can enlist the aid of a colleague. For example, the equipper could point to the skill steps on the flip pad as the role-play unfolds, while the colleague sits with the monitoring group members and helps them remain on track.

The role-playing should continue until all group members have had an opportunity to perform the social skill. With an average-sized group of six to eight members, this can usually be accomplished in a single session. However, we have typically used social skills training as the "split" EQUIP curriculum component, with the social skills training split across two equipment meetings (see chapter 6).

Discussing the Skill

After each social skill role-play, group members provide feedback on the performance of each step. The leader should encourage the group to support the coactor and to provide feedback ("How well was step _____ followed?") for the primary person in the role-play. The feedback should be honest ("_____ needs to know what he should work on improving in the follow-up practice"); specific ("What particular things went well or were left out?"; "Exactly how could _____ have done that differently?"); and constructive (a negative comment should always be followed by a suggestion for improvement). At minimum, a poor performance can be praised as a "good try" as it is being critiqued for its real faults. Where time permits, the group should encourage the member to try again with another role-play.

In ideal circumstances, the role-plays can even be videotaped; following each role-play, the actors can observe themselves on tape. Self-observation can help the actors reflect on their own verbal and nonverbal behavior and its impact on others, and it can help their peers provide accurate feedback.

Although the social skill steps have been formulated to apply to as wide a variety of situations as possible, some elements of some steps may not be applicable to some situations proposed for the role-plays; by the same token, some situations may require elaboration of some of the steps if constructive social action is to be accomplished. In these instances, the leader and the group may work together to modify the steps.

Practicing the Skill

When all group members have completed role-plays and received feedback, the group plans for follow-up practice using the Social Skills Practice Sheet. Such constructive social behavior among group members yields the additional dividend of contributing to the group's development as a positive culture. Members are reminded to help one another complete the practice in order to avoid the agreed-upon consequences for not doing so.

Follow-up activities should always be labeled as practice rather than as homework. (The term *homework* has negative connotations and is best avoided.) While distributing the practice sheets, the leader should remind the group that one cannot learn any skill without practicing it. Whenever possible, group members should complete question 1 (parts a through d) before leaving the session. Group members complete questions 2 and 3 after they have accomplished the practice activity; they are then required to bring the completed practice sheet to the next session.

EQUIP Social Skills

Skill 1—Expressing a Complaint Constructively

Skill 2—Caring for Someone Who Is Sad or Upset

Skill 3—Dealing Constructively with Negative
Peer Pressure

Skill 4—Keeping Out of Fights

Skill 5—Helping Others

Skill 6—Preparing for a Stressful Conversation

Skill 7—Dealing Constructively with Someone
Angry at You

Skill 8—Expressing Care and Appreciation

Skill 9—Dealing Constructively with Someone
Accusing You of Something

Skill 10—Responding Constructively to Failure

Skill 1—Expressing a Complaint Constructively

SKILL STEPS

Describe the situation for the group.

Step 1

Identify the problem. How are you feeling? What is the problem? Who is responsible for it? Did you contribute—or are you contributing—to the problem in any way?

Discuss how you can recognize a problem—by how someone treats you or what they say to you; by the way you act toward someone or what you say to them; by the way you feel inside.

Step 2

Plan and think ahead. To whom should you express your complaint? When? Where? What will you say (see step 3)?

Discuss when is a good time to tell that person—when the person isn't involved with something else, when the person is alone and seems calm. Advise participants to wait until they have calmed down before approaching the person.

For steps 3 and 4, participants will need a partner.

Step 3

State your complaint. In a calm, straightforward way, tell the person the problem and how you feel about it. If you've contributed to the problem, mention how you may be partly at fault and what *you* are willing to do.

> *Point out that if the person gets angry, you can talk about the problem some other time. The person is less likely to get angry if you are strong enough to apologize for your role in the problem.*

Step 4

Make a constructive suggestion. Tell the person what you would like done about the problem. Ask the other person if he or she thinks your suggestion is fair. If the *other* person makes a constructive suggestion, say that you appreciate the suggestion or that it sounds fair.

> *Participants can mention how their suggestion would help the other person, too. To help clear up any remaining hard feelings, participants may wish to ask the person how he or she feels about the suggestion.*

SUGGESTED SITUATIONS FOR USING THIS SKILL

1. The teacher gives you an assignment that seems too difficult for you.

2. Your parents won't let you go to a movie with a friend.

3. Your friend usually chooses what the two of you will do.

4. Your friend has spread a rumor about you.

5. You are always doing the hardest work in the kitchen. None of the other workers is helping you out.

6. You just bought a pair of sneakers and left the store, and now you realize the salesperson shortchanged you.

7. You just found out who stole your sneakers.

8. You share a room at home with your brother, who is always using your things without asking you.

9. You are having lunch at the facility, and you just took the first bite of your sandwich. Something tastes really spoiled.

10. You are being restricted for being disrespectful. You feel that the staff provoked you and that the restriction is unfair.

11. Your teacher keeps giving you work that is too easy. It's the same work over and over again, and you are really bored.

12. Your counselor always seems to have time to talk with the other residents in your unit but never seems to have time to talk with you.

13. At home, your mother always wants you in by 10:30 P.M., but you don't want to come home that early.

Skill 2—Caring for Someone Who Is Sad or Upset

SKILL STEPS

Describe the situation for the group.

Step 1

Watch the person (but don't stare). Does he or she look or sound sad? Upset? How strong might the feelings be?

Participants will need to pay attention to signs that the person may be sad or upset—hunched-over posture, expression on face, tone of voice. (Maybe you know something about what's troubling the person, maybe you don't.)

Step 2

Plan and think ahead. Ask yourself: Should I walk over to the person? Now? Or later?

Emphasize that if the person seems very angry or upset, it may be best to wait until the person has calmed down.

For steps 3 and 4, participants will need a partner.

Step 3

Start a conversation. Walk over to the person. Say something like "What's up?" "How are you feeling?" "Want to talk about it?"

Step 4

Listen and "be there." Listen to what the person says. Encourage him or her to talk. Say something like "So you're kinda bummed out." After the person seems done for the time, say something like "I'll be around if you want to talk some more about it" or "Let me know if there's anything I can do."

Participants should not interrupt unless it's to encourage the person to say more.

SUGGESTED SITUATIONS FOR USING THIS SKILL

1. A neighbor's family member has been ill.

2. Your dad or mom is slamming doors and muttering to himself/herself.

3. A friend hasn't been chosen for a game, or a classmate just watches a game instead of asking to join.

4. A resident who is a friend of yours tells you that he has just received a letter from his girlfriend and she has broken up with him.

5. A friend has just told you that his brand-new sneakers have been stolen.

6. A resident you know in another unit is upset because her parents, who have promised to visit for the last 3 weeks, have not shown up.

7. A new resident in your unit is homesick.

8. A resident who is a good friend of yours tells you that he has just learned that his girlfriend is pregnant.

9. A resident in your unit has just told the unit that his mother died of cancer last night.

10. Your sister just failed her GED exam.

11. Your closest friend just found out that his parents are getting separated.

LEADER NOTE

Be particularly alert to provide coaching on step 4, listening. Many young people will move right into giving advice or suggestions, having scarcely listened. Emphasize at the outset how important it is just to listen and to restrict what you say to words that will encourage the person to elaborate on his or her feelings. Also stress the importance of being available. We were especially impressed with the following "practice" of this social skill reported by an EQUIP group member on the practice sheet:

> Mr. M. came up to me and asked about some kid we got.
> I told him everyone is messing with him. Mr. M. said,
> "Well he wants to kill himself." I went and talked to him.
> Asked what was wrong and does he want to talk? He said
> no. I said, "Well, I'm in your dorm if you ever want to talk
> or need anything."

Skill 3—Dealing Constructively with Negative Peer Pressure

SKILL STEPS

Describe the situation for the group. Have participants start role-playing the situation with the partner or partners, then freeze the role-play.

Step 1

Think, "Why?" Think about what the other person or persons are saying. What is it they want you to do? Why do they want you to do it?

Step 2

Think ahead. Think about the consequences if you do what they want you to do. Who might get hurt? How might you feel if you go along? How *should* you feel if you go along?

Step 3

Decide what you should do. What reasons will you give the person or persons (this will help with step 4)? What will you suggest to do instead (this will help with step 5)?

Instruct participants to continue the role-play.

Step 4

Tell. In a calm, straightforward way, tell one of the persons what you have decided. Give a good reason—for example, how the pressure makes you feel or who might get hurt if you do what they want.

*Encourage participants to tell their decision to one person only.
Giving a good reason for not going along may help the group
rethink what they should do.*

Step 5

Suggest something else to do. This could be something less
harmful but still enjoyable, or something responsible.

SUGGESTED SITUATIONS FOR USING THIS SKILL

1. A group is teasing someone or planning to take something
   that belongs to someone else, and they want you to go along
   with them.

2. A group is planning to vandalize a neighborhood and wants
   you to come along.

3. Three residents have just asked you to go AWOL with them.

4. Several members of your unit tell you that they're going to steal
   cigarettes from a resident who is a member of another unit, and
   they want you to be the lookout.

5. You've just been released home and it's your first week in
   school. Some of your old friends have decided that they are
   going to skip the day and not go to school. They have just asked
   you to come with them.

6. Three friends pull over in a car you think they may have stolen.
   They ask you to get in and go for a ride.

7. You are at a party at a friend's house and some of the other
   guys ask you to help search for any liquor in the house.

8. Three residents are pressuring you to goof off like they are.

9. An old friend of yours has just asked you to join him and
   another friend in snatching a purse from an old lady who is
   walking down the street.

10. Two other unit members come to you and ask you to join
    them tonight in beating up a new resident whom no one
    seems to like.

LEADER NOTE

Point out that this social skill is a crucial tool for helping group members with an Easily Misled problem. It is also important to stress that blaming irresponsible behavior on negative peer pressure involves a Blaming Others thinking error. Note also the use in step 2 of thinking ahead to consequences and TOP (anger management, chapter 4).

Skill 4—Keeping Out of Fights

SKILL STEPS

Describe the situation for the group.

Step 1

Stop and think about why you want to fight.

Tell participants that, if they need to, they can breathe deeply, count backward, or think calming thoughts to calm down. They can also consider whether they did anything to contribute to the problem.

Step 2

Think ahead. Ask yourself, "If I fight, then what will be the consequences?"

Encourage participants to remember to think about consequences for others (TOP, chapter 4), including people who are not on the scene but who will be affected later on: How will they feel? What will they do? How will you feel? What are the likely consequences later on for you?

For step 3, participants will need a partner.

Step 3

Think of a way to handle the situation besides fighting and do it. Should you walk away for now? Give a displeased look? Talk to the person in a calm, straightforward way? Ask someone for help in solving the problem?

Ask group members: "Is the other person calm enough or reasonable enough to talk to? Are you calm enough yet to talk? Who might be able to help you resolve the situation constructively (teacher, parent, friend)?" Point out that in some situations, such as self-defense or the defense of an innocent victim, you may have no choice but to fight.

SUGGESTED SITUATIONS FOR USING THIS SKILL

1. Another resident has just come up to you and demanded that you give him cigarettes.

2. You just found out who stole your sneakers.

3. Another resident has just bumped into you and made you spill your drink and drop your food tray on the floor.

4. Another resident has just directed a racial slur at you.

5. Another resident tells you he has rights to the chair you are sitting on.

6. You lost your privileges because someone told your counselor that you were smoking cigarettes in the bathroom, and you just found out who told.

7. A resident to whom you loaned a pack of cigarettes is now refusing to pay you back.

8. Your mother's boyfriend is drunk and getting a little nasty.

9. A new resident comes up to you and calls you a name.

10. In a baseball game, you have just come up to bat. The other team's pitcher calls you a chickenshit.

LEADER NOTE

If an occasion does not arise for practicing the skill, group members may be given the option of completing the Social Skills Practice Sheet with information from a past incident. Again, note the use in step 2 of the thinking ahead, TOP techniques (anger management, chapter 4).

Skill 5—Helping Others

SKILL STEPS

Describe the situation for the group.

Step 1

Think, "Is there a need?" Decide if the other person might need or want your help.

Participants will need to think about the needs of the other person: What is the person doing or saying, or what is happening, that makes you think the person needs help?

Step 2

Think of the ways you could be helpful. Which way would be best?

Encourage participants to ask: Does the person need something done? Need someone to listen? Need to hear words of encouragement? Should someone else help?

Step 3

Plan and think ahead. Ask yourself, "Is this a good time for me to offer help?"

Participants should ask themselves whether the person could use the help better later. If so, they will need to be sure they are not supposed to be doing something else at the time they offer help.

For step 4, participants will need a partner.

Step 4

Offer to help. Ask the other person, "Need some help?" or "Want some help?" or go ahead and offer to help in some way. If the other person says yes, follow through with the help.

Stress that it is important to make the offer sincerely, allowing the other person to say no if he or she does not really want help. Point out that participants should not feel hurt or offended if the person says no or asks someone else for help. If they do help, they should ask themselves how they feel when they help others. When they are being helped? Point out that helping others is what EQUIP is all about.

SUGGESTED SITUATIONS FOR USING THIS SKILL

1. Your friend has a drinking problem.

2. A sick friend needs to keep up-to-date with schoolwork.

3. The person who is sitting next to you in math class is having trouble understanding the assignment.

4. You are walking down the street and see a lady standing beside her car, which has a flat tire.

5. Two unit members got into a dumb argument, and now it looks as though they are about to get into a fight neither of them wants.

6. A friend of yours wants to go to the movies but doesn't have enough money.

7. Your teacher needs help arranging chairs in the classroom.

8. Your brother is probably not going to finish his chores in time to leave for a date.

LEADER NOTE

It is important to help group members comprehend that sometimes helping people means doing something against their wishes—for example, saying no if they want you to get drugs for them or harm someone.

Skill 6—Preparing for a Stressful Conversation

SKILL STEPS

Describe the situation for the group.

Step 1

Imagine yourself in the stressful situation. How will you feel at the start of the stressful situation? Who is responsible for the situation?

Participants might feel tense, anxious, defensive, impatient, and so on.

Step 2

Imagine the other person in the stressful situation. How might the other person feel at the start of the stressful situation? Why?

This step can be related to TOP self-talk; see chapter 4.

Step 3

Plan what to say. Practice saying it in a calm, straightforward way.

Tell group members that if they can think of any way they have been contributing to the stressful situation, they can mention that while practicing saying what they want to say.

Step 4

Think ahead to how the other person might feel. What might
he or she say in response about what you will say?

*Ask participants: "Will the other person respond constructively
to what you plan to say? If not, can you think of anything
better to say?"*

SUGGESTED SITUATIONS FOR USING THIS SKILL

Preparing to ask for something important or to seek some important goal in the conversation:

1. You have an appointment tomorrow to talk to your school's
   football coach about trying out for the team. He is known to
   be a very tough guy.

2. You have a job interview with the facility's vocational specialist
   at 2:00 P.M.

3. You want to ask a person you like for a first date.

4. You need to talk to your teacher about your wish to drop a subject.

Preparing to reveal or explain something upsetting to someone:

5. You prepare to tell your parent about a school failure.

6. You have been caught smoking a joint, and you know you will
   have to speak about it to your counselor, who is coming in on
   the next shift.

7. You have to go talk to a staff person, your teacher, to discuss an
   earlier incident in which you have been disrespectful and have
   cursed at her or him.

8. You have to talk to the facility nurse (or to your partner) and
   say that you think you may have VD.

9. You have to telephone your parent this afternoon and say that
   you got into a fight, so the parole board may hold you for several months.

10. You are sitting outside the facility director's office, waiting to
    talk about your escape attempt last night.

LEADER NOTE

No partner is needed for the role-play because this social skill is restricted to preparation. Note the use of thinking ahead (TOP; anger management, chapter 4), especially in step 4.

Skill 7—Dealing Constructively with Someone Angry at You

SKILL STEPS

Describe the situation for the group. Participants will need a partner (or partners) for all of the steps.

Step 1

Listen openly and patiently to what the other person is saying. Nod your head or say "mm-hmm." If you need to, ask the angry person to tell you specifically what things you said or did that made him or her upset.

Stress that it is important not to interrupt or fidget. If group members feel themselves getting angry, they can breathe deeply or tell themselves to stay calm. Ask them to put themselves in the angry person's place (TOP, chapter 4) and remember that defending themselves at this point will only make the person angrier.

Step 2

Tell the person you understand why he or she is upset or that he or she has a right to be angry. Think of something you can agree with—say that the person is right about that.

If participants can't agree with any part of what the person is saying, they can agree that they do sometimes make mistakes or hurt people and that they regret this when it happens.

Step 3

Apologize or explain. Make a constructive suggestion to correct the problem.

Tell participants that if they are mainly at fault, then they will need to apologize for the hurt they caused and say that they plan to do better (and mean it!).

SUGGESTED SITUATIONS FOR USING THE SKILL

1. Your teacher is angry with you because you were disruptive during class.

2. Your parent is angry about the mess you've left the house in.

3. Your friend is angry about the fact that you called him a name.

4. A resident in your unit is angry because you cut in front in the dinner line.

5. It is 2:00 A.M. and you have just arrived home. Your parent is very angry because you were supposed to be home no later than 10:30 P.M.

6. A resident in your unit has just gotten heavily sanctioned. You started the fight that made this happen, and the person is very angry with you.

7. Some of the members of your unit are angry because you fouled an opposing player, the player scored, and your unit lost the basketball game.

8. The cook who is serving the food is angry with you because he just heard you tell another resident how bad it tasted.

9. A resident threatens you and the rest of your unit, saying he'll get even with the person who took his snack.

10. Another resident in your unit is angry with you because you borrowed his leather coat for your home visit and you have come back from the visit without it.

LEADER NOTE

To make the role-play more realistic, have several group members at once play the angry role and/or have several other group members "pump up" the role-player.

Skill 8—Expressing Care and Appreciation

SKILL STEPS

Describe the situation for the group.

Step 1

Think, "Would the other person like to know that you care about and appreciate him or her?" How will the person feel?

Explain that the other person may become embarrassed or may feel good.

Step 2

Plan and think ahead. What will you say? When and where will you say it?

Point out that it is often easier to express care and appreciation when others aren't around.

For step 3, participants will need a partner.

Step 3

Tell the person how you feel in a friendly manner.

SUGGESTED SITUATIONS FOR USING THIS SKILL

1. You thank a teacher for something he or she has done.

2. You tell your parents that you love them.

3. You tell your friends that you like them and want to continue being friends.

4. Your counselor or group member has helped you work out a serious problem.

5. You have been on the unit for about 45 days. Your parents have just arrived for their first visit. You are really excited about seeing them.

6. You have really made a lot of progress in your reading, and it's time for you to be released from the program. You must say good-bye to your reading teacher.

7. Your partner has just told you over the phone that he or she loves you.

8. You are on emergency home leave because your grandmother, who has spent the most time raising you, is very sick. You are visiting her in the hospital.

9. Your little brother, who is 10 years old, is getting high every day. You really care for him a lot.

10. You are leaving the facility after a year and have to say good-bye to another resident, who has become the best friend you ever had.

11. It is your first week home after being released from the facility. You have not seen your best and oldest friend for a year, and now you spot your friend walking toward you on the street.

12. Your mother has just given you a new coat for your birthday.

Skill 9—Dealing Constructively with Someone Accusing You of Something

SKILL STEPS

Describe the situation for the group.

Step 1

Think, "How do I feel?" If you are upset, stop and say to yourself, "I have to calm down."

If necessary, group members can also take a deep breath or count to 10. If the other person is very angry, they can tell the person that they understand how he or she feels, or that he or she has a right to be upset.

Step 2

Think, "What is the other person accusing me of? Is he or she right?"

Explain that it is important to be honest with yourself about the situation. This step amounts to using TOP; see chapter 4.

For step 3, participants will need a partner. Two responses are possible: one if the accuser is right, the other if the accuser is wrong.

Step 3

If the accuser is right: In a calm, straightforward way, say you're sorry. Offer to make up for what happened or say you won't do it again.

If the accuser is wrong: In a calm, straightforward way, tell the accuser that what he or she said isn't true or that you didn't do it. You may mention that you're sorry the person got the wrong impression, that this is a lot of false talk, or that you would like an apology.

> *Stress the importance of being sincere, not "slick." If the accusation is true, participants will need to think about how to make up for what happened—for example, by earning the money to pay for a lost or broken item, giving back a stolen item, or giving the person something else of their own.*

SUGGESTED SITUATIONS FOR USING THIS SKILL

1. A teacher has accused you of cheating.

2. Your parent accuses you of breaking something.

3. A friend accuses you of taking something of hers.

4. A neighbor accuses you of breaking his window.

5. Your parent accuses you of having hurt your sibling's feelings with your remark.

6. A friend accuses you of having lied.

7. A store owner accuses you of taking a new pair of pants from the store.

8. Your teacher accuses you of being lazy and never finishing your work.

9. Your counselor accuses you of always getting others to do your dirty work for you.

10. Your friends accuse you of always thinking of yourself first.

11. Your father accuses you of taking money from his wallet.

12. Your mother accuses you of being just like your father, a
    no-good bum.

LEADER NOTE

Anger reducers (described fully in chapter 4)—such as calming self-talk, deep breathing, and counting—are a helpful addition to this skill.

Skill 10—Responding Constructively to Failure

SKILL STEPS

Describe the situation for group members.

Step 1

Ask yourself, "Did I fail?" Decide if you have failed.

Explain that there is a difference between failing and not doing quite as well as you hoped.

Step 2

Ask yourself, "Why did I fail?" Think about both the thinking errors and the circumstances that contributed to your failure.

Ask: "Did you not try as hard as you could have? Did you have an overconfident or Self-Centered attitude? Were you not ready? Task too complicated for you? Just unlucky?" Encourage group members to avoid Assuming the Worst.

Step 3

Think about what you could do differently next time.

Ask: "Could you practice more? Change your attitude or way of thinking? Try harder? Ask for help?"

Step 4

Decide if you want to try again or get another chance and do better.

Step 5

If appropriate, make a plan to try again. Remember how you can do things differently.

Encourage group members to write down their plans. Stress that "plan" is another way of saying "think ahead."

SUGGESTED SITUATIONS FOR USING THIS SKILL

1. You failed a test at school.

2. You failed to complete your chores at home.

3. You failed to get the group to do the activity you wanted to do.

4. You spent 3 weeks trying to help your little brother learn how to ride a bicycle, and he still has not learned.

5. You asked someone for a date and were turned down.

6. You have been working on building a bookcase, but it just doesn't come out right.

7. You wanted to do at least 30 pushups in a row, but you could only do 23.

8. You have just been told that your grades are not good enough for you to be advanced to the next grade level.

9. You applied for a job and you really wanted it a lot, but you just found out someone else got it.

LEADER NOTE

Responding Constructively to Failure is an important aid for helping group members with a Low Self-Image problem and an Assuming the Worst thinking error.

PART 2

The EQUIP Program

CHAPTER 6

Program Implementation

This chapter deals with the place of the curriculum, or equipment (chapters 3 through 5), in the EQUIP program and with other topics pertinent to program implementation. Our thesis has been that antisocial youths can be motivated to help one another but that they cannot do so effectively unless they are appropriately equipped; EQUIP provides the needed equipment or psychoeducational curriculum. Research has indicated that many antisocial adolescents tend to be especially unequipped in certain areas: maturity of moral judgment, anger management (along with the related area of accurate or undistorted thinking), and social interaction skills. These limitations represent serious handicaps for youths attempting to help one another. A youth with Stealing and Lying problems, for example, can scarcely be helped by a group whose thinking on such matters is immature and distorted; in such a group, the EQUIP curriculum stimulates a more mature understanding of respect for property and the value of truth, while imparting techniques for monitoring and correcting self-serving distortions or rationalizations. Similarly, a youth with Aggravates Others and Inconsiderate of Others problems can scarcely be helped by a group of youths who lack skills for dealing with these problems—and many of whom are chronically aggressive themselves. Hence, the EQUIP curriculum teaches the would-be helpers how to reduce anger and respond constructively to provocations. In short, the helpers gain helping skills.

Of course, equipping the youths to help one another also means helping each one directly. Our message to young people, however, is not direct help to each youth but rather help to the *group* so that the group can help its *members*. The spirit of EQUIP, then, is adult guidance and empowerment of youths toward more effective mutual help—just as an athletic coach, in teaching various skills, guides and empowers team members to help one another by using their complementary strengths and thereby to succeed. EQUIP taps into a traditional strength of mutual help programs: the appeal to the individual to start making a positive contribution to others, "the only route to true strength, autonomy, and a positive self-concept" (Vorrath & Brendtro, 1985, p. 6).

The primary value of equipment meetings lies in their support for mutual help meetings, which should always be at least as frequent as the equipment meetings. In this spirit, we emphasize to the group the importance of getting the tools it needs to help its members, and hence the need to reserve some of the meeting time for equipment meetings. If time and personnel permit, equipment meetings can be run at times other than the scheduled times for mutual help meetings.

If the group is to be convinced of the need for equipment meetings it must already be motivated to some extent to attempt mutual help (see the discussion on beginning the curriculum under "Implementing and Maintaining EQUIP," later in this chapter). Ideally, the equipment curriculum should be introduced at a point when the group is moti- vated and hence receptive to the appeal for equipment—that is, not yet frustrated and discouraged by the *lack* of equipment.

As the motivated group becomes equipped, the equipment in turn often strengthens the motivation to help. We believe this feedback takes place for two reasons. The first is positive reinforcement: A group that is acquiring and using therapeutic tools is typically becoming more effective and successful—that is, experiencing rewards for its behavior— and such rewards render the helping behavior more likely to occur.

Second, the very nature of the EQUIP curriculum strengthens the motivation to help or care for others. In social decision making (moral education, chapter 3), the first problem situation (the Martian's Adviser's Problem Situation) leads the group to discover the values of caring, safety, and trust that they hold in common and to desig- nate those values as group goals. Group acquisition of skills for monitoring and correcting self-serving cognitive distortions (chapter 4) should reduce egocentric bias and enhance empathy or mutual caring within the group. Finally, motivation to help is obviously fostered as the group learns social skills such as Expressing Care and Appreciation, Car- ing for Someone Who Is Sad or Upset, and Helping Others (chapter 5).

An equipped group is a positive group. Indeed, the equipment helps to define *positive*: A positive group is mature in its moral understand- ing, accurate or undistorted in its social attitudes and beliefs, and skilled in managing anger, caring for others, and handling difficult social situations. A positive group, both motivated and equipped, not only *knows* the good and *can do* the good, but *does* the good—lives up to its responsible, caring potential—and feels good about it. At this stage, the stage of positive youth culture, the group shows a comfort- able confidence that is not easily shaken when problems develop; instead of seeing interpersonal problems in the group as frustrations to be avoided or inappropriately attacked, the group treats the problems as opportunities to use the acquired skills for growing and for helping its members.

The equipment curriculum, then, presupposes but also promotes young people's motivation to help one another as the group becomes more effective, positive, and caring. The following sections deal mainly with practical considerations for implementing the equipment curriculum within the EQUIP program. These sections describe or discuss the following: EQUIP course arrangements and possible modifications; fundamental themes and interrelationships of the course agenda; specific ways in which the course equips the youths to give mutual help; functions and desirable attributes for the course and mutual help group leaders; and various other program implementation topics (selecting youths for the program, starting the group, managing member turnover). The chapter concludes with suggestions for a structured format to be used in the final session.

COURSE ARRANGEMENTS

Although moral education, anger management/cognitive therapy, and social skills training were discussed separately in chapters 3 through 5, in an actual curriculum cycle or "course" these components of the EQUIP curriculum are arranged in alternation. Interspersing the components in this way heightens interest and permits certain helpful interrelationships and themes to emerge as the curriculum components develop concurrently.

Recall that a typical EQUIP program entails approximately seven youths meeting daily, Monday through Friday, with each meeting lasting between 1 and 1½ hours. Before the EQUIP curriculum is introduced, all of these meetings are mutual help meetings (including specialized variations such as life story meetings and prerelease meetings). Once the EQUIP course begins, we recommend that two (not more) of the five daily meetings become equipment meetings. If this schedule is observed, the EQUIP course can be completed in 10 weeks.

Table 6.1 outlines the main features of the course on a 10-week agenda. Note that social decision making occupies the right-hand column of the agenda, even though it was presented first in the book. When EQUIP is implemented, we recommend a weekly sequence of anger management–social skills–social decision making for several reasons. First, starting each week with anger management helps "sell" the need for the equipment meetings. In our experience, the problem most frequently reported in mutual help groups is Easily Angered; hence, the need for tools with which to help group members manage anger is obvious to most of the group.

Second, social skills is the easiest component to "split" across two meetings. In a given week, with a total of 3 hours for equipment,

TABLE 6.1

The 10–Week EQUIP Curriculum: Agenda and Main Features

WEEK	ANGER MANAGEMENT	SOCIAL SKILLS	SOCIAL DECISION MAKING (MORAL EDUCATION)
1	**Evaluating anger/aggression** Reevaluating, relabeling Anger management, not elimination	**Expressing a Complaint Constructively** Think ahead what you'll say, etc. Say how you contributed to problem. Make constructive suggestion.	**Martian's Adviser** Planet A seen as self-centered Planet B labeled truly strong Making the group Planet B
2	**Anatomy of anger (AMBC)** Self-talk (mind) as source of anger Early warning signs (body) Anger reducing self-talk	**Caring for Someone Who Is Sad or Upset** Notice and think ahead. Listen, don't interrupt. "Be there."	**Jerry, Mark** Loyalty, commitment Value of close friendships Breaking up in a considerate way Getting even is immature
3	**Monitoring/correcting thinking errors** Gary's Thinking Errors exercise	**Dealing Constructively with Negative Peer Pressure** Think, "Why?"	**Jim** Can't trust "friend" with a stealing problem

		Think ahead to consequences. Suggest something else (less harmful).	Stealing wrong even if from stranger
4	**More anger reducers** Deep breathing, backward counting, peaceful imagery Anger reducers to "buy time"	**Keeping Out of Fights** Stop and think. Think ahead to consequences. Handle the situation another way.	**Alonzo, Sarah** Shouldn't let friend steal (car, store items) Harm from stealing True friend wouldn't put you on the spot Closing gap between judgment and behavior (relabeling, using social skills)
5	**Thinking ahead to consequences** Thinking ahead or if-then thinking Types of consequences (especially for others) TOP (think of the other person)	**Helping Others** Think, "Is there a need?" Think ahead how to help, when, etc. Offer to help.	**George, Leon** Should tell on drug-dealing brother, friend planning to go AWOL Others could get killed Important to send drug dealers to jail

Table 6.1 (continued)

WEEK	ANGER MANAGEMENT	SOCIAL SKILLS	SOCIAL DECISION MAKING (MORAL EDUCATION)
6	**Using "I" statements for constructive consequences** "You" statements (put-downs, threats) Use of "I" statements instead of "you" statements	**Preparing for a Stressful Conversation** Imagine ahead your feelings, the other person's feelings (TOP). Think ahead what to say. Think ahead how the other person might reply.	**Dave** Shouldn't deliver drugs for friends Sister's life may be at stake Closing gap between judgment and behavior (relabeling, correcting thinking errors, exhorting)
7	**Self-evaluation** Self-evaluation, self-reflection Talking back to thinking errors Staying constructive	**Dealing Constructively with Someone Angry at You** Listen openly and patiently. Think of something you can agree with, say the person is right about that. Apologize or explain, make a constructive suggestion.	**Juan** Should tell on suicidal friend Suicide is Self-Centered thinking error Existential/spiritual concerns

			Sam
8	**Reversing** Things you do that make other people angry Reversing exercise (correcting Blaming Others error)	**Expressing Care and Appreciation** Think if the person would like to know you care. Think ahead what you'll say, when, etc. Tell the person how you feel.	Should tell on friend who shoplifted Important to prosecute shoplifters Store owner is not to blame (Blaming Others)
			Reggie
9	**Self as victimizer** Victims and Victimizers exercise Consequences for victims One's own victimization is no excuse for victimizing others TOP (think of the pain your actions have caused others)	**Dealing Constructively with Someone Accusing You of Something** Think how you feel, tell yourself to calm down. Think if the accuser is right (TOP). If the accuser is right, apologize/make restitution; if wrong, say it isn't true, it's a wrong impression, etc.	Should reveal violent dad's drinking Should do what's best for family Wouldn't want someone to lie to you But mother wrong to put Reggie on spot
			Antonio
10	**Victimizer and grand review** The Mind of Victimizer exercise Conclusion of consciousness raising	**Responding Constructively to Failure** Ask yourself if you did fail. Think what you could do differently. Decide, plan to try again.	Shouldn't help friend cheat Can't trust "friend" with cheating problem Correcting thinking errors

each component of the course can require between ½ hour and 1½ hours. Sometimes, then, anger management may take the entire first session. Usually, however, there will be time left over to begin the scheduled social skills lesson. The leader introduces and models the skill, getting feedback from the group; the group discusses situations in which the skill would be helpful; and then group members begin role-playing the skill. Typically, several group members will have done their role-plays and received feedback by the end of the meeting. A plan is in place, then, for the beginning of the week's second equipment meeting. The remaining group members will complete their role-plays, and the group will make preparations for practicing the skill.

Third, social decision making seems to be most effective when it follows social skills training. We believe the social skill role-plays "warm up" the group for discussing and providing justification for moral values. The role-play situations typically entail moral values; the role-plays, by rendering the situations vital and vivid, help the group grasp the reality and relevance of the problem situations that are central to this component of EQUIP.

COURSE MODIFICATIONS

Although we recommend conducting the EQUIP course for 3 hours a week over a 10-week period, in reality the length of the course will depend on many factors. For example, the course may take 15 weeks for a group that has more than seven or eight members and does not always have two equipment meetings per week. We have also had courses run longer than 10 weeks for groups that became very involved in certain components (such as the problem situation discussions). The guiding principle for conducting the course is service to and respect for the peer group process. For example, if an equipment meeting leader borrows time from mutual help to keep to a 10-week curriculum schedule, the group is likely to get the message that their mutual help work is less important than the curriculum. In general, the equipment meetings should accommodate to the mutual help meetings, and not the other way around.

Besides accommodating interruptions and delays, an EQUIP course may be modified in other ways. For example, in the social decision making component, Weeks 2, 4, and 5 each include not one but two problem situations; the group leader may choose to omit one if time is tight or use both, even if it means extending the course schedule. Another possibility is to allocate some extra time to complete a given week's curriculum material. If a group progresses rapidly and has time left over, it is possible to supplement the EQUIP curriculum (e.g., with additional social skills; see chapter 5). EQUIP can be adapted or expanded for diverse settings (e.g., schools) or populations (e.g., sex offenders); these modifications are discussed in chapter 8. Finally, despite our rationale for the anger management–social skills–moral education sequence, we do not rule out the possibility that a different sequence may be more appropriate for some contexts.

AN INTERRELATED AGENDA

The EQUIP course as presented in Table 6.1 represents an interrelated agenda, with relationships across the components becoming increasingly evident as the course progresses. The social skill Expressing a Complaint Constructively introduces the group to thinking ahead as a cognitive "step" weeks before it is introduced in anger management as an anger-reducing self-instructional technique. The social skill Dealing Constructively with Negative Peer Pressure, taught in Week 3, heightens awareness of right and wrong in such situations and hence promotes group prescriptions of and support for moral conduct in Weeks 4 through 10 (when most of the problem situations discussed entail negative peer pressure). Reciprocally, the problem situation discussions promote the application of social skills such as Helping Others. The best way to help a friend must be considered carefully when the requested "help" would mean joining in a car theft (Alonzo's Problem Situation), letting the friend steal or cheat (Sarah's, Antonio's Problem Situations, respectively), or keeping quiet about the friend's or relative's drug trafficking, AWOL, or suicide plans (George's, Leon's, Juan's Problem Situations).

A fundamental theme that pervades all three EQUIP components is that of becoming less self-centered—spontaneously taking the perspectives of others. In the anger management component, this theme emerges in the TOP (think of the other person) and think ahead techniques, as well as in exercises centered around identifying and correcting thinking errors (Gary's Thinking Errors; Figure 4.2) and taking the victim's perspective during the consciousness raising of the final 3 weeks (Reversing, Victims and Victimizers, and The Mind of a Victimizer; Figures 4.7, 4.8, and 4.9, respectively). Perspective taking is prominent in social skills as well. It is an explicit step in a number of the skills (e.g., "How might the other person feel at the start of the stressful situation? Why?" in Preparing for a Stressful Conversation or "Think, 'What is the other person accusing me of? Is he or she right?'" in Dealing Constructively with Someone Accusing You of Something), and it is involved at least implicitly in others (e.g., "Did you contribute—or are you contributing—to the problem in any way?" in Expressing a Complaint Constructively). Perspective taking completely captures the spirit of a social skill such as Caring for Someone Who Is Sad or Upset.

Finally, the social decision making component provides a label for the self-centered group condition (Planet A), permits the discovery of perspective taking as a common ideal value (Planet B), and encourages perspective taking in difficult social situations such as a conflict of loyalties (Jerry's Problem Situation) or the need to end a relationship (Mark's Problem Situation). In Alonzo's Problem Situation, concerning car theft, a clever probe question—"Let's say the car is *your* car"—induces the group to take the victim's perspective. Sometimes the group is influenced toward the right decision when it takes the perspective of someone not immediately present in the situation, as when the group—considering that the life of one's drug-dependent sister may be at stake—decides against making a drug delivery to her neighborhood (Dave's Problem Situation) or decides that stealing a tape deck is wrong even if from a stranger's car (Jim's Problem Situation).

EQUIPPING THE GROUP FOR EFFECTIVE MUTUAL HELP

As we have noted throughout this book, the EQUIP course equips the mutual help group in various ways. A simple but important example is the "think ahead" concept, learned in the anger management component and used as a cognitive step in the social skills component. "Think ahead" (as well as TOP and "check yourself") then become effective on-the-spot reminders that group members can use with one another. Another example: Although the problem reporting in the mutual help group covers from the start both behavior problems and thinking errors, group members' competence in reporting, identifying, and correcting thinking errors is enhanced significantly by EQUIP's anger management and social decision making components. The nature of thinking errors and ways to detect and correct them are explicitly studied in Week 3 of anger management. The problem situation discussions also provide rich opportunities for thinking errors to be heard and corrected. Indeed, we ensured that those opportunities would arise by embedding thinking errors in the discussion questions. For example, the questions in Alonzo's Problem Situation entail errors of Minimizing/Mislabeling ("What if Rodney tells Alonzo that stealing a car is no big deal, that plenty of his friends do it all the time?") and Blaming Others ("What if Rodney says to Alonzo that the keys were in the car, that anyone that careless deserves to get ripped off?").

Following is a summary of some ways in which the EQUIP course components relate to the behavior problems addressed in mutual help meetings.

Inconsiderate of Others. Of course, this general problem pertains to the self-centeredness theme noted in the previous section; we described the various ways in which the EQUIP curriculum encourages perspective taking.

Authority Problem. Adolescents with Authority Problems are helped by learning anger-reducing techniques (anger management). It is especially important for these youths to learn, and be reminded to use, the social skill Expressing a Complaint Constructively. The group should encourage them to practice this skill with staff members with whom they have actual complaints.

Misleads Others. Because a Misleads Others problem stems from a self-centered approach to dealing with other people (treating others as objects to be manipulated rather than as subjects in their own right), the perspective taking that pervades the EQUIP course should counteract Misleads Others behaviors. In addition, because the behavior problem often involves Minimizing/Mislabeling and Blaming Others ("He's the one who did it, not me"), the group can point out those thinking errors. The group can also remind the individual of the group consensus on the importance of trust and honesty in relationships.

Easily Misled. Easily Misled problems are directly addressed by the Week 3 social skill, Dealing Constructively with Negative Peer Pressure. Mature moral judgment concerning responsible conduct in such situations is developed in Weeks 4 through 10 of the social decision making component.

Aggravates Others. Aggravates Others is a problem of "proactive" (gratuitous, unprovoked, etc.) aggression. This problem is explicitly targeted in anger management beginning in Week 8 (when group members list "things you do that make other people angry"; Figure 4.6).

Easily Angered. Easily Angered or "reactive" aggression is targeted in Weeks 1 through 6 of anger management, when group members learn to notice early warning signs of anger and to use anger reducers. This learning is then used in conjunction with social skills such as Keeping Out of Fights, Dealing Constructively with Someone Angry at You, and Dealing Constructively with Someone Accusing You of Something.

Stealing, Lying. Adolescents with stealing and lying problems often Minimize, Mislabel, and Blame Others for their behavior. Their distorted belief that stealing or lying is "okay if you can get away with it" is also indicative of immature moral judgment. These youths can be helped especially by the cognitive therapy (anger management) and social decision making components of the curriculum.

Fronting. Fronting is the problem of putting on an act (pretentiousness, bluffing, clowning, etc.) rather than being genuine or showing real feelings in interpersonal relationships, including interaction with the group. For example, youths may front or verbalize that they are handling their problems when in fact they are not. (On the other hand, a certain amount of shallowness is inevitable as youths begin to conform to positive behavior; youths at this point should not be accused of fronting). Fronting is not specifically targeted in the EQUIP curriculum, but it may be ameliorated through the problem situation discussions of the importance of honesty and trust in relationships. Furthermore, as the EQUIP group itself grows more cohesive, mutually caring, and trusting or "safe," fronting problems may subside.

Inconsiderate of Self, Low Self-Image, Alcohol or Drug Problem. Because EQUIP targets youths with externalizing disorders, it provides fewer tools for helping group members with self-destructive problems. Nonetheless, many adolescents whose internalizing problems are just as severe as their externalizing problems have been helped considerably by learning to identify their thoughts of hopelessness and ruin as mistakes (Assuming the Worst) in need of correction and to use the social skill Responding Constructively to Failure when things once again do not go their way. Where the self-destructive problem is alcohol or drug dependency, EQUIP can be supplemented with compatible alcohol or drug rehabilitation programs (see chapter 8).

THE GROUP LEADERS: COACH AND EQUIPPER

We believe that the need for teaching is fairly widely recognized in the guided mutual help/adolescent peer group movement. In the preface, we mentioned Potter's frustrations and initiatives in this connection. In chapter 1, we described Positive Peer Culture (PPC) practitioner Dewey Carducci's conclusion that antisocial adolescents must be taught skills for helping one another solve problems. Needless to say, we agree with that conclusion emphatically. Indeed, we believe the teaching component is so important and distinct that it deserves a separate name (equipment meeting)—and even separate personnel.

Whereas the leader of the mutual help group (the coach) coaches, the leader of the equipment group (the equipper) teaches. Mutual help group coaches, like athletic coaches, operate from the sidelines. Their interventions are designed to maximize the players' positive teamwork without disrupting them or distracting their attention from the activity at hand. For example, the mutual help coach might interject at an appropriate point (e.g., "The group may want to share with Bob the thinking ahead concept"), just as a basketball coach might interject a message like "Keep your eyes on the basket."

Of course, the distinction between coaching and teaching is not cut-and-dried: Much of the coach's guidance is a subtle form of teaching, and much of the equipper's teaching amounts to guiding the group (through social skill role-plays, problem situation discussions, etc.). Furthermore, both leaders are typically more effective when they use the ask-don't-tell technique, and even the equipment meetings should be "owned" or conducted by the youth group to the maximum extent feasible. Nonetheless, there is an important difference: Although the coach has a certain social interaction format to help establish, it is only the equipper who has a didactic curriculum to teach.

Although they do not make the coach-equipper distinction, Vorrath and Brendtro (1985) describe three personality types among group leaders: the "demander," the "soother," and the "stimulator."

> The *demander* is the adult most comfortable in an authoritarian role. Usually he sets clear expectations, is willing to confront youths if they fail to meet these expectations, and is viewed by young people as firm, strong, and not easily manipulated. ... The *soother* is skillful at building interpersonal relationships and in communicating a warm, relaxed tone to students. ... The *stimulator* is usually adept at motivating students toward creative and productive activity. He serves as a catalyst in the program as he transfers his ... enthusiasm to young people. (p. 62)

Both the mutual help coach and the equipment leader should possess some mixture of the attributes of all three personality types (in addition to other attributes described in chapter 7). Both successful mutual help and successful equipment learning require at times the firmness of the demander, the warmth of the soother, and the enthusiasm of the stimulator. The "pure" demander, soother, or stimulator can be disastrous. For example, demanding devoid of soothing amounts to anger or hostility and invites power contests.

Instead, the power plays of a negative youth "must be met with composure, rationality, and quiet but firm adherence to a position of absolute responsibility" (Yochelson & Samenow, 1977, p. 545). One offender described his frustration in trying to provoke such a group leader: " 'It's like throwing a punch at a guy who isn't there' " (p. 546). Conversely, soothing must be tempered with firmness. The group leader who soothes by doing favors, making concessions, and giving unqualified compliments is seen as weak and totally accepting, quickly losing credibility as a demander and becoming manipulated or exploited.

The demander-soother distinction is reminiscent of the classic distinction in social psychology between the "task-instrumental" and the "socioemotional-expressive" leadership styles (Bales, 1958). It is possible that the demander or "task-instrumental" style is more relevant to the equipment meeting because there is a curriculum that must be taught. On the other hand, one could also point out that mutual helping is a task as well. Perhaps the equipment meeting leader simply must be a little more obvious about the task-instrumental demands. Both leaders must stimulate or motivate young people toward creative and productive activity.

We recommend that different staff members conduct the two kinds of meetings, especially because the equipment meeting leader may need to be someone with a more task-instrumental orientation. This arrangement relieves the mutual help group coach of a considerable additional burden. Even more advantageous is an arrangement whereby a different staff member teaches each component of the EQUIP curriculum. In such an arrangement, it is important for the leaders to function as a team. For example, each equipment teacher would know the other components well enough to substitute for another teacher if necessary. All staff members working with a group would participate in treatment team meetings pertaining to that group (see chapter 7). Ideally, coaches and equippers would sometimes lend a hand in guiding one another's groups. Of course, there are limits to the size of an effective treatment team; on the other hand, a small team risks becoming an elite cadre that can quickly lose the broad institutional support necessary for a successful program. In general, the broader the staff involvement in EQUIP, the better.

IMPLEMENTING AND MAINTAINING EQUIP

As previously noted, a group should be at least somewhat motivated to attempt mutual help before the EQUIP curriculum is introduced. Such a group is receptive to the EQUIP course. An optimally receptive group would be one that has already developed into a positive, cohesive, caring peer culture. In practice, however, the best that one can hope for might be a group that is growing beyond the forming or storming stages and into the norming stage, in which group members begin to disapprove of negative behavior. Delaying introduction of the course means running the risk that the unequipped group will become frustrated in its helping attempts and resort to coercive behaviors they know all too well. Therefore, we recommend starting an EQUIP course between 2 and 4 weeks after daily mutual help meetings have begun with a full-sized group.

The mutual help group should be prepared from the start to anticipate the equipment meetings, which will enhance the effectiveness of mutual help. Indeed, how should the EQUIP program itself be introduced to the youths? How should the youths be selected in the first place? How are the group meetings initiated and maintained? These are questions of program implementation.

Starting a Youth Group: "Seeding" and Intake Assessment

"Seeding" is the term used by Vorrath and Brendtro (1985) for the transfer of several youths from an ongoing group program to membership in a newly created group; ideally, a new positive group culture will develop as the experienced youths in effect socialize the new group (one is reminded of the time-honored strategy for extending the life of bread dough by transplanting starters into new batches):

> If the proper persons are selected, seeding new groups can be a very rapid and efficient way to start groups, but the students selected must be strong [and, we would add, equipped] enough to fill this teaching role in a helpful way without putting down peers who do not yet know how to participate in a positive group process. (p. 45)

Seeding can be used to start a youth group where there is no preexisting mutual help group. Specifically, one can seed a new group with adolescents in the facility or school who are (1) at least relatively nonoppositional and positive (i.e., relatively high functioning) and (2) popular or at least not disliked by their peers. Agee (1979) describes her youthful starters as "the stronger ones, the ones who could handle the negative peer pressure for breaking their unspoken rules to never cooperate with any adult or any system" (p. 66). Redl and Wineman (1957) describe them as " 'regular enough' guys so they can't be easily warded off through simple ridicule and contempt" (p. 171). We recommend selecting five or six such relatively high-functioning individuals with whom to start a core mutual help group, then adding new members (the "next best" available) one at a time, several weeks apart. The core group should learn the PPC problem list and the thinking errors (see chapter 1) and learn how to use them in a mutual help meeting. As the core group expands to the standard six or seven to nine (maximum) members, the core members are responsible for teaching EQUIP's basic operational features to the new members. Once a readiness for change is established and the positive group culture is sufficiently strong and equipped, seeding ends; at that point, the group can absorb and help new, initially negative members without suffering serious deterioration.

To help identify promising youths to include in the core group, the staff team may decide to use one or more standard measures. Two helpful assessment instruments are the Sociomoral Reflection Measure–Short Form (SRM-SF; Gibbs et al., 1992) and the Inventory of Adolescent Problems–Short Form (IAP-SF). The Social Reflection Questionnare for the SRM–SF is presented in Appendix A; the complete text of the IAP–SF is reproduced in Appendix B. These instruments assess, respectively, moral judgment maturity and social skills competence. We also recommend Gibbs et al.'s (1995) How I Think (HIT) measure of criminogenically distorted thinking, from which sample items are presented in Table 6.2. (This last measure is available from Dr. John C. Gibbs, The Ohio State University, Department of Psychology, Columbus, Ohio 43210-1222.) If the EQUIP setting is a juvenile correctional facility, it may be possible to administer the SRM-SF, IAP-SF, and/or HIT during each youth's intake period. Selecting youths who are relatively high functioning on these measures should ensure at least some positive potential for the starting group. Even where a facility's youth population appears to be uniformly low functioning, it is likely that some youths are at least in some respects "positive"; it is worthwhile to begin a group with these youths. If administration of assessment measures is not feasible, informal judgments of the treatment team may suffice. Youths who are extremely withdrawn and nonverbal, seriously retarded, or who have extremely disorganized personalities (autistics, schizophrenics) generally are not appropriate candidates for inclusion in group programs (Vorrath & Brendtro, 1985).

Introducing EQUIP to the Youths

Introducing the youths to the EQUIP program is the responsibility of the administrator (superintendent or principal) as well as the EQUIP treatment team staff, who should plan for a several-hour orientation meeting with prospective "core" group members. Because it is crucial

TABLE 6.2

How I Think Questionaire Items: Four Categories of Cognitive Distortion

SELF-CENTERED

If I see something I like, I take it.
If I lie to people, that's nobody's business but my own.
If I really want to do something, I don't care if it's legal or not.
When I get mad, I don't care who gets hurt.

MINIMIZING/MISLABELING

If you know you can get away with it, only a fool wouldn't steal.
Everybody lies. It's no big deal.
You have to get even with people who don't show you respect.
People need to be roughed up once in a while.

ASSUMING THE WORST

You might as well steal. If *you* don't take it, somebody *else* will.
I might as well lie—when I tell the truth, people don't believe
  me anyway.
People are always trying to hassle me.
You should hurt people first, before they hurt you.

BLAMING OTHERS

If somebody is careless enough to lose a wallet, they
  deserve to have it stolen.
People force me to lie when they ask me too many questions.
When I lose my temper, it's because people try to make me mad.
If people don't cooperate with me, it's not my fault if someone gets hurt.

---

to present a united front to the youths, the administrator's presence is vital: It will demonstrate that commitment to EQUIP exists at all levels, that staff are working closely with administration and have administration's full support.

In preparing the introduction, staff should think of adolescent offenders as currently negative but potentially positive. On the one hand, most youthful offenders have limitations in moral judgment, cognition, and social skills; on the other hand, they typically show positive potential as well. Their moral judgment may be relatively mature in some areas—for example, they will probably evaluate as "important" moral values such as keeping promises, telling the truth, helping others, saving a life, not stealing, and obeying the law, and they are likely to choose a hypothetical world that is nonviolent and caring. If their cognitive distortions are corrected and perspective taking is cultivated, some degree of empathy and caring begins to emerge.

Accordingly, the introduction to EQUIP should be tough but positive. It should stress that the youths will have an opportunity, through peer group meetings, to help their peers identify and resolve problems and, in so doing, to help themselves. The administrator should be the first to make introductory comments, which might go something like this:

> This program, EQUIP, is going to provide you with a really important opportunity, an opportunity to identify thinking and behavior problems and to resolve them. You'll be working on problems in a group that we call a mutual help group— you'll be helping one another. It will be your responsibility, in fact, to help one another work on problems.

> We want each of you to know that we believe in you. Each of you is a very important person. Yes, you've had problems in the past, but we believe that your potential for the future is very good if you work hard to take advantage of this opportunity. We all know of people who have overcome tremendous obstacles because they were determined to succeed. What happened to them in the past proved to be less important than the attitude they decided to take in the present toward the future. They knew it was up to them, just as it is up to you.

> You as a group are very important in EQUIP. For each of you, your first responsibility is to contribute to what the group is trying to do. The group comes first. The staff and I are available, but don't come to staff or me expecting to get around the group. We are going to be thinking about the group first, about how we can support what the group is trying to do, how the group is trying to develop.

> The basic type of meeting for the group will be the mutual help meeting. But there will also be "equipment" meetings, when the group will get equipment for helping group members more effectively. As the group grows and becomes more effective—that is, as you make progress in identifying and working on your problems in thinking and behavior—you will gain more freedom and control over your everyday world here. You will be *earning* that freedom. You will still

be helping others, but more and more you will be able to help yourself to think responsibly and act responsibly.

I said the group comes first. Even more, public safety comes first. Everyone has to be safe. You may gain more freedom and control, but you will not be given license to hurt other people. Rules to ensure everyone's safety will be enforced by the staff. Also, any punishment for negative behavior will be done only by the staff. You and the group are very, very important, but still our motto will be "public safety first," for everyone's sake. For example, only very responsible, very trustworthy groups will go off campus for service activities.

Many of the administrator's points should be repeated by staff. It may be effective in opening comments to liken the EQUIP group to an athletic team:

You all are going to get a chance to start a good team, a winning team. You'll have a coach, who will help you to help your teammates get better, and the coach will encourage you to be strong enough to let your teammates help you, too. We call this program EQUIP because you'll also have another person, an "equipper," who will give you the equipment you'll need to do well. But neither the coach nor the equipper can play the game for you. It will be up to you to help your teammates— and at the same time help yourself—to get good enough to win. And it won't be easy; there's no gain without pain. It will take a lot of time and effort and strength to help your teammates and yourself. It will take will power and learning how to use the right equipment to keep from getting frustrated. When you make mistakes, it will take patience and self-control to learn how to correct those mistakes and learn from them. When your teammates show problems, you'll learn not to feel put down and become angry but instead to keep respecting them, to see the problems as opportunities to really make changes instead of seeing them as setbacks for the group. You do have the power to help teammates change for the better, and in the process to change for the better yourself.

Now, the team we're talking about is a group, and the game we're talking about is life. The power to change for the better is the power to take control of your life, to work on your problems, and to stop hurting and start helping other people and yourself. Helping instead of hurting is something everyone wants, as you'll find out in EQUIP.

The equipment you'll learn for changing includes techniques for managing anger, for correcting negative mistakes in group members' and your own thinking, and other things.

Respecting your teammates means respecting other group members. For example, you will respect your group members' trust in you—that as they become strong enough to open up and share their problems, what they say will be kept within the group. In the same way, you'll want them to respect your trust. For another example, if a group member has been lying or stealing, you won't call him a liar or a thief; you will respect him as a person with a lying or stealing problem, a person who must be challenged and equipped to correct that problem. And you'll be big enough to accept challenges and equipment yourself.

You are the core group. As this core group becomes strong in EQUIP, some new members will join in to make the group bigger. Who will explain EQUIP to the new members? . . . That's right, the core group will.

Following the opening comments, the introduction should provide a comprehensive explanation of the program, with concrete illustrations of the major features and ample opportunity for the youths to ask questions. Many of the illustrations can be adapted from the EQUIP curriculum. For example, the Martian's Adviser's Problem Situation is an excellent vehicle for driving home the common goal of rising above self-centeredness to achieve a safe, caring, mutually helping group. The exercise Gary's Thinking Errors (Figure 4.2) dramatizes the nature of thinking errors and the reasons it is essential to identify and correct them. The problem list (Table 1.1) should be read and discussed. Staff should walk the group through the phases of a mutual help meeting (introduction, problem reporting, awarding of the meeting, problem solving, and summary) and have several youths role-play a sample social skill (e.g., Keeping Out of Fights). Although staff should attribute to the youths the desire for positive change, the youths should also be made aware that the staff will communicate regularly with responsible authorities (e.g., the committing juvenile court) on their participation and progress.

Establishing Ground Rules

Both at the first mutual help meeting and the first equipment meeting, the ground rules should be clarified. Goldstein et al. (1980) express one important group rule as follows:

It's really important in this group that only one person talks at a time and that we all try to listen to what is being said. We've got, let's see, _____ people in the room, and if we all talk at once, we're not going to learn anything more than what it's like to live with _____ people talking at one time. (p. 143)

"Listen to what others have to say" is the first ground rule for discussions in equipment meetings; other rules should also be introduced for mutual help meetings: If you criticize another group member, give him or her a chance to answer; never put down or threaten anyone; stay on the subject when you disagree; and—especially important—never talk to anyone outside the group about what's said in the group. Deborah Harrison, social services director at Rosemont Center in Columbus, Ohio, has her EQUIP group members sign at the outset a confidentiality statement adapted from Hastings and Typpo (1984), which reads in part as follows:

When we are confident in someone, we trust that person to understand what we are saying and feeling. We trust that person to respect our opinions and feelings.

It is important to remember that everybody owns his or her own feelings. That is why we have the rule "Do not tell anybody outside the group what someone else says in the group." It is not fair to tell someone else's feelings because those are his or her feelings, not yours. . . . It is not OK to talk outside the group about another group member's feelings, questions, or behaviors. . . .

In general, the rule is:

WHAT IS SAID IN GROUP, STAYS IN GROUP. Do not tell other people outside the group about things that someone else said or did in the group.

We will keep each other's confidences. We will respect each other.

Sign your name here _____ Date _____

Managing Membership Turnover

One perennial problem facing EQUIP programs is turnover in group membership. At least in a placement facility, departures from and arrivals to the group may be beyond the control of the treatment team. Fortunately or unfortunately, a youth who has been actualizing his or her positive potential in the EQUIP group is precisely the youth most likely to receive an early release. New arrivals (preferably, no more than one or two per week) are then needed to replace the departing members. During an equipment curriculum cycle lasting 10 weeks, it is likely that at least some group members will have participated in only portions of the EQUIP curriculum. Within certain guidelines, the determination of when to reinitiate an EQUIP cycle can be left to the discretion of the treatment team. If the rate of turnover has been so great that the majority of the group is new by the end of the cycle, we recommend initiating a new cycle immediately. In this case, it is important to convey a positive message to the full-fledged "veterans" of the course to counteract any feeling that they are merely repeating instruction in skills they already have; instead, they are getting the opportunity to perfect their skills—very much like basketball players who repeat drills to "overlearn" their skills so they will play their best under stress. Especially if appealed to in this fashion, the "veterans" can be expected to teach new members some of the EQUIP concepts and skills informally (e.g., appropriate completion of the daily logs) in settings outside the meetings—in the dormitory, on the grounds, at school, and so on. Giving effective informal help provides an additional opportunity for group members to be useful to others—and in the process to redefine their self-concepts in a way that justifies self-respect and self-esteem.

If turnover has not been a severe problem, the group may not need equipment again for several months. In general, however, we do not recommend allowing more than 3 months to pass between the end of one curriculum cycle and the beginning of the next. In the interval between cycles, the equipped and mature mutual help group could engage in activities such as community service projects.

THE FINAL SESSION

The final session of an EQUIP course should include, first, a "grand review" that spans all three curriculum components and, second, concluding comments that motivate group members to use the equipment to help others and reform their own lives. Figure 6.1 presents the exercise Darkness or Light? which is helpful for both aspects of the concluding session. This exercise lists 33 thoughts, skills, or behaviors drawn from all EQUIP components and characterizable as either negative (immature, distorted, unbalanced, destructive, irresponsible, etc.; "darkness") or positive (mature, accurate, balanced, constructive, responsible, etc.; "light"). Group members are given the list and instructed to check and discuss whether each entry should be placed in the "darkness" or the "light" column. The exercise is a structured vehicle for an overall review of a good sampling of course elements.

FIGURE 6.1
Darkness or Light?

Thought, Skill, or Behavior	Darkness?	Light?
Planet A	_____	_____
Noticing an early warning sign of anger	_____	_____
Constructively expressing a complaint	_____	_____
Apologizing if you're partly responsible for a problem	_____	_____
Stealing and thinking it's okay because you didn't steal from anyone you knew	_____	_____
Caring for someone sad or upset	_____	_____
Using put-downs and threats	_____	_____
Stealing a car with the excuse that the owner left the keys in the car	_____	_____
Taking deep breaths when angry	_____	_____
Making a Self-Centered thinking error	_____	_____
Doing it to others before they do it to you	_____	_____
Doing for others only if they'll do for you	_____	_____
Preparing for a stressful conversation	_____	_____
Selling harmful drugs	_____	_____
Giving in to peer pressure to hurt someone	_____	_____
Suggesting a less harmful alternative to a negative act your friends want you to do	_____	_____
Responding constructively to others' anger	_____	_____
Thinking ahead to consequences	_____	_____
Using self-evaluation	_____	_____
Using "I" statements	_____	_____
Keeping out of fights	_____	_____
Victimizing others and using the excuse that you were a victim	_____	_____

Figure 6.1 (continued)

Thought, Skill, or Behavior	Darkness?	Light?
Delivering drugs for a friend	_____	_____
Blaming the victim	_____	_____
Thinking whether the other person is right when you are accused of something	_____	_____
Expressing care and appreciation	_____	_____
Not telling on a suicidal friend	_____	_____
Thinking like a victimizer	_____	_____
Covering for your shoplifting friend	_____	_____
Responding constructively to failure	_____	_____
Helping a friend cheat	_____	_____
Showing how you would want to be treated in the way you treat others	_____	_____
Planet B	_____	_____

The darkness/light dichotomy provides a metaphor that is valuable both for a grand review and for an inspirational conclusion. If group members have retained "Planet A" and "Planet B" from the first social decision making session as vocabulary handles for negative and positive elements, then designation of the list entries as darkness or light should be fairly easy. The group should also understand readily that darkness and light are being used to describe not only group conditions but *any* thought, skill, or behavior.

Appeals to the common expression "seeing the light" in the context of the EQUIP course can inspire soul-searching among the youths ("What kind of person do I want to be?" "What kind of impact on others and the world do I want to have?" "What do I want my life to amount to?"):

Basically, we've been talking about two kinds of lives. There's the Planet A, victimizing life that's destructive, where you hurt other people and yourself, and then there's the Planet B, responsible life that's constructive, that involves *helping* other people and yourself. And in these equipment meetings the group gained tools for helping group members change from a life of victimizing other people and making excuses to a life of caring about others and being strong enough to be honest and responsible: Tools, that is, for helping group members see the light—you know, to see that we're here in this earthly life to try to help other people, to try to contribute to things positively. Once you've seen the light, you say, "Ah, so *that's* what life's all about." And if you haven't seen the light, then you're still in, what? . . . That's right: darkness. And in the dark is where all that hurt and hate and destruction and victimizing go on. And once you've seen the light, it's a choice. It's up to you to choose what kind of life you're going to live, whether you're strong enough to choose the light that you see.

Furthermore, the light metaphor inspires hope and optimism:

Any time you start to think that the things in the first column are stronger than the things in the second column, that darkness is stronger than light, remember this: Light dispels darkness. Darkness is what happens when there's no light. When you're in a dark room and you open a door into a lighted room, the darkness doesn't spill over into the lighted room. Instead, what happens? . . . That's right, light from that lighted room spills over into your dark room and dispels some of that darkness. And this group has been opening that door into the lighted room, the responsible life, where there's something stronger, something better than that darkness. Group members have not only seen the light but have been opening that door wider and wider, getting more and more light in their lives. And with the group's help, group members are preparing to walk through that door when they're released, not only the door to the outside but the door to the *inside*, to what it's all about, to the responsible life.

We believe the light metaphor is inspiring at least partly because of its spiritual significance. It is perhaps no coincidence that persons reporting near-death experiences often recall relating to a loving light and reviewing their lives in that light (Lundahl, 1993). In any event, if the EQUIP course has inspired some members to seek religious or spiritual support for newly developed positive values, they should be encouraged to do so (see chapter 2). Many institutions offer religious education programs as well as voluntary activities (Bible studies, community service projects, etc.) that can contribute significantly to the spiritual development of youths.

CHAPTER 7

Developing a Positive Staff Culture

If an institution treating antisocial youths is to be effective, its mode of management should match and support its treatment modality (Babcock & Sorenson, 1979). An institution implementing EQUIP, then, should attempt to match its new treatment modality—an effective and positive youth culture—with an effective and positive *staff* culture. The parallels in principle are strong. To be effective in developing their positive culture, young people must work in accordance with the following five principles:

1. *Mission:* A clear sense of mission (to achieve a Planet B environment in which group members can be helped)

Principles 2 through 5 enable the group to accomplish its mission. The group must have:

2. *Empowerment:* Genuine group decision-making autonomy to the maximum extent feasible, along with the ability to accept direction from staff

3. *Equipment:* The skills and other resources needed for helping group members

4. *Unity:* The ability to work as a cohesive, unified entity, especially with resistant, negative group members

5. *Feedback:* Systematic guidance (i.e., suggestions from peers and staff—most directly, the coach and the equipper)

Correspondingly, if staff are to be effective as they develop a positive treatment team, they must follow the same five principles:

1. *Mission:* A clear sense of mission as articulated in a mission statement, statement of philosophy, and program description

Principles 2 through 5 enable the group to accomplish its mission. The treatment team must have:

237

2. *Empowerment:* Participatory management of EQUIP program implementation, along with the ability to accept direction from the administrator

3. *Equipment:* The appropriate techniques for helping youths or working with colleagues

4. *Unity:* The ability to work as a cohesive, mutually helping entity, especially with youth groups in the early stages of group development

5. *Feedback:* Guidance in the form of systematic and accurate information concerning the therapeutic progress of the individual youths and their group

In this chapter, we will elaborate upon these five principles as they pertain to the development of an effective and positive staff culture.

PROGRAM MISSION, PHILOSOPHY, AND DESCRIPTION

Program Mission

Just as the Martian's Adviser's Problem Situation (chapter 3) stimulates the beginning youth group to construct a group mission (i.e., to achieve a Planet B environment in which group members can be helped), group discussion should stimulate the beginning EQUIP staff to achieve a clear sense of mission. The group discussion should lead to formulation of a mission statement such as the following: "To impart motivation and skills so that youths can effectively help one another think and behave in ways that are responsible rather than harmful to themselves and others."

Program Philosophy

An effective staff should have a clear sense not only of mission but also of underlying philosophy. Although a statement of program philosophy should be refined through staff discussion, its basic shape and content should come from the administrator. A program philosophy might comprise the following sections: characterization of the treatment population, overview of treatment, and expectations for staff.

Characterization of the Treatment Population

For an EQUIP program, a preliminary philosophical statement concerning the typical treatment population (adolescents with antisocial behavior problems; for variants, see chapter 8) can be drawn from literature reviews and from other chapters in this book. A statement concerning an adolescent treatment population should address the youths' positive potential, their limitations (which need remediation), and their accountability for their own behavior.

Positive potential. The philosophical statement concerning antisocial youths should begin by emphasizing their positive potential. Almost all juvenile offenders evaluate as "important" or even "very important" such moral values as keeping promises, telling the truth, helping others, saving a life, not stealing, and obeying the law (Gregg et al., 1994). In addition, almost all have a biologically rooted predisposition to empathize with others (Hoffman, 1981), a need to loved and be loved, and a need to feel worthwhile to others and themselves (Glasser, 1965). When faced with a choice of hypothetical worlds, they are likely to choose a world that would be nonviolent and caring. They are also likely to suggest responsible decisions with regard to many hypothetical social problem situations.

Limitations. The second component of the philosophical statement should render faith in this potential more realistic by acknowledging the limitations that impede its actualization. Most recidivist youthful offenders are developmentally delayed in moral judgment; limited in their resources for self-control and constructive social behavior; and self-centered as well as self-servingly distorted in their social attitudes, beliefs, and thoughts. Their potential empathy and caring for others tend to be neutralized by self-serving distortions as well as by the antisocial norms of their subculture. The backgrounds of many antisocial youths include dysfunctional families characterized by "(a) low levels of family affection and high levels of family conflict, (b) the use of ineffective and inept parental control strategies, and (c) antisocial [criminal] behavior in the parents" (Henggeler, 1989, p. 48; see also Holden & Ritchie, 1991)—in other words, by abuse and neglect. These environmental circumstances often interact with serious biological risk factors (e.g., low autonomic activity/reactivity) and temperamental style factors (e.g., high impulsivity, hyperactivity) in early childhood (Caspi, Henri, McGee, Moffitt, & Silva, 1995; Caspi & Silva, 1995; Magnusson, in press; Sampson & Laub, 1994; see review by Hartup & van Lieshout, 1995). Such factors have contributed to these adolescents' failure to live up to their potential for positive values, feelings, and constructive satisfaction of needs.

Accountability. Finally, in addressing the treatment population, the philosophical statement might emphasize young people's

accountability for the consequences of their behavior. Their acknowledgment of the importance of basic moral values implies a personal
awareness on some level that their harmful actions have been morally
wrong. Although abuse and neglect, along with individual variables,
certainly contribute to the likelihood of subsequent antisocial
behavior, there is no automatic or absolute linkage; such factors are
predisposing stresses but generally do not directly *cause* or *coerce*
behavior harmful to others (Kierulff, 1988). Other youths—sometimes
siblings—likewise hurt through dysfunctional family circumstances of
abuse and neglect do not "take it out on the rest of the world" but
instead struggle to make largely responsible choices. Antisocial
youths are irresponsible insofar as their way of fulfilling their needs
deprives others of the opportunity to fulfill *their* needs (Glasser, 1965).
Finally, although abusive and neglectful parents should be held
accountable—and the social conditions/policies that help give rise to
such parenting should be reformed (see Damon, 1995)—in many
instances the self-centered and irresponsible behavior of the youths
themselves "place[d] considerable stress on the family system"
(Henggeler, 1989, p. 42; Samenow, 1989; Vuchinich, Bank, & Patterson,
1992). In practical terms, failing to insist upon accountability typically
means allowing excuse making, a strategy at which many antisocial
youths have become adept (Barriga & Gibbs, 1995; Redl & Wineman,
1957). Conveying "greater expectations" (Damon, 1995) and insisting
on accountability means respecting and believing in these youths as
persons capable of change—that is, in the youths' positive potential.

Overview of Treatment

The overview of treatment section of the philosophical statement
might reflect the section on the treatment population in a twofold
restatement and elaboration of the program mission: (1) to actualize the
positive potential of youths with antisocial behavior problems by
equipping them with the skills and resources for eliminating or
overcoming their limitations and (2) to insist on accountability—
that is, consistently to make clear to the youths that their past adversities
in no way absolve them of responsibility for their choices. A tough-
minded articulation of the second element is an Ohio Department
of Youth Services (1990) victim awareness program directive that all
staff serve as "the voice of the victim" and help juvenile offenders
"look at themselves for what they are, primarily irresponsible people
and lawbreakers who must stop blaming others for their situations,
stop minimizing what they have done, and own their behavior" (p. 35).

Regarding the first element of the mission, young offenders
learn to actualize their potential by attempting and becoming

equipped to help one another. The thesis of EQUIP is that antisocial youths can become motivated to help one another but cannot do so effectively unless they are appropriately equipped. EQUIP provides the psychoeducational curriculum that antisocial youths need if they are to remedy their limitations.

Expectations for Staff

Finally, the philosophical statement should address expected standards for staff members and their approach to the treatment population at the institution. Our expectations for staff resonate with those expressed in the Annsville Youth Center program description and philosophy (Goldstein & Glick, 1987), and this section borrows liberally from that document. Preconditional to the development of a therapeutic environment is the development of a secure environment. Accordingly, staff and administration are responsible for providing young people with an environment that is "safe" or secure, both physically (e.g., with appropriate and clean living conditions, adequate food and clothing) and psychologically (e.g., with clearly established norms for behavior, structured activity and routines, predictability in relationships).

Beyond the expectations related to the establishment of a secure environment is the general expectation that the staff approach to youths reflect the overview of treatment: Staff members must have faith in the youths' potential for positive change, be realistic about the youths' need for remediation in order to actualize that potential, and resist any interpretation of the youths' needs as excuses from accountability. Especially given the paucity of affection and scarcity of positive role models in the typical antisocial youth's background, staff must convey genuine concern and model constructive behavior when working out conflict situations with young people and with colleagues.

In working with the youths, staff will continually be involved in *directive behavior* (i.e., telling youths what to do, where and when to do it, and how to do it), *therapeutic behavior* (e.g., telling youths to "check yourself," "think ahead," or "live up to Planet B"; or identifying and counseling against youths' Assuming the Worst or other thinking errors), and *supportive behavior* (e.g., listening to youths and providing support, encouragement, and other reinforcement). The professional staff person is adept at applying the appropriate mix of these behaviors as a function of the particular situation and the individual youth. Directive behavior will, of course, be especially prominent when staff are dealing with a new admission.

If staff members are to develop a positive and effective staff culture, they should attempt to cultivate in one another the following attributes:

Involvement: Ability to develop and demonstrate a commitment to one's treatment team and to EQUIP in general

Initiative: Willingness to accept responsibility and to contribute more than may be required by one's role or function

Understanding of self: Working knowledge of one's own feelings, values, beliefs, abilities, limitations, and needs

Understanding of others: Willingness to explore and listen to what others (e.g., coworkers) feel, believe, think, and need

Communication: Ability to share and receive information or data with and from coworkers

Listening ability: Ability to listen carefully to what others say and mean, to ask appropriate questions if necessary for better understanding, and to attend to instructions and necessary information

Participation in decision making: Willingness to invest time and energy in the shared decision-making process

Forthrightness, openness, responsiveness to feedback: Willingness to say what is on one's mind, confront peers constructively to enhance job performance, and respond nondefensively to constructive feedback from others or to opportunities to learn from mistakes; in other words, a constant desire to improve and help others to improve

Perseverance: Ability to sustain commitment to (and not abandon) youths or staff with whom one is working, possess or develop patience and endurance, work under stress without giving up, and follow through with the implementation of team decisions

Program Description

The treatment program translates the mission and philosophical statements into a strategic plan of action. Like the institutional philosophy, the treatment program should be introduced by the administrator (or someone designated by the administrator). As the Annsville Youth Center program exemplifies (Goldstein & Glick, 1987), the program description should detail who the target population is and how they will be treated. Population information might include the ages of youths appropriate for admission, the geographical areas from which they are referred, the ethnic characteristics of the institutional population, the youths' academic and vocational profiles, and the types of criminal activities best addressed by the institution. It is also important to indicate personal attributes that may preclude or diminish prospects for successful treatment given the institution's intervention program.

EQUIP and other vehicles for intervention with the institution's population should also be described. Hence, the program description should include a summary of the EQUIP mutual help and equipment meetings, as appropriate to the particular institutional setting. The equipment meeting curriculum (chapters 3 through 5) addresses limitations in the areas of moral judgment maturity, anger management (along with the related area of accurate or undistorted thinking), and social interaction skills; applications may vary from one institution to another.

In general, the program description covers the institution's system of contingent rewards and punishments; counseling, educational, health, and residential services; and recreation, religious, and other available resources. "System of contingent rewards and punishments" refers to the institution's particular level or point system for determining the extent to which a given youth earns—or loses—privileges or benefits while in residence. Valuable though level systems can be, administrator and staff should keep in mind the crucial distinction between managing populations or achieving compliant behavior through extrinsic rewards and punishments and helping youths to develop responsible thinking and acting through a treatment program such as EQUIP.

As indicated earlier, safety and security are crucial preconditions for a viable treatment environment. Indeed, apart from introducing the program philosophy and description, the administrator's chief responsibility is to create an environment that is safe and secure for both staff and residents or students. Hence, the administrator should communicate to both staff and students the requirements for safety and security and the consequences for violations. Furthermore, the administrator must be prepared to follow through by pressing charges against a violating student or staff member if that is warranted. The importance of safety and security and the consequences for violations are communicated both orally and through written policies, procedures, and directives. Safety and security issues may also suggest items for inclusion among the evaluation criteria for satisfactory staff performance.

Written policies concerning safety and security include expectations for institutional behavior—for example, youth movement (includes movement between program areas, demeanor, and conversation); language (tone of voice, use of profanity); wake-up routine (personal hygiene, cleanup, breakfast); mealtime procedures (receiving and returning trays); cleanup routines (chores, inspections); classroom behavior (attendance, punctuality, curriculum assignments, school decorum); vocational programs (use of equipment, stipend jobs); quiet time (leisure time); group and individual counseling; recreation (assigned activities, participation); off-campus trips/activities; bedtime (personal hygiene, relaxation, lights out); snacks; residential and living areas; and infirmary and sick call procedures. The effectiveness of the EQUIP program is undermined unless resident behavior in these areas is properly routinized and managed.

EMPOWERMENT THROUGH PARTICIPATORY MANAGEMENT

Just as the youth group is empowered to help its members and even to make recommendations to staff on important matters such as release decisions, the staff group or treatment team must be empowered to participate in important decisions pertaining to the treatment program. In correctional facilities, staff treatment teams span traditional departments (classroom, clinical, dormitory) to encompass all staff having regular significant contact with youth group members. The treatment team should "have the authority to create, compile, and act upon youth-related information in the areas of: level system, case communications, [and] program referrals . . . specific to the needs of each youth" as well as "the authority to plan and implement incentive and seasonal activities for their caseload" (Potter & Luse, 1988, p. 2). First and foremost, the staff team is responsible for the implementation of the EQUIP program. Providing the staff with a scientifically based, well-structured intervention such as EQUIP is in itself a tremendously empowering action on the part of the administrator.

A key feature of empowerment is respect for the considerable time demands faced by staff as they seek to develop a positive youth and staff culture. Hence, staff must be allowed to operate with a minimum of time-consuming administrative or bureaucratic requirements (e.g., demands from other administrative department heads, security personnel, or community representatives). It is the administrator's responsibility to keep such distractions to a minimum. For example, all calls for meetings should be challenged: What is the purpose of the meeting? Who will be involved? Could the issue be handled with a memorandum? Whether handled by meeting or memorandum, will time spent on the issue help the staff or the youths? "Departmental meetings, clinical meetings, section meetings [and] cottage meetings . . . all consume large blocks of time that might better be spent in other ways" (Vorrath & Brendtro, 1985, p. 126).

Of course, some staff meetings are necessary and extremely important. The treatment team meeting, lasting 1½ to 2 hours, must be held at least once a week. These meetings are organized and professional; attendance and participation are mandatory for all members. The team selects a meetings chair (typically the group coach), as well as a secretary to record notes on the agenda item decisions in a team log (usually a rotating responsibility). Issues discussed pertain to the operation of EQUIP, the functioning of the youth group, or the treatment progress of individual group members. The chair is responsible for preparing the agenda (in response to staff and administrator input and case communication needs of which the chair may be aware), and for ensuring that the team meeting follows the agenda.

Far from being a nuisance, the treatment team meeting is a vehicle for staff empowerment; the team meeting belongs to the staff just as the mutual help meeting belongs to the youths. Although it is usually valuable for the administrator to attend at least part of the meeting to show support (and sometimes to provide information— e.g., the outcome of a grievance), the administrator should not interfere with the staff's progression through the agenda. Where the need arises for the administrator to schedule an administrative meeting with the team, that meeting should never interfere with or replace the team meeting. When Potter was at the Maumee Youth Center near Toledo, Ohio, a highly effective tool for empowerment was a regularly scheduled meeting of team representatives with administrators. An administrative meeting is an opportunity for the treatment team to share any and all concerns, problems, or proposals for improvement; like the treatment team meeting, it should involve organized, professional discussion with an agenda and time line.

Apart from calling of unessential meetings, one of the most time-consuming and disempowering actions by an administrator is direct intervention in a youth or group problem or complaint. If the administrator believes that an issue requires attention, he or she should discuss the issue first with the staff and only then consider contact with the youths. (Of course, if the problem or complaint involves a disturbance, the administrator or the observer of the disturbance must investigate immediately to ensure that everyone is safe and that applicable procedures are being followed.) Furthermore, any written documentation ensuing from a youth problem or complaint should be made through standard feedback recording systems, discussed later in this chapter. Written reports outside the routine systems are time-consuming, are often resented by staff, and may not be accessible for later use in guiding the youths.

Direct intervention by the administrator—bypassing the treatment team—is disempowering, then, because it is preemptive; moreover, it is often counterproductive therapeutically. Carducci and Carducci (1984) illuminate the issue from the point of view of the teacher in a school setting:

> No . . . administrator, or any other support or ancillary adult is to get involved in any discussion with a student in a holding room or area. They are to listen to no excuses or explanations [Minimizing/Mislabeling, Blaming Others, etc.], nor are they to do any "problem-solving" with the student. Those activities are reserved for you [the treatment team] and the student must be told to deal with you [the treatment team]. . . . There is a very good reason for stressing the importance of other adults not getting involved. . . . Most acting-out youngsters are masters at excusing their own behavior [Minimizing/Mislabeling] and projecting blame for it onto others [Blaming Others]. The problem was with you [the team] and only you know the particulars. You are responsible for resolving the problem with the student [or the group]. If the student gets an opening, he will seduce the unsuspecting, "helping" adult into an endless stream of excuses, red herrings, rationalizations, accusations that you have been unfair, and pleas of innocence—until the whole process is so diluted, muddied, and convoluted that your hope of getting him to face up to responsibility for his own behaviors [and thinking errors] will be all but lost. (p. 51)

Nonetheless, because some problems or complaints may be legitimate, it is advisable to have a formal youth grievance procedure in place. We suggest that the steps in this procedure be modeled on the steps of the EQUIP social skill Expressing a Complaint Constructively (see chapter 5): In writing, on a standard form, the youth should (1) identify the problem, (2) plan a constructive complaint (the team should include a brief paragraph telling the youth to consider carefully what should be stated), (3) state the complaint, and (4) make a constructive suggestion for a remedy. Structuring the grievance procedure in accordance with Expressing a Complaint Constructively gives the youth an acceptable avenue for practicing this social skill. Staff members may even feel a sense of achievement that the youth is learning to act constructively by using a social skill they taught. In general, the experience of being part of a group that provides valuable help to others is no less a self-esteem builder for staff than it is for youths.

A supportive, actively responsive administrator is crucial to the treatment team's successful implementation of EQUIP in any setting: "Find a school with a healthy moral environment and a program for teaching good values and you'll find a principal who is leading the way or supporting someone else who is" (Lickona, 1991, p. 325). An effective leader draws upon the experienced input of his or her staff—that is, follows a participatory management model:

> The participatory model of administration solicits input from all staff at all levels within the institution [for example, at the staff-administration meetings suggested earlier] and cuts across supervisory lines as well as organizational units. The result, when properly managed, is an environment in which morale of staff is high, there is ownership of task and accomplishment, productivity and performance level of staff are above standard, and there is an abundance of new ideas and creativity. The administrator who adopts a participatory model of administration must have a tolerance for dialogue and debate of issues, not be threatened by challenges from subordinates, and be non-threatening to subordinates who desire to participate. Further, the administrator must be willing and able to change position, alter opinions, consider alternatives, and reverse decisions (based upon input from staff) without compromising policy or authority. (Goldstein & Glick, 1987, p. 258)

Input from an empowered team to a supportive administration provides the basis for the "dialogue and debate of issues" that is the heart of participatory management.

EQUIPPING THE STAFF

Empowerment of staff means very little if staff members do not receive appropriate training or equipment enabling them to fulfill their treatment mission. Equipping the staff is the responsibility of the administrator. Just as the administrator introduces EQUIP to the prospective youth group, he or she also introduces EQUIP to staff members, describing the EQUIP program and associated staff expectations. Essentially, the introduction paraphrases the program mission, philosophy, and description. Although the style of presentation may vary as a function of agency type or group size, the basic content of the introduction should include the points addressed in the following sample script:

> Welcome to our EQUIP program, a treatment program that is scientific, organized, and structured. The mission of EQUIP is to give the youths motivation and skills so that

they can effectively help one another think and behave in ways that are positive rather than harmful to themselves and others. This is our mission, yours and mine and all members'. EQUIP is the treatment modality we will use to fulfill our mission. Achieving our mission with these youths will be more like a marathon than a sprint. The EQUIP program has multiple components because that's what it takes to treat these youths' long-standing, multiple problems. We all wish we could use some quick fix, but unfortunately, there is none that's effective. EQUIP takes more time and planning than does a quick fix, but the research shows that EQUIP is effective.

To help us better understand our mission, we will now complete an exercise that we also use with groups of young people. The exercise is called The Martian's Adviser's Problem Situation *[see chapter 3]*.

The ensuing discussion of the reasons for recommending Planet B should give staff a clear grasp of the "positive culture" aims for both youths and staff groups. Indeed, this exercise should enable staff members to endorse common positive values (caring, safety, trust) and thereby to develop a positive staff culture.

[Stress positive potential.] Fortunately, to fulfill our mission, we don't have to start from scratch because, as you'll find out, most of the young people also pick Planet B when they do this exercise. In other words, it is important to recognize the positive potential of these kids here at _____ . Like their socially appropriate peers, almost all juvenile offenders believe that keeping promises, telling the truth, helping others, not stealing, and so on, are important moral values.

[Acknowledge limitations.] It's great that most of our kids know what's ideally right, but it's not so great that they don't live up to their ideal values. Of course, we have to be realistic. Research shows that most juvenile offenders are immature in their moral judgment; poor at managing their anger; self-servingly distorted in their thoughts, attitudes, and beliefs; and unskilled in constructive social behavior. EQUIP is a scientifically designed and validated program for remedying these limitations. You'll be finding out about equipment meetings; these are meetings in which some of you will be equipping the youths with the tools they need for overcoming these limitations so they can effectively help

one another and themselves. You'll also be learning about mutual help meetings; these are the meetings in which the youths will be trying to help one another. The young people first come together in mutual help meetings. We start the equipment meetings soon enough to rescue and enhance the mutual help meetings: Because our youths have the limitations I mentioned, they eventually get frustrated—and before they start resorting to put-downs and threats instead of constructive helping behaviors, we'll be starting the equipment meetings to give them the helping tools they need.

[Emphasize accountability.] The fact that the youths have these limitations does not mean that they aren't accountable for their thinking and behavior. As we said, most of them do know better, at least in the abstract. Furthermore, although many of them are hurting from abuse and neglect, they have been irresponsible in choosing to make bad situations even worse by doing things like taking their hurt out on the rest of the world. In some ways, our primary clients are the victims or potential victims of these youths' irresponsible and harmful behavior. Our efforts must be directed at reducing the youths' perceived license to harm others, in addition to overcoming other limitations.

One of the most valuable things about EQUIP is the fact that it provides a language that we and the youths can use for getting a handle on these irresponsible types of thinking and behaving. In the training that's coming up, it will be important for you to learn and begin using this language. For example, a youth's perceived license to harm others is called a Self-Centered thinking error, and there are other terms you will find helpful in identifying distorted, dangerous thinking. You will also learn some terms for getting a handle on behavioral problems, such as Authority Problem, Aggravates Others, Easily Misled, and so on. When a youth exhibits a thinking error or a behavior problem, the staff has an opportunity to guide the group toward helping that youth recognize, own, and correct the error or problem. In other words, in EQUIP, we go beyond control to do therapeutic intervention every chance we get.

As part of the training in the coming weeks, you may be visiting other agencies where positive and effective mutual help group programs similar to EQUIP are in place. It will also be important for you to read your copy of *The EQUIP Program* as well as our program booklet *[entailing description of the specific institution's mission statement, program philosophy, and program description]*. These visits and this reading should help you learn more about the language of EQUIP and the mutual help and equipment meetings.

Certain staff expectations are part of EQUIP. You will be expected to behave in a professional way and not to exhibit thinking or behavioral problems of your own. More positively, you will be expected to show involvement, initiative, openness, listening ability, perseverance, and other characteristics of professional conduct that you'll be reading about in your EQUIP book and program booklet.

Other staff training activities will follow the administrator's introduction. These activities should be "hands on" as much as possible. In addition to discussion of the Martian's Adviser's Problem Situation, which formed part of the introduction, other exercises representative of the EQUIP curriculum should also be utilized so staff will have a concrete grasp of the functioning of the equipment meetings. For example, six or seven staff volunteers should be chosen to form a simulated youth group while the other staff members observe; appropriate handouts should be distributed and one of the social skills should be modeled, tried, and discussed (see chapter 5). As another example, the same or a different staff subgroup might discuss Gary's Thinking Errors (see Figure 4.2) for an introduction to the four thinking error categories. In the same spirit, a staff subgroup should be walked through the procedural format for the mutual help meetings (see chapter 2).

THE UNIFIED MUTUAL HELP TREATMENT TEAM

To develop an effective EQUIP program, the treatment team must become unified. Presenting a cohesive, unified front to the resistant, negative youth is just as important for staff members themselves as it is for the youth group. Vicki Agee and Bruce McWilliams (1984) explain the rationale for team unity as practiced at the Closed Adolescent Treatment Center, a maximum security correctional facility for violent juvenile offenders in Denver, Colorado:

The [team] concept requires that staff work so closely together as to appear almost to be a gestalt organism. For one thing, they must role model cooperative interpersonal relationships to the peer group, and for another, the violent juveniles are obviously dangerous, and safety is achieved through cohesion. . . . In an ideal family, the parents present a united front to their offspring. In the therapeutic community the same thing must occur. Violent juvenile offenders usually have much experience at being able to split staff (and their own parents) and set them up against each other in an effort to divert attention from their negative behaviors. Ideally, in a team setting, there are very strong values against allowing this to happen, and attempts to do so are promptly confronted. (p. 289)

Working closely together, then, promotes both therapy and security. Again, this cohesion is no less important for the staff than for the youths. Only through mutual support and help can staff effectively accomplish basic tasks. These basic tasks pertain to therapy—for example, administering and interpreting standardized assessments, creating individualized treatment plans, evaluating the progress of individuals and the group, preparing case communications (to the judge, parole officer, children's services agency, etc.), and planning incentive activities. They also pertain to daily operations—for example, preparing daily schedules, ensuring conformity with them, and covering for team members on leave.

Staff members help one another in diverse ways. Groups (whether staff or youth) are composed of individuals with different interests and strengths; working together means appreciating complementary interests and strengths and weaving them together to accomplish a task. Consider, for example, a treatment team that is offering as a reward a social activity—for instance, a dance. The group coach and/or equipper might guide the young people through making arrangements for the dance (inviting guests, handling introductions at the dance, resolving scheduling conflicts, etc.), a cottage parent who happens to be a musician might offer to provide the music, and a teacher might offer to serve as a chaperon. As youths and staff cooperate in a joint undertaking, cohesiveness becomes not only an intragroup but also an intergroup concept. Such creative interaction reveals many facets of staff members' and youths' individual personalities—facets not normally seen in daily institutional life—and all become more human to one another.

Just as the youths in their group reach decisions through consensus, so should the treatment team. For staff to become of one mind on an important issue may require considerable time; it always requires an open, inviting group climate. It is crucial in staff decision making that all team members be treated as equals. Although egalitarian decision making may take time and patience, the investment more

than pays for itself in the resulting enhancement of group cohesiveness (mutual understanding and appreciation, as well as shared sense
of accomplishment) and lasting group ownership of the decision. A
cohesive group in which everyone has meaningful input is a group with
an intrinsic desire to make its decisions work. It is also a group that
offers every member an opportunity for personal and professional
growth.

In this light, supervisors who are treatment team members must
generally refrain from making their status salient by "pulling rank."
As Vorrath and Brendtro point out, "True teamwork seldom is achieved
if many hierarchical relationships exist within the team" (1985, p. 129).
Just as the youths' mutual help coach must not coerce a group to make
a particular decision, the supervisor as team member must follow
the same rule.

Nonetheless, unilateral or "command" decisions may occasionally
be necessary when time and circumstances legitimately require immediate action, a prospect for which staff should be prepared during
training. When such an occasion does arise, the administrator
should explain the circumstances surrounding the decision as well
as the rationale for it and should reassure staff that unilateral decisions
will be held to a minimum. In Potter's experience as administrator,
respecting staff by providing such explanations and reassurances—
and living up to those reassurances—is crucial if the egalitarian,
mutual help spirit is to be preserved.

Staff meetings resemble youth meetings not only in their importance and their egalitarian spirit but also in their decision-making
format. Recall that mutual help meetings entail problem reporting
and identification and problem solving (proposing solutions, developing a plan, and later evaluating the outcome). For staff, the problem
reporting/identifying/solving process can be similarly structured in
terms of the following sequence:

1. Identify the problem (be as concise as possible).

2. Examine the problem, or pattern of problems, and the
   causes (may lead to redefining the problem).

3. Propose and clarify possible solutions.

4. Select the best solution and develop a practical plan for
   implementing it.

5. Commit to the plan and, subsequently, carry it out (include
   evaluation of outcome on future meeting agenda).

6. Evaluate the outcome. Was the problem solved? How efficiently?

Awareness of the problem-solving sequence can make decision-making meetings more orderly, effective, and efficient. Meetings where staff give short shrift to problem analysis (steps 1 and 2) typically fail to develop appropriate and responsive plans for solving problems (steps 3 through 5).

ACCURATE AND SYSTEMATIC FEEDBACK

For an EQUIP youth group that spends much of the day together (in group meetings, classes, dormitory living, recreation, etc.), opportunities for obtaining and sharing feedback are plentiful. However, such opportunities are not so plentiful for staff members; hence, they must establish a system for obtaining, sharing, and using accurate feedback concerning how well the youths in the group are identifying and resolving their problems in their everyday activities. Such information is important not only for the treatment team but also for program integrity and for use in the preparation of case communications to external personnel such as judges, parole officers, or parents. For example, the group coach needs opportunities to obtain accurate feedback if he or she is to know when and what kind of intervention is needed with a particular youth group member. Consider a situation in which a youth with multiple thinking errors and behavior problems denies having any current problems in a mutual help meeting. If the group fails to confront this member, what should the coach do? Obviously, without relevant feedback, the coach would not even know that the youth was avoiding certain problems. On the other hand, if the coach is equipped with accurate and systematic feedback concerning this youth's current thinking error and behavior problems, he or she can make an appropriate, timely intervention in the course of the meeting (e.g., during problem reporting).

Informed interventions send a strong message to the youth group that staff members are involved and actively using a shared feedback system. A group that is struggling with a resistant peer will be encouraged by this sign that staff are indeed observing, recording, and sharing information about the group (a demonstration of staff attributes such as involvement and communication, described earlier). Furthermore, insofar as the negative group member realizes that the alert treatment team will probably pick up on a lying problem (as well as other problems), that youth may be more forthcoming in reporting thinking errors and behavior problems during mutual help meetings. Feedback, then, is a key to achieving the staff unity discussed earlier.

Although the residential youth group has a natural feedback advantage, that feedback often lacks in quality. Particularly because a new group lacks equipment, members may form impressions about one another that are partial and inaccurate. Just as, to be effective, a youth group must work to improve the quality (comprehensiveness, accuracy) of the shared feedback about group members, an effective treatment team must do likewise. Without collating and sharing feedback from diverse program areas, staff members may resemble the proverbial blind men attempting to describe the elephant. Shared feedback leads to an accurate grasp of the overall picture concerning a youth's problem dynamics.

The composite assessment of a given youth's progress in identifying and solving his or her thinking error and behavior problems, however, is only as good as the diverse feedback that makes up the overall picture; in other words, a summary of gossip is still gossip. Hence, it is essential that the feedback transcend casual or subjective impressions. The following are sources of more objective information.

Standardized or validated assessment instruments. Certain points in a youth's institutional residence (intake, midpoint, prerelease) afford the opportunity to administer standardized instruments for assessing the youth's status or progress in terms of physical health, academic and vocational skills, social skills, and other relevant areas of social functioning. A number of standardized tests are available for such assessment (see, for example, Goldstein & Glick, 1987, pp. 283–288). Noted earlier in this book has been the value of using reliable and valid diagnostic measures such as the How I Think questionnaire (Barriga & Gibbs, 1995; Gibbs et al., 1995), the Inventory of Adolescent Problems–Short Form (Appendix B), and the Sociomoral Reflection Measure–Short Form (Basinger, Gibbs, & Fuller, in press; Gibbs et al., 1992; see Appendix A).

The EQUIP language. In our experience, staff, youths, and families find the vocabulary used in this book for describing cognitive distortions and problem behaviors to be readily understandable, authentically descriptive, and helpful in pointing toward appropriate treatment directions. For example, a youth who reports a Self-Centered thinking error and/or an Inconsiderate of Others problem with respect to his family would clearly benefit from learning a social skill such as Expressing Care and Appreciation. In contrast, merely to write that a youth "has an acting-out problem" or "does not get along with peers or staff" provides very little descriptive power or treatment direction.

Daily activity reports and youth behavior reports. The EQUIP language figures in completion of daily activity reports. The daily activity form may be used by various staff members (e.g., a teacher or a recreational leader) and provides a fairly concise description of the youth group's behavior. Following are typical yes/no questions on the form:

Did the youths belonging to an EQUIP group enter on time?

Did they enter together?

Did they start their activity in a timely fashion?

Were they task oriented?

Were any thinking errors or behavior problems exhibited?

If youths exhibited problems, did they themselves or peers respond appropriately (e.g., checking themselves or being told to check themselves or to think ahead)?

Did they complete the task and clean up the area on time?

In addition to the yes/no questions, space is also typically allotted for short narratives of incidents—for example, "Bob showed an Aggravates Others problem by whistling while others were trying to work." Although insignificant in isolation, such an act may be revealed as part of a systematic pattern if feedback from other program areas contains corresponding narratives—for example, "Bob stood in front of the TV when everyone else was watching it" and "Bob often held the ball instead of passing it." A separate form requiring more extensive reporting may be used when a serious negative incident occurs. Positive patterns indicating therapeutic progress are also indicated on the daily activity reports.

Daily activity reports should also be completed in connection with therapeutic events planned by staff or by the youth group. For example, the hypothetical youth with the Self-Centered and Inconsiderate of Others problems may be encouraged by his peers to develop a plan whereby he will share this realization and practice the social skill Expressing Care and Appreciation the next time his family visits. If the youth is inexperienced in such positive behavior— and hence nervous—he may ask one or two peers to accompany him, a request that could become part of the plan. In addition to the peers, a staff member may also be present. The success with which the youth corrects his thinking errors and effects constructive behavior is obviously valuable information that should be recorded by staff and shared with the treatment team.

Summary reports. The daily activity reports feed directly into summary reports. For example, a youth's treatment team teacher may receive individual daily activity reports from the youth's other teachers, summarize the content of those reports, and take a summary report to the team meeting. Such a summary report provides the team with a more comprehensive representation of progression or regression in the youth's social functioning. The treatment team secretary transfers the summary information into the minutes so staff can determine the level of the individual's and the group's functioning and plan for responses in the coming week. For example, for a group in the forming stage, the treatment team may decide to give support for positive group members.

The EQUIP team log. Daily activity reports and summary reports feed into the team log—the ongoing central record of the activities of the youth group and the staff team. The team log can be a notebook with pages numbered and dated as used by staff. The recommended form is a permanently bound log that cannot be disassembled without the tampering being easily noticed. The team log should be housed in a secure place with limited youth access but ready access for all staff. All entries should be appropriate and professional recordings of descriptive feedback or practical communications between staff. Personnel other than staff team members or administration should have input into the team log only indirectly, through consultation with a team member or administrator who may then make an entry.

In general, an effective and positive staff culture is achieved through application of the same principles that underlie a positive youth culture. If any group—youth or staff—is to be positive, provide help, or otherwise fulfill their mission, the group must be empowered, equipped, unified, and informed.

Chapter 8

Program Adaptations and Expansions

More than a program, EQUIP is an intervention strategy to impart motivation and skills so that adolescents can effectively help one another think and behave in ways that are responsible rather than harmful to themselves and others. EQUIP is most readily implemented in a setting that already has in place either a mutual help group or a psychoeducational skills curriculum. For example, facilities, schools, centers, and homes that comprise the National Association of Peer Group Agencies use adult-guided peer-helping groups for treatment purposes. In our observation, however, such agencies often do not have in place separate meetings dedicated exclusively to teaching a psychoeducational curriculum and self-monitoring skills. As we have argued throughout this book, those meetings are crucial if the youths are to be effective in helping one another; such agencies should consider adopting the EQUIP curriculum and daily logs. Furthermore, the portion of the EQUIP curriculum devoted to cognitive distortions modifies and enriches even the mutual help format: We believe that the problems reported during mutual help meetings should include not only behavior problems (Easily Angered, Authority Problem, etc.) but also cognitive problems or thinking errors (Self-Centered, Minimizing/Mislabeling, etc.).

Some agencies or schools use psychoeducational programs such as Goldstein and Glick's (1987) Aggression Replacement Training (ART) in a youth group format but do not otherwise attempt to develop the group into a positive therapeutic culture. Yet youths often are most amenable to psychoeducation if it is presented in terms of equipping them to teach or help others. In our opinion, ART programs could benefit, at the very least, from inclusion of the innovations, reorganizations, and refinements presented in chapters 3 through 5. (In light of recent research [Gregg et al., 1994], we recommend our chapter 3 property problem situations, even for mainstream schools.) Equally important would be to cultivate in the youth group a culture genuinely amenable to treatment (chapter 2)—and a correspondingly positive culture among the staff (chapter 7).

In this chapter, we discuss adaptations and extensions of the EQUIP strategy. Although EQUIP often can be readily implemented as presented in this book, in some contexts it must be adapted for optimal effectiveness. For example, how must EQUIP be adjusted to become appropriate for female adolescents with antisocial behavior problems? Preadolescents? Young adults? In our experience, the basic strategy is adaptable to these populations.

In other contexts, EQUIP may not be implementable in its entirety, even with adjustments. Does EQUIP apply to settings where the youths' average stay is a matter of days or weeks rather than months? Where the group treatment occurs during the day only? Where the clients in group treatment are the youths' parents or families? Where there can be no group treatment but only individual therapy? Aspects of EQUIP are applicable to all of these contexts; these will be described under the subsequent discussion of partial applications.

In the final section of this chapter, we consider ways to expand the EQUIP strategy or bolster the EQUIP program to serve broader goals or more severely affected populations. Can EQUIP be integrated with cooperative learning programs to encompass educational goals as well as therapeutic ones? Can EQUIP be combined synergistically with substance abuse treatment programs? Can the program's equipment be bolstered to render EQUIP effective in treating even severe juvenile offenders (i.e., whose offenses are murder or rape)?

We conclude with a plea for accountability—this time, *program* accountability. However EQUIP is adapted or expanded, its effectiveness and the accuracy of its implementation should be monitored and evaluated with great care.

ADAPTATIONS

If appropriately adapted, EQUIP may well have substantial value with many types of client populations. Although ultimately EQUIP's value or effectiveness is an empirical question, three likely candidate populations are female adolescents, preadolescents, and young adults with antisocial behavior problems.

Female Adolescents

Traditionally, female adolescents with antisocial behavior problems have tended to be incarcerated for "covert" (theft, prostitution) or drug-related offenses and to evidence internalizing disorders (withdrawal, depression, suicidal ideation) along with their externalizing disorders.

Offer, Marohn, and Ostrov (1979) found empty-borderline or depressed-borderline psychological subtypes of juvenile delinquency represented within all four subtypes of the delinquents they studied at a forensic hospital; however, males provided the optimal cases for the predominantly impulsive and narcissistic subtypes and females provided the best illustrations of empty-borderline or depressed-borderline psychological subtypes of juvenile delinquency. For example, Offer et al. wrote the following about the depressed-borderline exemplar, Martha:

> The overriding pattern of Martha's ten-month hospitalization might be seen as self-incrimination. She expressed the feeling that she "blew the whole world away" when she made an elopement attempt, and was sincerely astonished and elated when other patients did not reject her for trying to elope. She continually . . . referred to herself as a "bitch" and an "animal." She was constantly confessing misdeeds—she turned in drugs [and] a knife mistakenly left in her room by her parents, and she informed the staff of several planned elopement attempts. . . . She falsely accused herself of stealing someone else's food in the community meeting. . . . [After starting a fire that engulfed her room and threatened her life, Martha] stared blankly, was completely immobilized, and made no attempt to help herself. (p. 78)

Given the greater prevalence among females of internalizing along with externalizing disorders (Dodge et al., 1990; Barriga, Harrold, Stinson, & Gibbs, 1995), it is not surprising that female delinquents' Assuming the Worst thinking error often includes exaggerated expressions of hopelessness and self-condemnation. With this qualification, use of the four thinking error categories is, in our experience, appropriate for female juvenile offenders. The main adjustment to the EQUIP program concerns the content of the curriculum materials, in which details such as character names and circumstances should be modified for females (see, for example, the suggested modifications to the problem situations in chapter 3). Also, where the externalizing behaviors are neither severe nor frequent, some of the consciousness-raising materials in the anger management curriculum (which assume conduct disorder or criminality as a life-style; see chapter 4) may be toned down or eliminated. On the other hand, not all curriculum materials require modification. We have found that female adolescents relate well to some of the male-oriented material, such as Gary's Thinking Errors (see Figure 4.2). Furthermore, the prevalence rate of serious externalizing or antisocial behavior problems among females may be increasing; a recent United States Justice Department survey found that the rate of arrests for severe felonies is increasing more rapidly for females than for males (Krauss, 1994).

At a treatment center for both male and female delinquents, should the EQUIP groups be segregated or integrated according to gender? Small mixed groups can permit academically talented girls to shine; in large groups, however, their internalizing problems may cause them to lose out to more assertive boys (Fader, 1976). We agree generally with Carducci and Carducci's (1984) argument that mixed-sex youth groups in delinquency treatment institutions should be initiated only when a caring culture is already in place:

> Briefly, delinquency is largely a product of male cultures, and delinquent males will relate more quickly and fully to their male peers. Inappropriate behavior is often stimulated by [the male] adolescent need to impress the girls and vie for them. Conversely, girls develop their sex roles in relation to each other, with peer support and encouragement. They need to be girls with other girls, to develop their identity before risking it with the boys. . . . Although problems of relating to the opposite sex present opportunities, and need to be dealt with sooner or later, in the beginning they will only dramatically escalate your difficulties. (p. 165; cf. Vorrath & Brendtro, 1985)

Preadolescents

Equipment meetings play an especially important role where EQUIP is used with at-risk preadolescents or children. Providing the psycho-educational equipment for mutual help is crucial because at-risk preadolescents are even less likely than antisocial adolescents to have the problem-solving skills needed for peer approaches (Brendtro, Ness, & Nicolaou, 1983). Indeed, with totally unskilled children it may be advisable to teach the entire EQUIP curriculum before starting the mutual help meetings. (The institution may also wish to adapt for children the social skills component of the EQUIP curriculum; cf. McGinnis & Goldstein, 1984; Stephens & Arnold, 1992.)

Brendtro et al. (1983) also note that, in comparison to adolescents, children tend to have shorter attention spans (hence the appropriateness of shorter meetings), greater need for clear structure (hence the importance of explicit conduct rules and immediate feedback about behavior and thinking problems), greater inclination to "tattle" on others (hence a continuing emphasis on the need for confidentiality), and more intense need for adult nurturance and guidance (hence a greater need for individual counseling apart from the group therapy). Finally, Brendtro et al. note that

> in a latency-age group with an age span of several years, very marked differences in size, developmental level, experience, cognitive understanding, and peer group orientation may exist. Staff may need to be more active to make sure older, more sophisticated children do not dominate and bully. (p. 217)

Groups with ages spanning several years can nonetheless be valuable; a relatively sophisticated or streetwise 9-year-old may benefit more through interaction in a group of similarly sophisticated 11- and 12-year-olds than in a group of same-aged but less sophisticated children. For example, such a youngster will learn the skill Dealing Constructively with Negative Peer Pressure (see chapter 5) if the role-play partners are similar to those he or she actually "hangs with" in the neighborhood.

Young Adults

There is in principle no reason why EQUIP cannot be used with young adult offenders, although some of the curriculum materials geared exclusively to teenagers should be either modified or deleted. In other words, many of the materials provided in chapters 3 through 5 may be adaptable to young adults. For young adults with long histories of frequent offending, EQUIP should be bolstered with the empathy-enhancing techniques described in the subsequent discussion of applications for severe juvenile offenders.

Similar to EQUIP in some respects is a group treatment program for adult career criminals already in operation at United States correctional facilities and psychiatric hospitals—namely, Yochelson and Samenow's therapy for "the criminal personality" (Samenow, 1984; Yochelson & Samenow, 1976, 1977, 1986). Like EQUIP, this program provides group support but emphasizes individual responsibility for change: "The change process calls for criminals to acquire moral values that have enabled civilizations to survive. The objective is to teach them to live without injuring others" (Samenow, 1984, p. 252). The program is based on a therapist-guided small group in which members report problems, are helped, and help one another. Group members are "at different points in the change process . . . so that a new man could see how others were functioning and the current members could see themselves all over again as they heard the questions, arguments, and excuses of a totally unchanged criminal" (p. 217). Central to the reporting and solving of problems is the identification and correction of thinking errors. At opportune points, the therapist helps group members to spot thinking errors, to put themselves in the place of others and see how their actions have injured others, to respond constructively to stress or adversity, and to use techniques such as thinking ahead to consequences and positive self-instruction.

Yochelson and Samenow's therapy differs from EQUIP in several respects, however. First, whereas youth participation in EQUIP may or may not be voluntary, participation in the Yochelson and Samenow therapy is not only voluntary but indeed the result of an admission process. Prerequisites for admission to the group are permitting oneself to be the subject of a diagnosis of criminal life-style and worldview and learning to monitor and record on paper one's thoughts in an objective fashion (a kind of personal journal that goes beyond the structured logs used in EQUIP).

The second difference concerns the referent for problem reporting in the mutual help meetings: Whereas EQUIP participants report problems in both behavior and thinking, in the Yochelson and Samenow therapy, problem reporting refers more exclusively to recent criminal thinking, based on recorded notes brought to the meeting. Criminal thoughts "flood the mind" (Samenow, 1984, p. 228) of the unchanged criminal every day. Samenow describes the case of Leroy, a burglar and armed robber admitted to the group:

> Having heard that Yochelson's group met all morning every day, Leroy wondered what in the world consumed so much time. He quickly found out. Discussion was not limited to events or problems. . . . A criminal considers himself having a "problem" only when he gets into a jam by doing what he isn't supposed to. So there was little point in limiting discussion to that. The heart of the meeting was the daily report of thinking. (p. 219)

Third, the therapist plays a more dominant role than in EQUIP, not only in the preliminary interview but also during the group session. In effect, the therapist runs the meeting, respectfully but assertively interjecting with "corrective concepts" (Samenow, 1984, p. 218) and other teaching as needed during the session.

> As reports were made, Yochelson listened carefully and, from the hodgepodge of thoughts, selected a focus. . . . One morning, [Leroy] reported being furious when he was called into an office and accused by a nursing assistant of being high on marijuana. He was especially outraged because he had used no drugs for a week, now that he was in the program. The thought flashed through his mind, "I'll bust the SOB's

head wide open." In the group meeting, Leroy's thought of assaulting the attendant was treated as seriously as if he had actually done it. Yochelson knew that unless such thinking was controlled, it would be only a matter of time before Leroy became violent. (p. 220)

In a recent set of staff training/client therapy videotapes (Schuman, 1994), Samenow models such group leader techniques. Although Samenow's group leadership is generally similar to Yochelson's, we were impressed with Samenow's extensive use of Socratic questions to stimulate group members' awareness of thinking errors. One particularly impressive technique involved eliciting the group's reactions to a videotaped interview segment in which a group member evidences errors in thinking. Simply hearing one's own or a group member's thinking produced some insight into thinking errors and provided a basis for the leader's subsequent Socratic questioning and teaching.

The directive leadership of the therapist means that the Yochelson and Samenow program does not seek to empower an autonomous group to the extent EQUIP does. Such empowerment is probably essential for influencing antisocial adolescents, who listen to other adolescents much more readily than to adults. However, for volunteering adults who have been prepared for group work with an active therapist, group empowerment may be less essential—the videotaped offender group did appear to develop into a positive, helping culture. We do suspect that the Yochelson and Samenow program could benefit from dedicating some meetings exclusively to learning "equipment" so that coverage of the needed skills could be more systematic and comprehensive.

PARTIAL APPLICATIONS

Whereas it is feasible to apply EQUIP in its entirety to female adolescents, preadolescents, or young adult offenders, it may not be feasible—even with adaptation—to apply the EQUIP strategy in certain other contexts or situations: for example, in short-term or day treatment centers, with families of offenders, and in individual counseling or one-on-one therapy situations. In these settings, however, partial applications may be feasible.

Short-Term Treatment

In a short-term residential setting such as a detention center or a house providing shelter care, the young person's stay may be a matter of days or weeks rather than months. Given such a limited time frame, the opportunity for meaningful treatment is obviously restricted. It is difficult to cultivate a stable group culture with continual turnover in group membership—difficult, but not impossible. The attempt to develop a positive culture is worthwhile, considering that even in a short-term setting a youth culture or social climate will develop. As Ohio's former Paint Creek Youth Center Director Vicki Agee once rhetorically asked, "If you don't have a positive youth culture, what kind *do* you have?" (personal communication, March 18, 1988). A group that has discovered some common values (through a discussion of the Martian's Adviser's Problem Situation; see chapter 3) should grasp what a positive group would be and will be more amenable than otherwise to learning at least portions of the EQUIP curriculum. (In short-term circumstances, Goldstein has selectively taught several of the social skills or only one of the curriculum components.)

An immediate contribution to the short-term facility will be the vocabulary associated with cognitive distortions and behavioral problems, as discussed in chapter 1. Simply introducing and teaching this vocabulary can give a more positive tone to the facility's social climate—among both youths and staff—because the terminology provides a common frame of reference that residents and staff can use to identify destructive lines of thought and action. A more positive social climate means a safer environment; personal safety must be a priority, especially at short-term nondetention facilities, which in many cases are not even permitted to lock up dangerous residents. Equipping residents with a language for describing the inaccurate and harmful elements in their thought and behavior also imparts a valuable tool that can be supplemented in the event that the court orders further treatment.

Although true mutual help meetings may not be practicable with a high-turnover population, the cognitive and behavioral problem language should be well learned. Teaching is the best vehicle for learning, and the group should be frequently engaged in teaching the vocabulary to new members.

Day Treatment

Thanks to longer average commitment periods, day treatment centers afford greater opportunities to apply EQUIP. Participation in an EQUIP group conducted at a day treatment center can be mandated as a part of an adjudicated youth's required activities during a probation or parole period, which usually lasts at least several months. In the case of parole, a parolee who participated in an EQUIP-type program while incarcerated could continue such participation at a day treatment center during the parole period. The responsible state youth service agency would then gain the opportunity to promote its mission of public safety and relapse prevention (i.e., reduction of the recidivism rate) by providing a continuum of services for adjudicated youths.

Where an EQUIP program is implemented at a school, participation lasts even longer, perhaps 8 or 9 months (see subsequent discussion of program expansions). On the other hand, day treatment settings by definition exclude the possibility of round-the-clock EQUIP groups and therapeutic communities as at a residential facility. This day-only limitation also means less control over completion of EQUIP activities, such as daily logs. Inclusion of the youths' families in the day treatment EQUIP program can do much to compensate for the limited control. Although EQUIP cannot be implemented in its entirety at a day treatment facility, an EQUIP group in day treatment should have the potential to be receptive to learning equipment, to practice using that equipment immediately in the community (an advantage of community-based programs), and even to become active users of that equipment in helping one another.

Families

Antisocial youths' families should be considered "full partners" (Brendtro & Ness, 1982, p. 323) in the youths' treatment (McCubbin, Kapp, & Thompson, 1993), yet these families are often in need of intervention themselves (Agee, 1979, pp. 5, 70; Azar, Robinson, Hekimian, & Twentyman, 1984; Heaven, 1990; Henggeler, 1994; Robin & Roehling, 1986). For example, therapists working with such families often hear thinking errors in parents' attitudes and beliefs concerning their children: A grandmother raising her grandson revealed an Assuming the Worst attitude as she lamented, "He's doing just like his daddy did; I couldn't do anything with his daddy either." Can *families* be equipped with less defeatist attitudes and other resources for helping youths more effectively?

Interestingly, Goldstein, Glick, Irwin, Pask-McCartney, and Rubama's (1989) application of Aggression Replacement Training (ART) to families seems to capture an important aspect of the EQUIP strategy insofar as considerable attention is given to techniques for motivating parents to become an equipped and mutually helping group. Goldstein et al. deal with ways to recruit families (of course, the family's involvement is sometimes court-mandated) and especially with ways to engage the recruited parent group in activities that heighten group autonomy, cohesiveness, and identity. For example, they recommend planning social gatherings involving food and opportunities for informal socializing, such as potluck dinners or bowling parties. Particularly important for group autonomy is having the group plan the event, select a member as coordinator, and cooperate on specific arrangements.

A cohesive group provides a receptive atmosphere for teaching the parents "skills dealing with self-control, parenting, marital relations, interpersonal relations, and supplementary competencies—skills designed to function in a manner complementary to or reciprocal with skills being taught to the delinquent youth in their own ART sessions" (Goldstein et al., 1989, p. 60). Meetings represent an interesting blend of mutual support and equipment activity. Goldstein et al. emphasize that the meetings should be more than conversation sessions; they should include the kind of sharing that leads to identification of needed skills:

> We have found that reviewing the week is a good way to see how use of the structured learning and anger control skills learned in previous weeks went when used in real-life settings. Furthermore, as persons relate new events and experiences, facilitators have the opportunity to spot an appropriate skill for presentation this week. For example, a person might relate apprehension about having to deal with a neighbor or child's teacher, in which case Preparing for a Stressful Conversation might be spotted as the skill on which to focus that evening. (p. 70)

Teaching ART (or EQUIP curriculum) skills to parents should enable them to achieve more positive and constructive relationships with their delinquent adolescents. At the very least, teaching the cognitive and behavioral problem terms to the parents will mean that the parents and children can speak a common therapeutic language.

It is also helpful to supplement ART or EQUIP by teaching parents how to conduct a family or "fairness" meeting (Lickona, 1983; Popkin, 1983; more personal and intense modes of parent-child reconciliation are described by Agee, 1979, p. 100). Like EQUIP, parental use of a fairness approach in a structured meeting demonstrates how "reason rather than power can be used to solve conflicts" (Lickona, p. 301) and provides further practice in expressing views, listening to others, and finding middle ground on issues. Fairness meetings can have three benefits:

> First of all, they challenge kids to take the perspective of the group—to think of what's good for the family as a whole, not just for themselves. That's an important part of [Kohlberg's] Stage 3 moral reasoning, and a step toward the Stage 4 ability to think of the good of society.

Second, such discussion bolsters kids' self-respect by giving them a say in family life, a forum where their ideas are heard and respected.

Finally, by sharing responsibility for solving family problems, kids are sharing responsibility for the making of a good family life. In a real sense, they become cocreators of the family. (p. 299)

Lickona stresses the importance, once "common ground" is found in a fairness meeting, of drawing up a contract. Such contracting would involve writing down the agreement, having all involved sign it, and planning for a follow-up meeting to discuss how the agreement is working out and to agree upon fair consequences for violations of the agreement. Where parents must deal with a youth who has drug abuse or other severe behavior problems, Lickona suggests using a fairness meeting to develop

a hard-nosed behavior contract that spells out, with clear consequences for violation, the behaviors you find unacceptable while your child is living under your roof. Kids should get the message, "If you want to be part of a family, you have to behave like a member of a family. Home is not a no-strings-attached proposition." (p. 403)

Individual Therapy

To some extent, EQUIP applies to therapy contexts that do not afford any opportunity for individual work. Two EQUIP themes that can apply to one-on-one therapy or individual counseling are (1) that anti-social behavior is, to a considerable extent, the result of distorted or erroneous thinking and (2) that the antisocial individual can choose to think and act in a noncriminal direction. Samenow (1993) stresses the importance of communicating, in both tone of voice and style of interaction, a respect for the client as a person who has the capacity to face the truth about him- or herself, accept individual accountability, and make a series of choices to change. The client's externalizing must be spotted and politely challenged at every turn. To a client who seeks to escape accountability by referring to "all the people who have done things and aren't locked up," the therapist might counter, "What does that have to do with you?" (cf. the reversing technique, chapter 2). If a client excuses a criminal act by saying, "I wasn't myself," the therapist might politely ask, "Who were you, then?" and suggest that the crime does not seem at all uncharacteristic—indeed, the problem that requires work is the iceberg of which the crime was the tip. If the client asks point-blank for a personal impression, the therapist should respectfully state the unvarnished truth—for example, "I think you are a person who takes shortcuts, steals, lies, and runs from problems."

Both to the client and to significant others (family, probation officers, etc.) who play important roles in the individual's life, the therapist should highlight the crucial questions for therapy: How does this person deal with life, especially with things that are disagreeable? Is the person constructive in the way he or she tries to grapple with problems? Does the person use the past as a guide to the future? How does he or she look at past events? What is the person's worldview? The significant others should be alerted that the therapy focuses on the issue of the client's character and integrity and that their assistance is needed if the client is to be held accountable for change.

The themes of correcting cognitive errors and choosing constructive alternatives are illustrated in Beck and Freeman's (1990) narrative of therapeutic interactions with a wife batterer (the thinking error terms used in EQUIP are noted in the narrative):

> Joe was asked to give concrete descriptions of the typical family tensions that bothered him. This included details on exactly what each person did and said, and his automatic thoughts about the situation. . . . Each circumstance in which Joe felt anger or irritation was listed as a problem situation in a choice review exercise. Joe and his therapist then tried to think of all of the different ways that he might react to the situation, listing the advantages and disadvantages for each way. . . . A crucial component of this process [of assisting him in making better choices] was helping him to recognize his negative thoughts as triggers for his angry feelings and aggressive behavior, instead of blaming his actions on something Becky [his wife] did or said [Blaming Others]. A second major component was clarifying for Joe how his underlying beliefs reflected rules for living that dictated mistrust of others [Assuming the Worst], and a conviction of personal infallibility [Self-Centered]. These attitudes included the notions that "Others are always trying to screw you over" [Assuming the Worst], "No one really gives a damn about me" [Assuming the Worst], and "I should always have the final say-so because I am right" [Self-Centered]. . . . For instance, Joe came home late one evening (after drinking) and found that Becky had already cleaned up from the evening meal and put the food away. He automatically

thought, "That bitch never fixes a decent meal for me" [Mislabeling, Blaming Others]. When he attempted to confront her about this, he thought, "She is ignoring me" [Self-Centered, Assuming the Worst], so he proceeded to force her to pay attention to him by hitting her. When he was asked to evaluate the validity of his first statement ("That bitch . . . ") and to identify other possible reactions, Joe recognized that this thought was a distortion, since Becky was in fact a very responsible homemaker. Joe and his therapist then discussed different ways that he might have handled this situation more peacefully. This discussion helped Joe to see that Becky and his children also had needs that had to be taken into consideration [correcting Self-Centered]. Although he didn't accept it wholeheartedly, Joe agreed to consider the therapist's suggestion that his heavy drinking interfered with more rational thinking and made Becky want to withdraw from him [correcting Self-Centered, Blaming Others]. (pp. 168–169)

As implied by our interpolation of the thinking error vocabulary, we believe that clients in this type of cognitive therapy might better monitor and correct their thinking errors if they were equipped with vocabulary to use as tools in that process—just as Beckian therapists equip "internalizing" (i.e., depressed) clients with vocabulary tools for the monitoring/correcting process. The exercise Gary's Thinking Errors (Figure 4.2) might be useful in one-on-one therapy for teaching the basic externalizing thinking errors; teaching the behavioral problem terms is helpful in the same way. Finally, aspects of the EQUIP curriculum and other techniques (reversing, relabeling, checking) can be taught to an individual client (who can then practice thinking ahead, TOP, checking him- or herself, etc.).

Identification and correction of thinking errors should also be helpful for treating clients whose externalizing disorder is specific to child molestation (e.g., Kahn & Lafond, 1988). The cognitive distortions found and used by Abel, Becker, and Cunningham-Rathner (1984) are classifiable in the EQUIP system. The following statements are classifiable as Blaming Others: "A child who does not physically resist my sexual advances really wants to have sex with me"; "When a child asks an adult a question about sex, it means that the child wants to see the adult's sex organs or have sex with the adult"; and "Children do not tell others about having sex with a parent because they really enjoy the sexual activity and want it to continue." Classifiable as Minimizing/Mislabeling are these statements: "Having sex with a child is a good way for an adult to teach the child about sex";

"An adult who only feels a child's body or feels the child's genitals is not really being sexual with the child, so no harm is being done"; and "My relationship with my daughter or son or other child is enhanced by my having sex with him or her." Again, these thinking error terms should be directly provided as tools useful for the client to learn and use in the change process.

EXPANSIONS

The EQUIP strategy can be not only adapted or applied partially but also expanded—merged or combined with other ideas or programs. We will focus on three examples. First, equipping youths to help one another is essentially the basis of cooperative learning techniques, which have become increasingly popular in school settings. Second, the EQUIP program and materials as provided in this book may not be powerful enough to penetrate the self-centered distortions of severe offenders; for juvenile murderers and repeat rapists, EQUIP may need to be supplemented with other programs that enhance victim awareness and empathy and thereby facilitate the self-accepted and self-maintained correction of criminogenic distortions. Finally, the EQUIP program may be combined with an EQUIP-like substance abuse treatment program supported by the National Institute on Drug Abuse.

Many of the therapeutic and educational interventions that we will review in this section represent new and creative suggestions for clinicians and researchers. Like EQUIP (Leeman et al., 1993), some of these interventions (e.g., certain cooperative learning programs) have been systematically evaluated and found to be effective. Careful evaluation research is needed for promising but as yet untested approaches. As Yalom (1985) writes, "Without the utilization of scientific rigor to test basic principles and relative treatment efficacies, the field [of group psychotherapy] remains at the mercy of passing fashions" (p. xii). Such evaluation research should be built into adaptations or expansions of EQUIP.

EQUIP and Corresponding Interventions in Educational Settings

Corresponding to EQUIP in the educational setting is cooperative learning, in which students learn to cooperate and cooperate to learn (Slavin, 1990). Cooperative learning is actually a rubric for a variety of classroom learning arrangements, from pairs or peer triads for learning, to small-group learning teams, to cooperative class projects.

Lickona (1991) characterizes cooperative learning as one of the most rapidly growing movements in contemporary education and describes the abundance of materials available for implementation. The relevance of cooperative learning for treatment of antisocial youths is evident in psychologist Marilyn Watson's conclusion following a review of cooperative learning outcome evaluation research: "The opportunity to be a contributing member of a just and benevolent peer group is conducive to caring about fellow group members, to developing more altruistic attitudes, and to a greater tendency to engage in spontaneous prosocial behaviors" (personal communication, February 21, 1995; cf. Goldstein, 1988). Equipping youths to help one another in the classroom represents an expansion of EQUIP from a treatment-only program to a treatment-and-academic-learning program.

The Power of Triads

In their excellent book *The Caring Classroom*, Dewey and Judith Carducci (1984) present their pioneering procedures for the use of cooperative learning with disruptive, unruly youths. They argue that their approach is applicable not only to classrooms serving students with severe behavioral handicaps or other conduct disorders but also to regular classrooms "because it addresses the needs of all students to be taught to cope, grow, and care, and be cared about" (pp. 9–10). At the heart of their cooperative learning procedure is the organization of the class into triads of students responsible "for academic progress . . . [for] support for self-control, [for] caring external control if necessary, and also for providing consistent, *ongoing* overt commitment to help and care about one another" (p. 82). Their argument for forming triads, as opposed to dyads or groups of four, sheds some light on the way the triads work together:

> If one member of a triad is tempted to misbehave, two
> can stop him where one could not. If a member does not
> understand a problem, he has two teachers within the triad—
> and if one of them needs a time-out, he still has one helper
> left. If two members do not understand a problem, the one
> who does understand it can teach until either one or both
> of the others has grasped it, at which point he either has a
> helper for ongoing teaching of the subject, or all three can
> go on to another issue. (p. 82)

To prepare a classroom for the formation of triads, the authors recommend that the teacher explain the following principles:

> If any member of the group has a problem, that problem
> will then belong to all three of them, and . . . they will be
> responsible for helping each other, with my supervision.
> Rather than talking with one person, I will be talking to the
> group; if I make a presentation of some academic material,
> it will be to the group, who will then be responsible for
> teaching each other. (p. 84)

In support of triads, Lickona (1991) quotes a teacher's experience of greater student accountability: "When I had them working in pairs, one would sometimes say to the other, 'Don't tell her I didn't do it, okay?' " (p. 190).

Of course, the teacher cannot establish the triads instantaneously. *The Caring Classroom* offers guidelines for establishing classroom control and for composing the triads. The recommended procedures for bringing a disruptive student under control include obtaining a commitment from the student to change his or her behavior, removing the student to a time-out area or holding room, and holding a conference with the student that includes a parent and a school administrator. An additional procedure available once the triads are functioning is use of positive peer pressure—for instance, saying to the entire class, " 'I wonder if others are bothered by John's behavior. It seems to me he is making it rough for the whole class. ' . . . If there is agreement with your statement, ask for suggestions from the peers as to alternatives. One acceptable suggestion might be that a couple of his classmates take John to the 'time-out' areas . . . and talk with him" (Carducci & Carducci, 1984; pp. 63–64).

Carducci and Carducci recommend allowing a week—generally of relative relaxation and getting acquainted—before forming triads so the teacher can learn as much as possible about each student. For example, in addition to taking standardized academic tests, students may be asked to make daily journal entries on topics such as "a time I felt happy," "an argument I had with a friend," and "the last time I helped someone." The journal entries typically afford insight into students' coping skills, social awareness, and particular difficulties or sensitivities. Also during this week, students are given the Positive Peer Culture problem list (see Table 1.1) and told to ask one or more fellow students to help them memorize it; the teacher learns about affinities among students by observing whom they turn to for help (information that can then be used in forming the dyads). We recommend, in addition, that the teacher (1) include the thinking errors list along with the problem list for the students to memorize (see Table 1.2); (2) consider including the assessment instruments described in chapter 6 of this book among the standardized tests administered; and (3) if necessary, consider extending the preliminary period in order to teach EQUIP techniques especially likely to be helpful to the triads—for example, checking, relabeling, and selected concepts from the curriculum (chapters 3 through 5). The teacher should confer with individual students concerning their test results and prepare for each student a diagnostic/prognostic folder that will be maintained throughout the year.

Carducci and Carducci then suggest how to form the triads, using the information gathered during the preliminary week: Rate the students "according to ability to give both academic help and support for coping behavior" (1984, p. 89) and, on the basis of the rank ordering, compose each triad with a high-, intermediate-, and low-functioning member. Wherever possible, the triads should be integrated with respect to ethnic origin or disability status: "As the students get to know each other, and appreciate each other's strengths through the work in the triad, the differences become no longer strange and frightening. Mutual respect, seeing each other as people, and treating each other with caring and kindness are the result" (p. 174; cf. Johnson, Johnson, & Maruyama, 1983).

Youth-to-Youth Service Programs

Related to EQUIP and cooperative learning are other initiatives that provide "ongoing, firsthand experience in face-to-face helping relationships" so that students "come to bond with other people, value them, and discover the powerful rewards of touching another's life" (Lickona, 1991, p. 313). Lickona recommends that schools adopt a philosophy that places a priority on service—for example, through programs in which older students teach or simply relate to younger ones (although these relationships do not entail reciprocal help as in EQUIP, they *do* involve helping). In one-to-one "buddies" programs, "the older children are learning to care by caring; the younger ones are learning to care by being cared for" (p. 314). Similar programs are offered by Older Friends for Younger Children, a program sponsored by Big Brother/Big Sister, and Youth to Youth, a program sponsored by CompDrug (a Columbus, Ohio–based nonprofit corporation concerned with drug abuse prevention). Note the importance of equipping the helpers: "To increase the chances of success, schools typically provide a training program for the student tutors, giving tutors their own 'teacher's manual' and taking them step-by-step through specific lesson plans" (p. 314). Similarly, Youth to Youth offers training workshops and conferences to equip youths for preventive interventions with at-risk children. Organizations providing such preparation would be well advised to enrich their preparatory materials with adaptations from the EQUIP curriculum.

Equipping or training is especially important in a recent variant of Youth to Youth, in which gang members are hired to counsel younger youths about the negative consequences of joining gangs and to help mediate gang disputes. Los Angeles, Denver, Fort Worth, and other cities with serious gang problems have experimented with the approach. The programs are controversial because they entail monetary payment, which some critics characterize as bribery for good behavior. Granted, unpaid volunteers would be preferable (they would indeed be more likely to be intrinsically or altruistically motivated), and the monetary compensation should not be exorbitant (considerable research documents the potential detrimental effects of external incentives on internal motivational resources). In practical terms, however, volunteers simply were not forthcoming, and expecting completely intrinsic motivation may be unrealistic. Furthermore, denying these youths payment for appropriate behavior would seem to be hypocritical. After all, are not the critics paid for their "appropriate behavior" (i.e., their job performance as educators, politicians, journalists, and the like; Goldstein, Harootunian, & Conoley, 1994)?

Anecdotal evidence suggests that this version of equipping youths is helpful, perhaps because the younger youths look up to the gang members (or former gang members) as role models. According to Denver's program coordinator Richard Rainaldi, quoted in the *Columbus Dispatch*: "Guys who were shooting at each other last summer are now sitting down together and trying to figure out how to heal their community, talking about things like starting a small business and talking to kids" ("Fort Worth's Hiring," 1994). We would concur, however, with the caveat from Los Angeles gang unit detective Michael Vaughn, quoted in that same article, that gang youths must be carefully selected and extensively trained for such a program.

Bolstering EQUIP for Severe Juvenile Offenders

The outcome evaluation research on EQUIP indicated that the program does get through to many juvenile offenders: For example, in a 12-month follow-up, the EQUIP group's recidivism rate was one-third that of the control group (Leeman et al., 1993). The incarcerated delinquents in the Leeman et al. study evidenced the full range of offenses, from minor felonies to murder. EQUIP may be less likely to be effective for a group of predominantly severe offenders, however, unless it is strengthened or supplemented in some way. We propose that the most useful programs for strengthening EQUIP are those that reach the offender's empathic potential (Goldstein, 1988). We now review two such types of programs: victim awareness programs and group role-play techniques with severe juvenile offenders.

Victim Awareness Programs

Victim awareness programs are an excellent idea for all offenders, but they may be especially important as a supplement to EQUIP where severe offenders are concerned. Victim awareness programs are designed to inculcate a sense of accountability in offenders by inducing them to put themselves in their victims' places. Because inducing perspective taking is central to EQUIP, the compatibility of victim awareness programs with EQUIP should be clear. Indeed, several of the exercises used in EQUIP's anger management curriculum are also found in victim awareness programs as formulated in Ohio and California, programs that we review here. Ideally, an antisocial juvenile would learn to take the perspectives of others and accept accountability not only through EQUIP processes (mutual help meetings, equipment meetings) but also in juvenile correctional facility classroom settings.

Incarcerated juveniles in Ohio and California are required to study victimization prior to release. The Ohio Department of Youth Services (1990) and the California Department of the Youth Authority (1994) victim awareness programs both teach the impact of crime on victims through a variety of materials and techniques. For example, both programs cover property as well as person offenses and present factual information on victimization that distinguishes myths (e.g., "Property crime does not harm anyone because insurance will take care of everything") from realities (e.g., "Many people do not have homeowner's or theft insurance. Even for those who do, not all items are insured, and there are deductibles and limitations to insurance policies"). Teaching such distinctions can reinforce EQUIP's effort to correct Minimizing and Mislabeling thinking errors. Both programs also use empathy-inducing questions based on specific depicted situations (the Victims and Victimizers exercise presented in Figure 4.8 is, in fact, adapted from the California curriculum) and other stimulations of victim awareness through video or film presentations, newspaper or magazine articles, guest speakers (especially recovering victims), letters or tapes from victims, role-plays, personal journals, homework, and reminder posters.

Features specific to one or the other program are also noteworthy. The Ohio program provides excellent material for teaching seven thinking errors (adapted from Yochelson & Samenow, 1977, and relatable to the four thinking error categories used in EQUIP). The Ohio program's emphasis on corrective cognitive therapy is clear in the suggestion that juvenile offenders be helped "to look at themselves for what they are, primarily irresponsible people and lawbreakers who must stop blaming others for their situations, stop minimizing what they have done, and own their behavior" (Ohio

Department of Youth Services, 1990, p. 35). Particularly helpful may be this program's suggestion of role-play and role-play reversal through letter writing—specifically, the suggestion that offenders write one letter (not to be sent) to each of their victims, showing empathy and remorse, and another letter to themselves as though they were a victim, talking about how they were affected by the crime and what having it happen meant to them. The potential of personalizing the victim in such ways for remorse or "grief work" by the offender is revealed in the following group leader notes from a group therapy session at Colorado's Closed Adolescent Treatment Center (Agee, 1979; see also the following discussion of crime reenactment role-play):

> Jeff states he is feeling good about himself but tomorrow is the first anniversary of his assault on the woman in the hospital parking lot. . . . Said he would like to make up to her for what he did. I (Group Leader) told him to write a letter to her, and that her first name is Sally (this is not her real name). On hearing the name, Jeff freaked. He began crying, got angry, began shaking. He finally was able to talk and said before he knew her name he could discount it. He said it "hit him hard" and that he was angry at me because he never wanted to know her name. He had seen what Jack and Keith went through since they knew about their victims. Once he knew her name, Sally became a person. Not knowing her name made her a "nonperson." He feared he would look her up and make up for what he did, or worse, get back at her for turning him in. He was fearful he would hurt her again. . . . He couldn't tell if he was angry at her or at himself. (pp. 98–99)

Agee notes that "the group leader must be very careful to see that the appropriate kind of support is given. The group members identify strongly with the emotions expressed and have a tendency to be too comforting [or even begin to offer rationalizations for what happened]. Although the youth's anxiety must be lowered somewhat, it must still remain high to motivate" behavioral change (1979, p. 97). In the present instance, the group should clearly and firmly identify the group member's thinking errors (e.g., Blaming Others: "get back at her for turning him in") and encourage him to continue feeling remorse and accepting personal accountability.

Also impressive in the Ohio program is the emphasis on victim awareness as a comprehensive view that should pervade the institution. All staff should take advantage of opportunities to "be the voice of the victim" in "teachable moments" that occur both inside and outside the classroom.

One suggested activity in the California victim awareness program relates well to the community service activities of mature EQUIP groups:

> A critical element of the Victim Awareness/Community Safety Course is student involvement in planning and implementing a Community Action Project. Students are encouraged to assist community crime prevention through involvement in projects which in some way directly contribute to Victim Assistance or crime prevention in local communities. Resources, time, security levels, and geography will influence the breadth and scope of these projects. The goals of Community Action Projects are to: create ownership, gain valuable skills, see other community members as "partners" versus "enemies or victims," and to build youth who are advocates. It is hoped that these "abilities" will transfer to the community upon release. (California Department of the Youth Authority, 1994, p. 2)

Crime Reenactment Role-Play

Like a victim awareness program, role-play activities can make an excellent contribution to any offender group treatment program. Indeed, in EQUIP, role-play is the primary vehicle for teaching social skills. The use of role-play in victim awareness programs was noted earlier. A particular type of role-play that deserves special attention entails the reenactment of a crime perpetrated by the offender. Crime reenactment role-play has proved to be a powerful tool for getting through to the violent offender—specifically, we believe, by eliciting in the perpetrator as well as in observing group members empathic distress (along with empathy-based guilt in the perpetrator). Crime reenactment role-play can be illustrated by its use in two group treatment programs for violent juvenile offenders: Colorado's Closed Adolescent Treatment Center (Agee & McWilliams, 1984) and Texas's Capital Offender Group program (Alvarez-Sanders & Reyes, 1994).

Closed Adolescent Treatment Center. In this setting, crime reenactment role-play was used as a therapeutically effective mode of problem reporting in a mutual help group setting:

> Larry, a 14-year-old, asked for the agenda. He was committed to the unit for the kidnap and rape of a two-year-old girl. Several times he had attempted to have group on his crime, but was unsuccessful in doing more than a very mechanical, emotionless relating of the details. By pre-arrangement, he had agreed to act out the crime on a large

baby doll in the hopes of bringing out more of the emotion in the situation. Larry proceeded to describe the situation in the room where he kidnapped the baby and talk about what was going through his mind. He saw the sleeping child as a good opportunity to have sex and thought about where he could take her where he would be undiscovered. He left the home with the baby, with his hand over her mouth so she couldn't cry. He went to a nearby park, and with considerable difficulty, raped the baby, and then left her there injured. He stated he had no interest in whether she lived or died, but did feel a little scared at what he had done.

When the role play with the baby was acted out, there was clearly shock and disgust among all the group members, both male and female, and also the Group Leader. All of the group members took some physical action wherein they were trying to distance themselves from Larry, such as scooting their chairs back. One girl (who had been sexually abused herself in childhood) screamed when another youth accidentally touched her as he moved his chair back. After some difficulty in getting started, the peers expressed their shock and disgust to Larry. He had frequently stated that he had no feeling for his victim, but in this group, he seemed to be stunned by the enormity of what he had done. He listened mutely to the feelings of his peers and appeared noticeably stricken when the Group Leader also told him of his feelings of disgust for what he had done. The group concluded in somewhat of a shocked state, and one of the girls in the group asked the Group Leader to please take the doll off the unit.

It was not until two or three months later that the effects of this particular group on Larry were seen. At that time, he had a repeat court appearance, and when asked by the judge what he felt for his victim, gave an extremely moving and [at least seemingly] honest statement which showed much awareness of the harm he had done to his victim. This was in sharp contrast to his earlier behavior in court when he had been very cocky and unrepentant. (Agee & McWilliams, 1984, pp. 292–293)

Agee and McWilliams attribute much of the impact of the emotionally charged session to Larry's experiencing his peers' and the group leader's visceral responses to his crime. Crime reenactment role-play can also benefit observing group members: Those "who themselves have difficulty with remorse can see someone else becoming aware of the consequences of their actions on their victims" (p. 293). This technique for enhancing victim empathy has gained increasing use with sex offenders (Hildebran & Pithers, 1989; Mendelson, Quinn, Dutton, & Seewonarain, 1988; Murphy, 1990; but cf. Hilton, 1993).

Capital Offender Group Program. Reenactive role-play has also been used as a more effective method of problem reporting in the Texas Youth Commission Capital Offender Group program, an intensive 4-month therapy designed "to break a participant's psychological defenses, to force him to see his victim's suffering, to help him discover his conscience and feel remorse" (Woodbury, 1993, p. 58). Participating in small mutual help groups, the capital offenders (specifically, juveniles incarcerated for murder) "are required to identify choices they made along the path which culminated in homicide in order to dispel the notion that the killing could not have been prevented and to enhance awareness of personal control over future actions" (Alvarez-Sanders & Reyes, 1994, p. 2). The incarcerated juveniles role-play many aspects of their own histories, including family relationships and the homicidal events themselves. In a role-played reenactment of a crime, the perpetrator must remain at the scene even though in the actual event he most likely fled. He is urged by the group and the leader to hear the pleas and "see" the blood of the victim (played by a group peer), to experience the victim's suffering (and thereby to experience empathic distress). In a second reenactive role-play, the perpetrator must literally put himself in the victim's place: This time the perpetrator feels what it is like to be the victim by taking the victim role. Alvarez-Sanders and Reyes report that the role-play activity has contributed powerfully to the program and report promising preliminary results.

The perpetrator's defenses might be further neutralized by a peer group equipped to identify the thinking errors. One of the Texas group members "showed no remorse for his crime and blamed his victim for embarrassing him—thus deserving to be killed. He said of the murder that it was 'no big deal, it was just another crime'" (Woodbury, 1993, p. 58). It would not be too difficult for an equipped group to detect the Blaming Others and Minimizing/Mislabeling errors in such problem reporting and thereby to expose the group member's self-serving rationalizations.

Supplementing EQUIP with Substance Abuse Group Treatment Programs

EQUIP can be not only merged with but also supplemented by other programs. Because antisocial behavior problems so often entail concomitant substance abuse problems, an especially valuable supplement to EQUIP is participation in Alcoholics Anonymous (AA), Narcotics Anonymous (NA), and/or Cocaine Anonymous (CA) small-group programs characterized by the National Institute on Drug Abuse (NIDA; 1993) as

> successful mutual help programs to support abstinence. For participants who have already achieved primary treatment goals, the testimony of others can be powerful reinforcement. Many people, in fact, seem to have a vital need for recalling the pain and damage of the past, acknowledging their growth and sources of strength—their own "Higher Power," the program's creed, and mutual help—and recommitting themselves openly to continued abstinence. For participants who are not abstinent, the meetings can provide real help in that direction, in effect, serving the purposes of primary treatment or pretreatment. (p. 12)

Fortunately, participation in such a program or programs is in fact often a condition of parole or probation where alcohol or drug addiction is implicated in an adjudicated youth's offense history.

Synergistic with AA or NA and focusing on relapse prevention is Recovery Training and Self-Help (RTSH; NIDA, 1993), a program for supporting recovery from addiction that features "a recovery skills training curriculum in combination with a guided peer support group" (p. 19)—in other words, the EQUIP idea. The skills training curriculum was added to the support group because "an aftercare group could do more than just talk about whatever came up at a given meeting and need not be limited to the ideas of whoever happened to be at that meeting" (p. 33). Representing the skills curriculum and support group components, respectively, are two weekly group meetings, each lasting 1½ hours: "fellowship meetings" (cf. EQUIP's mutual help meetings) and "recovery training sessions" (cf. EQUIP's equipment meetings). The skills training curriculum used in the recovery training meetings consists of guidelines or suggestions (e.g., "What to Do When You Have an Urge to Get High"); checklists (e.g., "The Ready-for-Work Checklist"); and "cases to consider," with comments to guide group discussion (cf. EQUIP's problem situations). The fellowship meetings are support group sessions in which the curriculum material "can be further explored and adjusted to personal situations" (p. 16). In addition to participating in fellowship and recovery training meetings, RTSH groups also engage in recreational activities and gain guidance and inspiration from contact with a network of senior recovering addicts.

PROGRAM EVALUATION

> Years ago, people thought that "good intentions" were
> sufficient—that if a child were surrounded by good people,
> the benefits would flow to him and be self-evident. However,
> the ballooning expense of both education and treatment,
> along with the obvious and frightening failures of education,
> has made a pained public suspicious. Their sensitivity has
> resulted in a sensitivity to the need to be accountable: What
> are we doing for children? What works? What doesn't? How
> can we prove it? (Carducci & Carducci, 1984, p. 180)

However EQUIP is adapted or expanded, the resulting program
should be monitored and evaluated on a continuing basis. Just as
EQUIP expects young people to be accountable for their behavior,
the public has a right to expect that programs for antisocial youths
be accountable for evaluating and demonstrating the effectiveness of
their treatment procedures. Indeed, development and use of valid
methods for assessing the effectiveness of one's therapeutic services
should be considered a professional responsibility.

A particular agency's plan for evaluating EQUIP's effectiveness
should be the product of a collaborative, democratic decision-making
process. Just as EQUIP youths are empowered to help others and to
change, EQUIP staff should be empowered to contribute significantly
to the evaluation plan that is best suited to their goals. Participation by
all involved staff members in the plan's development is the best way to
ensure that the plan will be understood, accepted, and implemented.

Although the specifics will vary, evaluation procedures should sat-
isfy certain basic requirements. The first requirement is to ensure that
the actual initiation and continued implementation do not depart substantially from the agreed-upon plan. To improve the prospect for
fidelity to the plan, or program integrity, it is important to specify the
plan as precisely as possible. Kazdin (1995) recommends that treatment
"be delineated in manual form that includes written materials to guide
the therapist in attaining the specific goals of treatment, and in the procedures, techniques, topics, themes, therapeutic maneuvers, and activities" (p. 92; cf. Luborsky & DeRubeis, 1984). We believe that this
book provides the core for such written materials, to be adapted,
applied, or expanded as appropriate to a given institutional setting.
Explicit and specific procedural materials, however, are not by themselves
sufficient to ensure program integrity. As Goldstein (1991b) points out,

> a wide and usually unpredictable variety of "emergencies,"
> "exigencies," "realities," and the like may arise. Caseloads

may expand. Workers may grow tired, lazy, or overburdened.
. . . Even if appropriately described, detailed, and exemplified
in an intervention procedures manual, the intervention plan
may fail to anticipate an array of crucial circumstances. Whatever
the bases for diminished intervention integrity, program
efficacy is likely to suffer. (p. 483)

Because of such possibilities, Kazdin (1995) recommends monitoring
to ensure that actual treatment conforms to prescribed procedures.

The second requirement is for standard measurement of the
presenting problems of the treatment population. As Kazdin (1995)
observes, "the failure to use standard diagnostic criteria or widely
used assessment devices makes it difficult to identify the severity of
child dysfunction relative to other samples and to normal (nonre-
ferred) peers" (p. 93). Furthermore, establishing a means for
measuring problem severity is a prerequisite for assessing whether a
program has been successful in reducing severity. In our implemen-
tations of EQUIP we have found the Sociomoral Reflection
Measure–Short Form (SRM-SF; Gibbs et al., 1992; See Appendix A),
the Inventory of Adolescent Problems–Short Form (IAP-SF; Appendix B), and the How I Think questionnaire (Gibbs et al., 1995) to be
very helpful pre-post assessment devices for this purpose. Goldstein
(1991a) refers to such measures as proximal—that is, "directly tied
to the content of the intervention" (p. 29). Proximal outcome evaluations are especially helpful as constructive feedback to staff on the
strengths and weaknesses of the program components. For example,
in our own preliminary implementation, minimal changes in moral
judgment as measured by the SRM-SF led to scrutiny of—and certain
improvements in—the social decision making curriculum. The fact
that major gains in social skills were highly correlated with degree of
self-reported institutional change improvement (Leeman et al.,
1993) suggested that the social skills component as then formulated
was already effective. Presumably dependent upon proximal effectiveness are more distal or derivative changes, such as a resultant decline
in a group's recidivism rate.

Ideally, assessing treatment effectiveness would entail comparisons
of a treatment group's pre-post changes with those of a matched or
randomly assigned control group (e.g., Leeman et al., 1993). Kazdin
(1988) acknowledges, however, that a scientifically optimal design
may not be feasible in many field settings where staff and financial
resources may be limited. Kazdin argues that where large-scale studies
are not feasible, detailed case studies entailing pre-post assessment
would represent an improvement over anecdotal reports or impressions.

A democratically agreed upon plan is also a democratically revisable plan. Carducci and Carducci (1984) recommend that plan revisions (whether for individual youths or the group) be expected and that periodic meetings expressly for this purpose be incorporated into staff operations (cf. Lickona's, 1983, similar recommendation for families, described earlier). After all, EQUIP is primarily an intervention strategy and program, and the growth of EQUIP will entail some unique features developed in accordance with the particular setting for its adaptation, partial application, or expansion. "Interventions cannot, nor should they be, automated or implemented unswervingly and unresponsively in a manner dictated by program manuals, and we are not championing such literalness of application here" (Goldstein, 1991a, p. 483). Nonetheless, we believe that once EQUIP takes the form of a concrete program with explicit directives, such a program deserves to be accurately implemented, faithfully maintained, and rigorously evaluated.

APPENDIX A

Social Reflection Questionnaire of the Sociomoral Reflection Measure–Short Form (SRM-SF)

Note. This questionnaire was originally published in *Moral Maturity: Measuring the Development of Sociomoral Reflection* (pp. 149–153) by J. C. Gibbs, K. S. Basinger, and D. Fuller, 1992, Hillsdale, NJ: Erlbaum. A rating form, scoring manual, and self-training materials for the questionnaire are included in that source.

Social Reflection Questionnaire

Name_____ Date_____

Birth date_____ Sex *(circle one)*:   male   female

INSTRUCTIONS

In this questionnaire, we want to find out about the things you think are important for people to do, and especially why you think these things (like keeping a promise) are important. Please try to help us understand your thinking by WRITING AS MUCH AS YOU CAN TO EXPLAIN—EVEN IF YOU HAVE TO WRITE OUT YOUR EXPLANATIONS MORE THAN ONCE. Don't just write "same as before." If you can explain better or use different words to show what you mean, that helps us even more. Please answer all the questions, especially the "why" questions. If you need to, feel free to use the space in the margins to finish writing your answers.

1. Think about when you've made a promise to a friend of yours. How important is it for people to keep promises, if they can, to friends?

   Circle one: very important   important   not important

WHY IS THAT VERY IMPORTANT/IMPORTANT/NOT IMPORTANT (WHICHEVER ONE YOU CIRCLED)?

_____

_____

_____

_____

SRM–SF (Code #_____)

2. What about keeping a promise to anyone? How important is it
for people to keep promises, if they can, even to someone they
hardly know?

Circle one: very important   important   not important

WHY IS THAT VERY IMPORTANT/IMPORTANT/NOT IMPORTANT
(WHICHEVER ONE YOU CIRCLED)?

_____

_____

_____

_____

3. How about keeping a promise to a child? How important is it
for parents to keep promises, if they can, to their children?

Circle one: very important   important   not important

WHY IS THAT VERY IMPORTANT/IMPORTANT/NOT IMPORTANT
(WHICHEVER ONE YOU CIRCLED)?

_____

_____

_____

_____

4. In general, how important is it for people to tell the truth?

Circle one: very important   important   not important

WHY IS THAT VERY IMPORTANT/IMPORTANT/NOT IMPORTANT
(WHICHEVER ONE YOU CIRCLED)?

_____

_____

_____

_____

5. Think about when you've helped your mother or father. How important is it for children to help their parents?

   Circle one: very important   important   not important

   WHY IS THAT VERY IMPORTANT/IMPORTANT/NOT IMPORTANT (WHICHEVER ONE YOU CIRCLED)?

   _____

   _____

   _____

   _____

6. Let's say a friend of yours needs help and may even die, and you're the only person who can save him or her. How important is it for a person (without losing his or her own life) to save the life of a friend?

   Circle one: very important   important   not important

   WHY IS THAT VERY IMPORTANT/IMPORTANT/NOT IMPORTANT (WHICHEVER ONE YOU CIRCLED)?

   _____

   _____

   _____

   _____

7. What about saving the life of anyone? How important is it for a person (without losing his or her own life) to save the life of a stranger?

Circle one: very important   important   not important

WHY IS THAT VERY IMPORTANT/IMPORTANT/NOT IMPORTANT (WHICHEVER ONE YOU CIRCLED)?

_____

_____

_____

_____

8. How important is it for a person to live even if that person doesn't want to?

Circle one: very important   important   not important

WHY IS THAT VERY IMPORTANT/IMPORTANT/NOT IMPORTANT (WHICHEVER ONE YOU CIRCLED)?

_____

_____

_____

_____

9. How important is it for people not to take things that belong to other people?

Circle one: very important   important   not important

WHY IS THAT VERY IMPORTANT/IMPORTANT/NOT IMPORTANT (WHICHEVER ONE YOU CIRCLED)?

_____

_____

_____

_____

10. How important is it for people to obey the law?

Circle one: very important   important   not important

WHY IS THAT VERY IMPORTANT/IMPORTANT/NOT IMPORTANT (WHICHEVER ONE YOU CIRCLED)?

_____

_____

_____

_____

11. How important is it for judges to send people who break the law to jail?

Circle one: very important   important   not important

WHY IS THAT VERY IMPORTANT/IMPORTANT/NOT IMPORTANT (WHICHEVER ONE YOU CIRCLED)?

_____

_____

_____

_____

APPENDIX B

Inventory of Adolescent Problems–Short Form (IAP-SF)

John C. Gibbs
The Ohio State University

Ann Swillinger
Ohio Department of Youth Services

Leonard W. Leeman and Susan S. Simonian
The Ohio State University

SaraJane Rowland and Connie Jaycox
Ohio Department of Youth Services

Inventory of Adolescent Problems–Short Form (IAP–SF)

The IAP–SF is designed to assess adolescents' social skills in problematic or stressful interpersonal situations. This appendix contains everything you will need for using the IAP–SF (except for the optional audiotape of the situations). Included are the interviewer's annotated copy of the Problem Situations; the Scoring Manual, which includes scoring rules and criteria; and the Score Sheet. The situations are male adolescent–oriented; the notes include instructions for adapting the situations for use with female adolescents. The IAP-SF would appear to have adequate reliability and validity for use with both male and female adolescents (see chapter 5 of this book; Paradissis, 1987; Shockley, 1987; Simonian, 1987; Simonian, Tarnowski, & Gibbs, 1991).

PROCEDURE

The preferred procedure for administering the IAP–SF involves the use of a tape recorder and two copies of the 22 IAP–SF situations. (In addition to the annotated copy provided here, a simple copy of the situations should be prepared for the subject.) The tape recorder should be used to provide a standard reading of the situations. Direct reading of the situations is also permissible, especially if a standard tone of voice is maintained from subject to subject. Following are the steps in the procedures.

1. *Open the interview.* After a few minutes of warm-up conversation with the subject, you (the interviewer) say:

   Now we'll listen to some situations that could happen to a teenager like you. We want to hear how you would handle these situations so that we can get to know you better. You might learn something about yourself, too. Please feel free to be honest. What you say will be used only for research or treatment purposes; it will not be part of your permanent record. I would like you to read along on your copy as we

---

Note. This measure is based on the Adolescent Problems Inventory (Freedman, Rosenthal, Donahoe, Schlundt, & McFall, 1978) and the Problem Inventory for Adolescent Girls (Gaffney & McFall, 1981).

listen to the tape. While we hear each situation, I'd like you to imagine yourself in this situation and think about how you'd respond if the person in the situation were really you and this were happening today. After I finish reading a situation, I'll ask you, "What do you say and do now?"

After you play (or read) each situation, pause for the subject's response. If a second tape recorder is available, you may wish to tape the subject's responses.

2. *Overcome a reluctance to respond.* Some subjects will object that they cannot imagine themselves in particular situations. Usually the subject will respond after some encouragement—for instance, "I know you'd probably never be in this situation, but please try to imagine what you would say and do if somehow you *did* find yourself in this situation." Similarly, if, on a situation item featuring a parent, a subject objects that he or she does not have a father (or mother) at home and so cannot reply, ask the subject to respond as if the situation had featured the parent figure appropriate for him or her. If the subject responds, "I don't know what I would do" and persists despite prompting, then enter a U for "unscorable" on the Score Sheet and move to the next item.

3. *Clarify vague or unfamiliar responses.* Once the subject responds, the response is sometimes so vague that it might be unscorable—for example, "I wouldn't do it." In such a case, initiate a neutral probing question, such as "Exactly what do you say, then?" or "What do you actually do, then?" Place a [Q] in brackets before a response that has been prompted by a query.

Some responses may seem vague because the interviewer is not familiar with the colloquialisms of the youth's cultural, regional, or age group. Such responses should be probed to clarify their meaning for the interviewer and scorer.

Another type of vague response is a self-report of words or actions that could be constructive if intended to be truthful but that may well be produced for self-serving, manipulative reasons. To clarify, ask the subject, "Do you mean that, or are you saying that to get over (i.e., to evade or manipulate)?" Astonishingly, juveniles will often freely acknowledge insincerity, permitting a scoring of the response as manipulation (usually a 2; see the Scoring Manual).

4. *Record the response.* Copy the subject's responses verbatim onto the Score Sheet. Make notes regarding tone of voice of the responses, especially when tone does not match verbal content. During a verbally assertive response, note if the tone is giggly or otherwise inappropriate. During a verbally conciliatory response, note if the tone is angry or antagonistic. Finally, note any tone that suggests exaggeration or putting on a front. Response content–response tone disparities affect response score (see the section on scoring rules in the Scoring Manual).

5. *Probe for tone of voice.* If the tone of voice is not evident, ask the subject to role-play tone of voice: "What is your tone of voice when you're saying that?" Note the tone of voice as indicated in step 4.

6. *Elicit contemporary responses.* If the subject indicates that the response represents what he or she would have done "before I got caught," ask, "What would you do today if you were on the outside and you were in this situation?" This occasion is one of the few where the hypothetical *would* should be used. Generally, say, "What do you say or do?" because the present tense encourages the subject to role-play realistically.

7. *Handle multiple responses.* Sometimes a subject will give several responses to a situation. If these multiple responses are based on a contingency—for example, "If it was summertime, I'd _____ , but if it was winter, I'd _____ "—then record all the responses (if there are more than two responses, the first two will be scored; see the Scoring Manual). If the multiple responses are not based on contingency—for example, "I'd say I'm sorry, or maybe I'd shoot him"—then ask the subject, "What do you think is the most likely thing you'd say and do?" (Again, under these circumstances, the hypothetical *would* may be used.)

8. *Make concluding observations.* At the conclusion of the interview, enter in the appropriate space on the Score Sheet your general clinical impressions of the subject. It is especially important to note any impression that a subject has been "putting on a front" in responding. Also, the IAP–SF situations may yield impressions of the subject's likely conduct in particular contexts that may be important for diagnostic, management, or treatment purposes. For example, does the subject seem to be at high risk for violence in dealing with members of the opposite sex (see situations 4, 13, 15)? Does the subject seem to have particular difficulty in dealing with adult authority (see situations 3, 5, 9, 11, 20)? Such impressions may also be noted.

IAP-SF Situations

Situation 1

You're visiting your aunt in another part of town, and you don't know any of the guys your age there. You're walking along her street, and some guy is walking toward you. He's about your size. As he is about to pass you, he bumps into you and you nearly lose your balance. What do you say and do now?

Note. If the subject *(S)* indicates that he would make a comment, ask about the tone in which he would make the comment. The female version substitutes *girl* for *guy*.

Situation 2

It's Friday night and you have the car, but you don't have any plans. The evening stretches ahead of you. You're bored and a little restless. You wish there were something to do. What do you say and do now?

Note. If *S* says, "I'd party," ask, "Could you explain more fully? What do you say and do when you party?"

Situation 3

It's 7:30 on a Saturday night, and you ask your father if you can go out driving around with some friends. He says no and is angry. He yells, "Nothing doing! You know what happens when you go driving around with those kids. You're staying home tonight!" What do you say and do now?

Note. If *S* says, "I'd stay home," ask, "But what exactly do you say or do now, facing your father?"

Situation 4

You've been going steady with a girl named Mary for about 3 months. It used to be a lot of fun to be with her, but it isn't anymore. There are some other girls you'd like to go out with now. You decide to break up with Mary, but you know she'll be very upset with you. What do you say and do now?

Note. If S says, "I would send her a letter," ask, "What do you say in the letter?" The female version of this situation refers to *a guy named Matt* instead of to *a girl named Mary* and makes other appropriate substitutions.

Situation 5

You walk into the kitchen one morning before school. Your mother takes one look at your clothes and says, "Oh, no! You're not going out of this house one more time looking like that! You march yourself right up those stairs and get on some decent things, or you're not going anywhere this morning, young man!" What do you say and do now?

Note. If S says, "I'd argue with her," say, "Exactly what do you say in the argument?" and "She still says no. What do you say and do now?" The female version substitutes *young lady* for *young man*.

Situation 6

One of your friends does some dealing on the street. Once in a while, he even gives you some pills or something for free. Now he says to you, "Listen, I've got to deliver some stuff on the south side, but I can't do it myself. How about it—will you take this stuff down there for me in your car? I'll give you some new stuff to try plus $50 besides for half an hour's driving. Will you help me out?" What do you say and do now?

Note. If S says that he'd say, "Do it yourself," ask, "What if the friend says he can't do it himself?" The female version of this situation replaces *he* with *she*.

Situation 7

One of your friends really likes a girl named Debbie and dates her some. You think she's pretty nice yourself. You went out with her Saturday night, and you both had a really good time. Someone must have told your friend because he comes running up to you in the school parking lot and says, "You dirty cheater! Bill just told me about you and Debbie. If you ever go out with her again, I'll knock your ugly face in!" What do you say and do now?

Note. The female version of this situation refers to *a guy named Dan* and makes other appropriate substitutions.

Situation 8

Your friend calls on a Saturday night to ask if you want to get together with him and some other friends. You tell him you've been grounded because you got home after curfew the weekend before. He says, "So what's the big deal? Just sneak out the back door and meet me in the next block. Your parents will never know you're gone." What do you say and do now?

Note. If S says, "I'd stay home," ask, "But what do you say to your friend?" In the female version, the friend is referred to as *she*.

Situation 9

Your father has been concerned for months about your getting home by midnight. Sometimes that's a problem because none of your friends has to be home before 1:00 A.M. One night you walk in at 1:30 A.M., and your father is sitting in the living room, looking mad. He says, "Where in the world have you been? Do you have any idea what time it is?" What do you say and do now?

Note. It is often important to probe responses to situation 9 for sincerity. If S says, "I forgot" or "It won't happen again," ask, "Would you say that to get over?"

Situation 10

You're walking along a side street with a friend. He stops in front of a beautiful new sports car. He looks inside and then says excitedly, "Look, the keys are still in this thing! Let's see what it can do. Come on, let's go!" What do you say and do now?

Note. The female version of the situation replaces *he* with *she*.

Situation 11

You're about an hour late getting to your part-time job in a supermarket because your car ran out of gas. You feel pretty dumb about that, and you know your boss will be mad because this is the busiest time of the day in the store. You punch in at the time clock, and the boss comes storming over to you and says, "You're fired! I've put up with you kids being late and not coming in one time too many. Starting with you, anyone who comes in late gets canned!" What do you say and do now?

Note. It is often important to probe responses to situation 11 for tone of voice. Also, if S says he would ask to talk to the boss later or in private, ask, "Okay, then what do you say?"

Situation 12

You have a friend who's a few years older than yourself. He's been in trouble with the law a lot, and he's even been to prison, but he's out now. You really like him a lot and respect him, and you wish he would like and respect you, too, because he's a popular person in the neighborhood. He comes to your house one night and tells you that he and another person are going to rob a place. He says, "You want to come along? We think you could be a big help to us." What do you say and do now?

Note. The female version replaces *he* with *she*.

Situation 13

You ask the girl who sits next to you in study hall if she'd like to come to a party at your house Saturday night. She says, "I'd like to, but my father won't let me hang out with anyone who has been in trouble." What do you say and do now?

Note. If S says he'd keep trying to talk her into it, ask, "Exactly what do you say to her?" The female version replaces *girl* with *guy* and *she* with *he*.

Situation 14

You're at a party, and all the people there are smoking joints. You used to do a lot of smoking yourself until you got caught last month. Everyone knows you used to smoke. Your girlfriend offers you a joint. What do you say and do now?

Note. If S says, "I don't smoke pot," ask, "If you did, what would you say and do now?" The female version substitutes *boyfriend* for *girlfriend*.

Situation 15

The girl you've been going out with just broke up with you. She said that you're okay but that she'd like to go out with other guys, too. You still like her, and you're hurt that she doesn't want to go out with you and continue to be your girl. You're in a terrible, miserable mood. You feel really down. What do you say and do now?

Note. The female version substitutes *guy* for *girl* and makes other appropriate substitutions.

Situation 16

You work as a clerk in a grocery store. The store isn't too busy, and a guy you know from school comes over to your cash register. He says, "Hey, I only have a dollar with me. Ring up these cigarettes and six-pack for a dollar, won't you? The manager is in the back of the store. He'll never know." What do you say and do now?

Note. If S says, "This is my job," say, "But what exactly do you say to your friend?"

Situation 17

You're playing basketball at school, and some guy you don't know well is standing on the sidelines. He starts teasing you, making fun of the way you play. What do you say and do now?

Note. The female version of this situation reads: *You're playing volleyball in gym class, and some girl you don't know . . .*

Situation 18

You're in a job interview, and you really want the job because the pay is good and the hours aren't bad. The interviewer seemed interested in you until he found out you were on parole. Now he says, "Our usual policy is not to hire anyone who's on parole. Nothing personal, but we've had too many problems with you kids in the past. Sorry." What do you say and do now?

Note. If S says he would try to talk to the supervisor, ask, "But what do you say now, to the job interviewer?" Also, it is often important to probe for sincerity in responses to situation 18. If S says, "I'm not like the other kids you've had here," ask, "Do you mean that, or are you saying that to get over?"

Situation 19

You were suspended from school for a week because you were caught in the locker room drinking one afternoon with several of your friends. You're back in school now, and it's been hard getting back in with the teachers. Just now, one of the teachers has surprised you in a little-used classroom, where you're catching a smoke, which is against school rules. The teacher says, "Okay, just what do you think you're doing in here, young man? Didn't you learn anything from your suspension?" What do you say and do now?

Note. If S says he'd just stand there, ask, "What do you do with your cigarette?" It is often important to probe for tone of voice and sincerity in responses to situation 19. If S says that he'd say, "I was just trying to calm my nerves," ask, "Would you say that just to get over?" The female version substitutes *young lady* for *young man*.

Situation 20

Your parents don't seem to like your friends. They say that they're dirty, or that they have no manners, or that they'll get you into trouble. Joe, a new friend with a bad reputation, has just left your house after his first visit to your place. After he's gone, your mother gets on his case, calling him a good-for-nothing and demanding that you not see him again. You know that Joe has become more responsible lately. What do you say and do now?

Note. If S says, "I'd say he's changed," ask, "Would you still see him?" The female-subject version substitutes *Jane* for *Joe* and makes other appropriate substitutions.

Situation 21

You're driving around with a good friend on a hot, muggy summer night. Your friend says, "I'm thirsty! I could really use a cold beer. I know a place that doesn't check IDs. How about going over and getting some booze?" What do you say and do now?

Note. If S says, "Go ahead," ask, "What do you mean by that?" or "What exactly do you say to your friend?"

Situation 22

It's early afternoon, and ever since you woke up this morning, you've been in a bad mood. What do you say and do now?

IAP–SF Scoring Manual

SCORING RULES

This manual provides scoring criteria for each problem situation. Using the criteria, rate the subject's responses on the following scale:

8 = high level of social skills (definitely constructive and appropriately balanced)

6 = socially skilled (probably constructive and somewhat balanced)

4 = neither socially skilled nor socially unskilled (no effect; would probably neither help nor hurt the situation)

2 = poor social skills (probably destructive and somewhat imbalanced)

0 = no social skills (definitely destructive and imbalanced)

Keep in mind the following scoring rules:

1. *Multiple criteria.* The word AND in a scoring criterion means that both requirements must be met for S to receive that score. The word OR means that only one of the requirements need be met.

2. *Multiple responses.* When S has given more than one response to a problem, average the first two scorable responses (even if the second response is in reaction to a query), and do not score any further responses. If an interviewer note designates one of the responses as "more likely" according to the subject, score that response only. If an interviewer note indicates that one of the responses represents what S used to do, score instead the response indicating what the subject would do at present. If the second response is contingent or ambiguous (see rule 3), then derive the mean score for the second response and average it with the score for the first response to obtain the overall score for that item. Determination of response unit can be difficult. One helpful criterion is that response material punctuated by a query [Q] is automatically considered to constitute at least two responses (provided that responses both before and following the query are scorable).

3. *Contingent or ambiguous responses.* When S has spontaneously given a contingent response scorable at different levels—or if S

has given an ambiguous response interpretable at different levels—average the first two levels. For example, one subject gave a contingent response to situation 7, regarding the jealous friend, as follows: "If we're real close I'd say nothing, but if not I'd say, 'If I date her again and you try to knock my face in, we'll be fighting.' " The response is scored as a 3, the mean of the first identifiable level (level 4) and the second identifiable level (level 2; see pp. 311–312). When *S* has given a response so ambiguous or so irrelevant (i.e., not directly pertaining to the immediate situation) that it fails to relate to any level, then enter a U for unscorable in the rating column for that situation. A U may also be recorded in the case of a persistent "I don't know" response. The entire protocol is unscorable if more than 3 of the protocol's 22 situation items are unscorable.

4. *Content vis-à-vis tone.* Consider not only the content but also the tone of *S's* responses, and deduct 1, 2, or 4 points where there is an inconsistency. In a situation calling for assertiveness (e.g., resisting an unethical temptation) as a criterion for social skills, both the content and the tone of the response should be assertive (but not aggressive); if the words are assertive but the tone is giggly or otherwise inappropriate, credit *S* with one point less than you would have had the tone matched the words in assertiveness—for example, assign a 5 rather than a 6. Deduct 4 points—for example, reduce the score from 6 to 2—where the tone is exaggerated, suggesting that *S* is putting on a front or being insincere. Finally, deduct 2 points where the scoring criterion calls for a conciliatory or apologetic response and such a response is given in content but not in tone (i.e., the tone is angry or antagonistic).

MEANING OF PROTOCOL SCORES

The IAP–SF yields four scores: an overall social skills score and three subscores (see Score Sheet). The overall score is the mean (or, alternatively, modal) rating (range from 0 to 8) based on all 22 protocol situations. The subscores are based on a recent factor analysis (Simonian et al., 1991) of the IAP–SF, which found three common factors (Deviant Peer Pressure, Immediate Response Demand, and Deferred Response Demand) among the situation items.

Because the mean rating is multiplied by 100 (see Score Sheet), an adolescent's social skills mean protocol rating can range from 000 to 800. An individual with an overall IAP–SF score of 600 or higher is socially skilled and would be very unlikely to have a deficient subscore (below 400). With a score below 600 on the IAP–SF, however, a differentiated profile of peer pressure and anger provocation scores may emerge and prove useful for management and/or treatment purposes. An 800 or 600 score means very or somewhat socially skilled, 400 is borderline, and 200 or 000 means somewhat or very unskilled. Modal score can be 0, 2, 4, 6, or 8; modal score is not entered where two or more response frequencies are identical.

The meaning of a "very socially skilled" response or a "very unskilled" response varies somewhat according to factor. In Deviant Peer Pressure situations, an 8 signifies a forthright resistance, typically with a moral explanation or a suggestion for a constructive alternative. In anger-provoking (Immediate Response Demand and, to some extent, Deferred Response Demand) situations, an 8 response is calm, reasonable, and respectful, offering an apology, acknowledgment of a legitimate criticism, an explanation, or a constructive suggestion where appropriate. "Somewhat skilled" or 6 responses are also forthright and calm but may be missing the element of explanation or apology. Scores of 2, or somewhat unskilled responses, are generally manipulative, deceitful, evasive, or tactless. These responses also tend to be verbally antagonistic in anger provocation situations and inappropriately submissive in Deviant Peer Pressure situations (hesitancy involves mainly questions concerning getting caught). A score of 0, or a very unskilled response, in Deviant Peer Pressure situations generally signifies an unconflicted and immediate willingness to join in antisocial or illegal activity. In anger provocation situations, a score of 0 generally signifies a very hostile or defiant, physically threatening, insulting, and/or vengeful response. Borderline responses (scored 4) are rather nondescript, evidencing neither constructive (scored 8, 6) nor destructive (scored 2, 0) social skills.

Because modal scores have somewhat different meanings according to factor, it is advisable to examine the factor subscores section on the Score Sheet to determine whether a disparity greater than 2 exists between the modal score frequencies. For example, an overall modal 0 may entail four 0s for Deviant Peer Pressure and a single 0 for one of the anger provocation factors. Where modal score is mainly attributable to one or another factor, that factor should be indicated in parentheses next to modal score—for instance, 0 (Peer Pressure).

Overall social skills assessment should take into account both mean and modal score, especially where a disparity is evident between the two. For example, a protocol with a modal score of 2 but a mean score of 341 would suggest a subject whose most typical social response is manipulative or antagonistic but who shows potential for higher levels of social skills under some circumstances. Conversely, a protocol with a modal score of 4 but a mean score of 262 would suggest a subject whose most typical response is borderline but who in many circumstances will produce an unskilled response.

SITUATIONS AND SCORING CRITERIA

Situation 1

You're visiting your aunt in another part of town, and you don't know any of the guys your age there. You're walking along her street, and some guy is walking toward you. He's about your size. As he is about to pass you, he bumps into you and you nearly lose your balance. What do you say and do now?

8—S ignores the boy and walks on (he may give him a displeased look), without saying anything.

6—S ignores the boy and walks on but only because of unfamiliarity (*Examples:* "I don't know how he'd react"; "I don't know whether he's trying to start a fight") OR makes a calmly assertive response (*Example:* "Watch where you're going" [in a nonhostile manner]) OR a simple polite response (*Examples:* "Excuse me"; "Pardon"); may attempt some tentative friendliness before walking on.

4—Response is unassertive or otherwise ineffective but not likely to provoke a fight (*Examples:* [In a nonhostile tone of voice] "Oh, I'm so sorry"; "Why'd you bump me?"; "Can't you say, 'Excuse me?' "; "I'd like an apology").

2—Response is insulting, antagonistic, or provocative (*Examples:* "Watch where you're going" [in a nasty tone]; "Excuse *you*! What's your problem?"), OR S hits back (see next response).

0—S pushes or fights the boy (irrespective of whatever else S says or does, except that hitting back if the boy hits first or continues verbal provocation is rated a 2).

Situation 2

It's Friday night and you have the car, but you don't have any plans. The evening stretches ahead of you. You're bored and a little restless. You wish there were something to do. What do you say and do now?

8—*S* becomes involved in a nonaggressive and legal, specifically goal-directed activity (*Examples:* taking a quiet drive in the country, seeing a movie, engaging in a sports activity, taking a girlfriend out for dinner, going shopping at the mall).

6—*S* visits a friend or friends or starts a party with friends (as long as party activities are nonaggressive and legal), OR *S* drives around to look for a party.

4—*S* just drives around and looks for something to do (no specific goal mentioned) OR goes home and goes to bed.

2—*S* picks up a girl (except if it's done in a bar, which is scored 0) OR engages in any activity that is not in itself law breaking but that might lead to antisocial or illegal behavior (*Examples:* just hanging out, driving around looking for action, picking up hitchhikers).

0—Any activity that by nature is aggressive, illegal, or antisocial (*Examples:* drinking, taking drugs, drag racing, going to a bar, making fun of people).

Situation 3

It's 7:30 on a Saturday night, and you ask your father if you can go out driving around with some friends. He says no and is angry. He yells, "Nothing doing! You know what happens when you go driving around with those kids. You're staying home tonight!" What do you say and do now?

8—*S* gives respectful and calm verbal response, either raising objection (*Example:* "We'd be home by midnight, and we wouldn't get into any trouble") OR agreeing to stay home because of what's happened before when *S* was driving (*Example:* "I understand why you feel that way").

6—*S* agrees, perhaps with an accommodating comment other than the one noted for a score of 8, OR *S* raises competent but less convincing objections that fall between 8 and 4 in quality (*Example:* "They've changed and don't want any trouble now"), OR *S* asks if he can go out with other friends.

4—*S* stays home without saying anything (may continue to be angry), OR *S* uses weak objections that are not likely to anger his father but aren't likely to change his mind either (*Examples:* "Give me a good reason"; "I don't see why not";

"We're just going out to have a good time"), OR *S* asks if he can go out with other friends.

2—Response is mildly antagonistic, angry, or provocative (*Examples:* "Why not?"; "I want to go out"; "You give me the same argument every night"; "You never let me go out") OR manipulative or pressuring (*Examples:* "Bribe him"; "Talk him into it"; "Try the other parent").

0—Response is very antagonistic or insulting, OR *S* goes out anyway against the father's wishes (announces he is leaving or walks or sneaks out of the house).

Situation 4

You've been going steady with a girl named Mary for about 3 months. It used to be a lot of fun to be with her, but it isn't anymore. There are some other girls you'd like to go out with now. You decide to break up with Mary, but you know she'll be very upset with you. What do you say and do now?

8—Response is gentle, sympathetic, and tactful but clear, not beating around the bush, AND *S* suggests they both date other people or still be friends (*Example:* "Mary, we've had some wonderful times together, and I like you an awful lot, but I'm beginning to feel tied down. I think it would be a good idea if we both go out with other people").

6—One or the other of the components of the response with a score of 8. Response may not be as sensitive/tactful or mutually oriented as 8 (*Example:* "I don't want to get attached. We need to break up"), OR *S* suggests he would take steps to restore relationship.

4—*S* asks Mary what she thinks about dating others for a while, OR gives an excuse of the "white lie" variety (*Example:* "My father says I have to go out with other people"), OR simply says he wants to break up or would like to date other girls.

2—*S* says he wouldn't break up with her after all OR will have someone else tell Mary for him OR will try to manipulate or provoke her into breaking off the relationship OR just stops seeing her and sees others without giving her any explanation, perhaps hoping she will get the message herself OR is blunt to the point of being tactless (*Example:* "I don't like you any more. I'm breaking up with you").

0—*S* uses a perhaps deliberately careless lie OR is very tactless, insensitive, and antagonistic (*Examples:* "I don't have time for you"; "I'm sick of you"; "I'll come back if I don't find anyone better"; "If you don't like it, that's your problem").

Situation 5

You walk into the kitchen one morning before school. Your mother takes one look at your clothes and says, "Oh, no! You're not going out of this house one more time looking like that! You march yourself right up those stairs and get on some decent things, or you're not going anywhere this morning, young man!" What do you say and do now?

8—*S* gives verbal response that is (1) respectful and calm, and (2) cooperative, reasonable, or conducive to discussion; may agree to change clothes (*Example:* "There's no dress code, and they're perfectly clean. This is the style nowadays. What do you think is wrong? But if you still want me to change, I will").

6—*S* is still calm, but response is somewhat less cooperative (*Examples:* "I feel I'm old enough to decide for myself"; "I'm comfortable"; "I bought them"; "I'd change to avoid an argument, but I'd be mad").

4—*S* simply changes clothes without saying anything OR uses a weak argument that is not likely to make the situation better or worse; may remain angry (*Examples:* "Why should you care what I wear?"; "Nothing else is clean"; "Aw, come on—I don't have any better clothes"; "This is what I wear").

2—*S* walks out of the room OR is rude and disrespectful (*Example:* "It's up to me, and if I want to wear it then I'll wear it"—doesn't change clothes), OR *S* attempts to manipulate mother, OR *S* simply stays home from school, OR *S* changes his clothes now but says (to the interviewer) he or she will put the old ones back on in school.

0—*S* indicates a physical threat OR is very disrespectful OR says he will skip school for the day and stay home OR walks out of the house in the unacceptable clothes (perhaps underneath the acceptable ones) OR sneaks out the window in the unacceptable clothes.

Situation 6

One of your friends does some dealing on the street. Once in a while, he even gives you some pills or something for free. Now he says to you, "Listen, I've got to deliver some stuff on the south side, but I can't do it myself. How about it—will you take this stuff down there for me in your car? I'll give you some new stuff to try plus $50 besides for half an hour's driving. Will you help me out?" What do you say and do now?

8—*S* assertively (but not in exaggerated fashion) refuses to deliver the pills AND gives moral explanation (*Example:* "No, drugs harm people").

6—*S* refuses assertively but without a moral explanation (*Examples:* "No"; "No, thanks"; "No, I don't take that kind of risk"; "Forget it").

4—*S* refuses by making up an excuse to get out of the situation this time but leaves himself open to further pressure in the future (*Examples:* "Can't, my car's in the shop"; "Sorry, I don't have time now").

2—*S* says he will drive the friend but won't actually deliver the drugs himself, OR *S* asks a question, suggesting that he will do it if the answer is right (*Examples:* "And what if I get busted with the stuff on me?"; "What if it's a setup?"; "What kind of stuff is it?"), OR *S* agrees to do it just this once.

0—*S* agrees to deliver the drugs. Score 0 even if *S* demands more money or asks for gas money for the errand.

Situation 7

One of your friends really likes a girl named Debbie and dates her some. You think she's pretty nice yourself. You went out with her Saturday night, and you both had a really good time. Someone must have told your friend because he comes running up to you in the school parking lot and says, "You dirty cheater! Bill just told me about you and Debbie. If you ever go out with her again, I'll knock your ugly face in!" What do you say and do now?

8—*S* attempts to calm the friend down and avoid a fight OR explains calmly that since they weren't going steady, he also had a right to take Debbie out OR expresses regret at hurting the friend's feelings (*Examples:* "Cool it a minute. Let's talk about this first"; "She's not your girl yet. You know I'd never take her out if you were going steady or something like that"; "Let's not let this break up our friendship").

6—*S* is reasonable and calm but unassertive in defending the right to date Debbie, OR *S* says his friend can have the person, OR *S* suggests that they let Debbie choose between them.

4—*S* attempts to avoid a fight but does not resolve the situation; however, he does not make it any worse (*Examples:* "Well, it's only one date"; "That's the way it is"; "She wanted to go out, and I'm going out with her"; "We like each other"; "I didn't mean to take her away from you" [not said to "get over"]), OR *S* just walks away.

2—*S* lies or minimizes (*Examples:* "I never went out with her"; "She asked me out"; "I took her out to see how she felt about you"; "I had a lousy time anyway"; "We just went out as friends" [said to "get over"]), OR *S* laughs, OR his response is likely to provoke a fight (*Examples:* "If you're looking to make it a big deal, go ahead"; "I'll go out with her again"; "You can't keep me away from her"; "If I do go out with her again, sounds like a fight"), OR *S* says he will fight if the friend swings first (*Example:* "Just try it!").

0—*S* is very antagonistic (*Examples:* "Fuck you, man"; hits the friend first; suggests they fight). If *S* fights but the friend swings first, score it a 2.

Situation 8

Your friend calls on a Saturday night to ask if you want to get together with him and some other friends. You tell him you've been grounded because you got home after curfew the weekend before. He says, "So what's the big deal? Just sneak out the back door and meet me in the next block. Your parents will never know you're gone." What do you say and do now?

8—*S* assertively (but not exaggeratedly) refuses to meet the friend AND either explains again that he is grounded (*Example:* "I can't. I'm grounded") or gives a moral reason (*Examples:* "My parents trust me"; "I respect my parents").

6—*S* refuses to meet the friend, but perhaps less assertively and without either of the additional components involved in the response given a score of 8; may suggest that perhaps he won't be grounded at a future time (*Examples:* "I can't"; "I'd better not take the chance"; "You're not the one taking the chance"; "I'd better not"; "If I sneaked out when I'm grounded, I'd be grounded for the rest of my life").

4—S does not give the friend a definite answer (*Example:* "Maybe some other time") OR makes up a weak excuse OR simply states that he would stay home.

2—S refuses with a lie to get his friend off his back (*Example:* "I can't. I'm sick") OR promises to meet the friend later and then does not OR attempts to manipulate parents into letting him go despite grounding.

0—S agrees to meet the friend or says that he will sneak out.

Situation 9

Your father has been concerned for months about your getting home by midnight. Sometimes that's a problem because none of your friends has to be home before 1:00 A.M. One night you walk in at 1:30 A.M., and your father is sitting in the living room, looking mad. He says, "Where in the world have you been? Do you have any idea what time it is?" What do you say and do now?

8—S is respectful, reasonable, and calm AND is apologetic or accepting of responsibility for having violated a rule (*Example:* "Dad, I realize you're upset because I'm so late, and I'm sorry").

6—Response includes one of the components of the response scored 8: S is respectful but less apologetic, or apologetic but less respectful; may ask father to understand, talk to father about getting curfew changed, or explain (truthfully) where he was or what he was doing (*Examples:* "You must have been late some times when you were a boy"; "I'm sorry. It won't happen again" [not said to "get over"]).

4—S goes to his room OR stands there without saying anything OR complains that the curfew is unfair; may ask what the punishment will be (*Example:* "Nobody else has to be in by midnight").

2—S lies about what happened OR provides (insincere) excuse or assurances to placate the father OR is implicitly disrespectful (*Examples:* "Forget it"; "I don't care"; "Whatever"; "I'm too young to tell time") OR leaves the room (with no intention to return soon thereafter).

0—S walks or runs out of the house OR hits father OR is very disrespectful (*Examples:* "Bye"; "Get out of my life"; "I don't give a fuck what time it is").

Situation 10

You're walking along a side street with a friend. He stops in front of a beautiful new sports car. He looks inside and then says excitedly, "Look, the keys are still in this thing! Let's see what it can do. Come on, let's go!" What do you say and do now?

8—*S* refuses assertively (but not exaggeratedly) AND either provides a moral explanation or suggests a constructive alternative (*Examples:* "Forget it—that's wrong"; "No way. How would you feel if someone took your car?"; "Hey, remember? We were going to shoot some pool"; "Let's just get to where we're going").

6—*S* refuses assertively but without giving a moral explanation or suggesting a constructive alternative (*Examples:* "No"; "What do you want to do that for?"; "We'd get busted in no time"; "I don't take that kind of risk"; "I'm not into that"; "None of my friends steals cars").

4—*S* says he will not do it but suggests that the friend can go ahead (*Examples:* "Maybe that's your thing, but it's not for me"; "I don't feel like it, but go ahead if you want to").

2—*S* considers the suggestion, perhaps asking about the risk (*Examples:* "I'm not sure I want to"; "What if we get busted?") OR accepts after a pause OR considers a ride home in the car.

0—*S* joins in stealing the car or "borrowing" it for a while OR tells his friend to take the car and pick him up somewhere else in a while.

Situation 11

You're about an hour late getting to your part-time job in a super-market because your car ran out of gas. You feel pretty dumb about that, and you know your boss will be mad because this is the busiest time of the day in the store. You punch in at the time clock, and the boss comes storming over to you and says, "You're fired! I've put up with you kids being late and not coming in one time too many. Starting with you, anyone who comes in late gets canned!" What do you say and do now?

8—*S* is polite and respectful AND apologizes AND explains (truthfully) what happened, OR *S* asks to talk to the boss about it later and then, at the later time, would be polite and respectful OR would apologize OR would explain (truthfully); may offer to work overtime (*Examples:* "Could we talk about this a minute? I'm really sorry I was late. I ran out of gas and that was stupid, but otherwise I'm doing a good job around here and I'm a reliable employee. I really would appreciate it if you'd give me another chance"; "Can I finish this day and then talk to you afterwards?").

6—Any one or two components of the response scored 8.

4—Response is ambiguous as to whether or not it is polite or truthful. *S* may promise that it won't happen again (unprobed for sincerity) OR accept being fired without saying anything or with exaggerated politeness OR simply leave, maybe because he or she would be mad (*Examples:* "I promise I won't be late again"; "It happens to everybody some time").

2—*S* announces that he's quitting, OR response is mildly disrespectful or rude, OR *S* concocts a manipulative excuse (*Example:* "I'm not like the others" [*S* acknowledges saying this to "get over" on the boss]).

0—*S* is very disrespectful or verbally threatening, or hits the boss, OR does something illegal, such as getting drunk or coming back at night to vandalize the store.

Situation 12

You have a friend who's a few years older than yourself. He's been in trouble with the law a lot, and he's even been to prison, but he's out now. You really like him a lot and respect him, and you wish he would like and respect you, too, because he's a popular person in the neighborhood. He comes to your house one night and tells you that he and another person are going to rob a place. He says, "You want to come along? We think you could be a big help to us." What do you say and do now?

8—*S* refuses, definitely and assertively, without making up excuses and without sounding self-righteous or pious; may say it's wrong, ask the friend to understand, or try to talk the friend out of it (*Examples:* "Look, I think you're a great person, and I like you a lot, but there's no way I want to get involved in that stuff"; "No, that's not my thing"; "No, that would be wrong"; "Please try to respect my feelings").

6—*S* refuses without elaboration or in a less definite or less assertive manner (*Examples:* "I just can't"; "Thanks anyway, but I'd rather not"; "Nope, I don't want to go to jail or get into trouble").

4—*S* does not give a definite answer OR simply says he wouldn't take the chance OR makes up an excuse of the "white lie" variety (*Examples:* "Sorry, gotta meet my girlfriend"; "I have some chores to do"); may suggest that the friend go ahead without him.

2—*S* asks about the chances of getting caught OR promises to do it later and would then back out.

0—*S* agrees to participate in the act, perhaps to drive the car or even just to go along without participating in the crime itself, OR *S* says he would hit the friend (*Example:* "I'd punch him in the face").

Situation 13

You ask the girl who sits next to you in study hall if she'd like to come to a party at your house Saturday night. She says, "I'd like to, but my father won't let me hang out with anyone who has been in trouble." What do you say and do now?

8—*S* asks if he can meet the father to explain the situation and demonstrate to him that he is responsible (*Examples:* "Could I meet your father and explain the situation to him?"; "He probably has some wrong ideas about what I'm really like. How about if I come over and talk to him?").

6—*S* asks if he can meet the father but is less clear with respect to the goal of explaining and demonstrating responsibility, OR *S* suggests that the girl convey to her father her (truthful) positive impression of him, OR *S* expresses regret (*Example:* "I'm sorry your dad thinks that way about me").

4—*S* accepts refusal passively, without taking any action to change the situation in his favor; response is quiet and not antagonistic (*Examples:* "Okay"; "I guess that's your decision"; "If you decide to come anyway, come"), OR *S* says he would make a good impression on the father (not probed for sincerity) OR suggests that he is responsible to the girl but not to her father OR asks if the girl has any friends who might want to come.

2—*S* questions her father's knowledge of him or expresses resentment of the father for making such a rule (*Examples:* "How does he know?"; "Who does he think he is?"; "Are you your father?") OR *S* denies, objects to, or questions the bad reputation label (*Example:* "What do you mean by bad reputation?"), OR the response is irrelevant or meaningless, OR *S* tells the girl to cajole her dad into coming around, to call the *S* behind her father's back, or lie about whom she's going out with or where she's going (*Examples:* "How would your father know?"; "So what?"; "Tell him you're going to study with a girlfriend, and I'll meet you downtown").

0—*S* is very disrespectful toward the girl or her father, perhaps cursing one or the other out, OR *S* suggests that the girl sneak out or overtly defy her father.

Situation 14

You're at a party, and all the people there are smoking joints. You used to do a lot of smoking yourself until you got caught last month. Everyone knows you used to smoke. Your girlfriend offers you a joint. What do you say and do now?

8—*S* leaves the party when he discovers others are smoking OR refuses, briefly and assertively (but not exaggeratedly); may explain honestly why he can't smoke or may give moral explanation (*Examples:* "No, I can't. I got caught and I quit that stuff"; "No, I don't want to, and you shouldn't either"; "No, that stuff can be harmful"; "This is my chance to prove I can stay off that stuff").

6—*S* refuses without any explanation, or if there is an explanation it is less definitive (leaving him open to further pressuring); may express anger at the girlfriend's attempt to pressure him (*Examples:* "I'm not in the mood"; "I don't need it"; "I'm too tired already"; "No thanks—I have to stay clean from now on"; "I don't want to get caught again").

4—*S* refuses but says his girlfriend can if she wants to OR gives an explanation implying that he would accept the joint at a future time (*Example:* "No, thanks—I have to be a super kid for a while") OR suggests that they wait until he is off parole.

2—*S* accepts if the girlfriend persists or if he can avoid getting caught, OR *S* suggests that they go smoke somewhere more private, where there is less risk of being observed or getting caught.

0—*S* agrees to smoke. Score a 0 even if *S* says he would only smoke once.

Note. If *S* says he would knock the joint out of his girlfriend's hand, consider the response unscorable.

Situation 15

The girl you've been going out with just broke up with you. She said that you're okay but that she'd like to go out with other guys, too. You still like her, and you're hurt that she doesn't want to go out with you and continue to be your girl. You're in a terrible, miserable mood. You feel really down. What do you say and do now?

> 8—*S* talks to somebody about the problem and how bad he feels OR makes a conciliatory or constructive comment to the girl (*Examples:* "I understand. Maybe it is best if we see other people"; "I still like you, but it's up to you"; "Maybe it's for the best"; "Sorry it has to end, but we had a good time"; "I hope we can still be friends"), OR *S* tries to date other girls he's met or knows of.

> 6—*S* gets involved in an activity that takes his mind off the problem or begins to do things with his male friends, OR *S* tries to meet other girls (*Example:* "There's other fish in the sea").

> 4—*S* tries once to convince the girl to keep dating him as his steady OR asks for an explanation (*Example:* "Why did you break up with me?") OR asks a mutual friend to talk to the girl OR accepts the situation and does nothing at all about it (*Examples:* "If that's what she wants"; "Whatever") OR doesn't talk to anybody for a while.

> 2—*S* repeatedly attempts to pressure the girl into liking or dating him again OR tries to make her jealous OR sounds resentful or defensive (*Examples:* "I'm through with you"; "Someday you'll want me back"; "I really didn't like you in the first place").

> 0—*S* gets drunk, looks for a fight, takes drugs, vandalizes property, or engages in any other illegal or antisocial activity to make himself feel better OR threatens the girl or the guys she's now dating OR plans harm to the girl or to the guys she's now dating.

Situation 16

You work as a clerk in a grocery store. The store isn't too busy, and a guy you know from school comes over to your cash register. He says, "Hey, I only have a dollar with me. Ring up these cigarettes and six-pack for a dollar, won't you? The manager is in the back of the store. He'll never know." What do you say and do now?

> 8—*S* says no assertively AND with a moral explanation OR suggests a constructive alternative *(Examples:* "No, it's not right"; "No, I feel trusted"; "I'll know"; "No—how would you feel if you owned this store?"; "It would come out of other people's money"; "Why don't you go home and come back when you have the money?").

> 6—*S* says no because of personal loss or risk *(Examples:* "They keep track"; "The money would come out of my pocket"; "Are you kidding? I'd lose my job") OR directs friend to return item *(Example:* "If you don't have the money, put it back") OR is otherwise assertive *(Example:* "You've got to have the money").

> 4—*S* simply says that he will not do it, with no elaboration, OR rings up the dollar and tells the friend to take one or the other (the six-pack or the cigarettes) AND offers to make up the difference this once.

> 2—*S* offers to lend or give the boy enough money for his entire purchase. A one-time-only qualifier earns the response a level 4 score.

> 0—*S* rings up the cigarettes and six-pack for a dollar and does not make up the difference with his own money. Score a 0 even if *S* says he would do this only once.

Note. "This is my job" could be an 8 or a 6, and so should be scored as a 7. Probing the response, as recommended, may yield a different score.

Situation 17

You're playing basketball at school, and some guy you don't know well is standing on the sidelines. He starts teasing you, making fun of the way you play. What do you say and do now?

> 8—*S* continues to play on court, ignoring remark and boy's presence OR uses banter or humor to defuse the situation, perhaps suggesting that the boy join him *(Example:* "Bring yourself on in here and let's see what you can do").

> 6—*S* makes a remark that may prevent a fight by showing that he is not hurt *(Examples:* "At least I'm out here playing"; "If you can do better, then come take my place").

4—Makes a remark not likely to improve or hurt the situation; "talks" to the boy with unspecified tone of voice (*Example:* "Why are you cracking on me?") OR leaves to avoid a confrontation.

2—*S* is insulting or provocative or, in a hostile fashion, challenges the boy (*Examples:* "Would you mind repeating that?"; "What's your problem?"; "Get your ass out of here") OR says he might hit the boy depending on what the boy does next; may say he will bring some buddies.

0—*S* immediately hits or fights the other boy.

Note. The response that *S* would defend himself if the boy starts to attack him is unscorable.

Situation 18

You're in a job interview, and you really want the job because the pay is good and the hours aren't bad. The interviewer seemed interested in you until he found out you were on parole. Now he says, "Our usual policy is not to hire anyone who's on parole. Nothing personal, but we've had too many problems with you kids in the past. Sorry." What do you say and do now?

8—*S* politely and reasonably asks for a chance or for the interviewer to reconsider; says (truthfully) that he has changed, that he has learned from his mistakes, or that he will do a good job OR offers to work on probation for a while to demonstrate his competence (*Examples:* "That's too bad. I think I could do a good job here, and I really would appreciate the chance to prove to you that being a parolee doesn't automatically mean you're going to be a problem"; "I think it's wrong to hold someone's past against them, especially when they are trying to improve themselves") OR asks the interviewer to put himself or herself in the intervie-wee's shoes.

6—*S* is polite and reasonable; may say policy is wrong (without further elaboration) or may accept interviewer's rejection without standing up for himself, OR *S* just isn't as clear or convincing as in responses scored 8 (*Examples:* "I have really changed"; "This time [with me] it's different"; "How am I going to show I've changed if I don't get a job [respectful tone]?"), OR *S* asks if he can be considered after parole period.

4—*S* may just leave, or response isn't likely to improve the situation or make it worse; may put on air of indifference (*Examples:* "That's behind me, but if you don't want to hire me, that's okay"; "Okay, call if you change your mind"; "I need the job badly"; "Why not?").

2—*S* is mildly sarcastic or antagonistic (*Example:* "I'll bring a lawsuit") OR attempts to convince interviewer he doesn't really have a record.

0—Response is very antagonistic, provocative, or insulting, or he hits the interviewer; may say he will return later and vandalize the store (*Examples:* "If that's the way you feel about it, you can stick the job up your ass!"; "Sorry, hell! You got a policy? Let me read it").

Situation 19

You were suspended from school for a week because you were caught in the locker room drinking one afternoon with several of your friends. You're back in school now, and it's been hard getting back in with the teachers. Just now, one of the teachers has surprised you in a little-used classroom, where you're catching a smoke, which is against school rules. The teacher says, "Okay, just what do you think you're doing in here, young man? Didn't you learn anything from your suspension?" What do you say and do now?

8—*S* ignores the provocativeness of the criticism (in other words, is respectful) AND acknowledges that what he was doing was wrong or accepts responsibility (*Example:* "Look, I know it's against the rules. I owe you an apology, and I won't let it happen again").

6—Response is less effective than those scoring 8, but still respectful. *S* uses a brief, humorous response OR explains why it happened (but does not apologize); may ask for another chance or say he hopes next time he will learn (*Example:* "It's been hard making the transition back into school, and I've been feeling uptight").

4—*S* makes a comment that may not make things worse but that does not help the teacher understand his motivation for smoking (*Example:* "I wish you'd have a smoking room around here"; "Lots of kids smoke in here, but you just caught me"; "It's not so bad"; "Okay, I'm caught"), OR *S* responds to the teacher's question about whether he learned anything from his suspension with a simple yes or no OR asks teacher whether the teacher will punish him OR puts out the cigarette, saying nothing.

2—*S* says he is smoking, with no further explanation, OR *S* asks the teacher not to tell or attempts to cajole or manipulate the teacher, OR *S* attempts to stonewall or ignore the teacher (*Examples:* "Yes, I learned something from my suspension"; "Nope, I didn't learn a thing"; "Guess I didn't learn how not to get caught"), OR *S* makes mildly sarcastic response (*Example:* "I'm smoking—what does it look like I'm doing?").

0—Response is openly defiant (*Example:* keeps smoking), threatening, vengeful, very antagonistic, or otherwise very disrespectful (*Examples:* hits teacher; "Why are you always on my back? I haven't done anything to you!"; "What the hell's it look like I'm doing [or other sarcastic remark]?"; "What're you going to do about it?"; leaves school; vandalizes school).

Situation 20

Your parents don't seem to like your friends. They say that they're dirty, or that they have no manners, or that they'll get you into trouble. Joe, a new friend with a bad reputation, has just left your house after his first visit to your place. After he's gone, your mother gets on his case, calling him a good-for-nothing and demanding that you not see him again. You know that Joe has become more responsible lately. What do you say and do now?

8—*S* acknowledges Joe's reputation AND either asks his mother to reserve judgment for a while (*Example:* "I know what you've heard, but let me bring Joe around some more and see what you think when you get to know him better") or suggests that Joe has changed (*Example:* "I know what you've heard, but Joe isn't like those other guys any more"), OR *S* acknowledges Joe's reputation AND reasonably and articulately argues that he is old enough to be trusted to choose responsible friends.

6—Response includes one of the components of level 8, OR *S* respectfully asks his mother what she doesn't like about Joe or respectfully suggests that everybody deserves a chance.

4—Content of response is same as in those responses scored 8 or 6, but it is less articulate and less convincing OR involves a poor argument, OR *S* says he will continue to see Joe while attempting to convince or placate his mother (*Example:* "Joe

won't influence me"; "I'm as bad as Joe anyway"), OR *S* asks
Joe to change further to please his mother, OR *S* simply
stops seeing Joe.

2—*S* is disrespectful (*Examples:* "Get off my back"; "Lay
off Joe—he never bothered you") OR attempts to ignore,
manipulate, or mislead his mother (*Example:* "Joe's never
been in trouble") OR says that he will continue to see Joe
but will try to appease his mother OR says his mother has
no right to pick or judge his friends.

0—*S* insults his mother's friends OR says that he'll continue
to see Joe, with or without his mother's knowledge (doesn't
make any effort to try to change his mother's mind).

Situation 21

You're driving around with a good friend on a hot, muggy summer
night. Your friend says, "I'm thirsty! I could really use a cold beer. I
know a place that doesn't check IDs. How about going over and getting
some booze?" What do you say and do now?

8—Response is an assertive (but not exaggerated) no with a
definitive moral explanation or personal comment (*Example:*
"Drinking is harmful. I'm not into that"), OR *S* suggests an
alternative plan or activity.

6—*S* says no but without a moral explanation (*Examples:*
"I'm not thirsty"; "I'm not in the mood"; "I don't think so";
"Count me out"; "I don't want to get into trouble").

4—Response leaves *S* open to continued pressuring within
the same episode (*Example:* "I have to be home now" [or
other white lie]), OR *S* refuses to have a beer himself but
either tells the other boy to go ahead without him or stays
with the other boy as he gets some, perhaps offering to drive
(*Examples:* "With our luck, the cops would be watching the
place"; "You go ahead, but I'll pass"; "You drink, I'll drive").

2—*S* agrees to have some beer but suggests they not drive
while they drink or suggests they not drink too much, OR
S asks a question, suggesting he'll do it if the answer is right
(*Example:* "Are you sure they don't check IDs?"), OR *S* offers
to drink the beer once the other boy has bought it.

0—*S* simply agrees to have some beer.

Situation 22

It's early afternoon, and ever since you woke up this morning, you've been in a bad mood. What do you say and do now?

8—S becomes involved in a directed and constructive activity in which he is not likely to get into trouble (*Examples:* something that helps someone else, a quiet drive in the country, a movie, a visit to friends, conversation with a friend, a sports activity), OR S tries to find out what made him angry or upset.

6—S looks for something to do, perhaps with a friend; activity is specified and not aggressive or illegal (*Examples:* engaging in a sport, eating, seeing a movie, listening to music or watching TV, or taking a shower in order to distract himself).

4—S keeps his mood to himself (that is, he tries not to let it show in or affect his behavior) OR proposes some unspecified and undirected activity (*Example:* "I'd go do something with a friend").

2—S goes back to bed (or some other equally passive-depressive solution); may express hope that some exciting external event will happen to improve his mood.

0—S does something antisocial or illegal (*Examples:* teasing people, talking back to people, assaulting someone, taking drugs, drinking).

IAP-SF Score Sheet

SCORING THE RESPONSES

Duplicate the IAP-SF Work Sheet on page 327 or use separate pages modeled on this sheet to write down the subject's responses. Remember to write [Q] before any response prompted by a query. The situation number for the first response is already provided on the Work Sheet. On the last line of the response, indicate the rating at the far right. Continue the numbering for responses 2 through 22, taking as many lines as necessary for each response.

CALCULATING THE OVERALL SOCIAL SKILLS SCORES

Once the responses have been scored, scan the ratings column on the Work Sheet for each social skills level, starting with 0 (0, 2, 4, 6, 8). Total the frequency for each level and enter on the appropriate line below. If a situation has been scored between levels (e.g., 5), then assign half-credit to the two adjacent levels (e.g., ½ to 6 and ½ to 4). Sum the frequencies. Multiply each level by the corresponding frequency and enter the products on the appropriate lines below. Sum the products. Divide the products' sum by the frequencies' sum. Multiply the resultant number by 100. The final number is the Overall Social Skills Score (Mean). Enter this number in the appropriate space on the Score Sheet (see p. 328). To get the Overall Social Skills Score (Modal), identify the highest frequency in the frequency column and enter the corresponding level in the appropriate space on the same page.

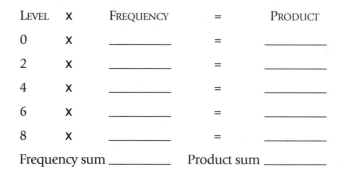

LEVEL	X	FREQUENCY	=	PRODUCT
0	X	_____	=	_____
2	X	_____	=	_____
4	X	_____	=	_____
6	X	_____	=	_____
8	X	_____	=	_____

Frequency sum _____   Product sum _____

CALCULATING THE FACTOR SUBSCORES
(COMPUTING MEAN RATINGS)

To calculate factor subscores, first enter the score for each situation (situation numbers appear at the left under each subscore category). Sum the scores for each category and enter those sums in the space provided. To derive the mean ratings, divide each sum of scores by the number of situations in that category.

IMMEDIATE RESPONSE DEMAND	DEFERRED RESPONSE DEMAND	DEVIANT PEER PRESSURE
1 _____	2 _____	6 _____
3 _____	4 _____	10 _____
7 _____	15 _____	12 _____
9 _____	22 _____	14 _____
17 _____		16 _____
18 _____		
Sum _____	Sum _____	Sum _____
$M =$ _____	$M =$ _____	$M =$ _____

Note. Situations 5, 8, 11, 13, 19, 20, and 21 either did not have an exclusive factor loading (Simonian et al., 1991) or did not have acceptable face validity exclusively for one factor.

IAP–SF WORK SHEET

RATING

1. _____

_____

_____

_____

_____

_____

_____

_____

_____

_____

_____

_____

_____

_____

_____

_____

SOCIAL SKILLS ASSESSMENT RESULTS

Code #_____ Overall Social Skills (Mean)   _____

Name _____ Overall Social Skills (Modal)   _____

Age _____ Deviant Peer Pressure Score   _____

Sex: Male Female   Immediate Response Demand Score _____

Date _____ Deferred Response Demand Score   _____

GENERAL TEST AND OVERALL CLINICAL IMPRESSIONS

_____

_____

_____

_____

_____

_____

_____

_____

_____

_____

_____

_____

_____

References

Abel, G. G., Becker, J. V., & Cunningham-Rathner, J. (1984). Complications, consent, and cognitions in sex between children and adults. *International Journal of Law and Psychiatry, 7,* 89–103.

Abramson, L. Y., Seligman, M. E. P., & Teasdale, J. D. (1978). Learned helplessness in humans: Critique and reformulation. *Journal of Abnormal Psychology, 87,* 49–74.

Achenbach, T. M., & Edelbrock, C. S. (1978). The classification of child psychopathology: A review and analysis of empirical efforts. *Psychological Bulletin, 85,* 1275–1301.

Agee, V. L. (1979). *Treatment of the violent incorrigible adolescent.* Lexington, MA: Lexington Books.

Agee, V. L., & McWilliams, B. (1984). The role of group therapy and the therapeutic community in treating the violent juvenile offender. In R. Mathais (Ed.), *Violent juvenile offenders* (pp. 283–296). San Francisco: National Council on Crime and Delinquency.

Ahlborn, H. H. (1986). *Dilemma session intervention with adult female offenders: Behavioral and attitudinal correlates.* Unpublished manuscript, Ohio Department of Rehabilitation and Correction, Columbus.

Akhtar, N., & Bradley, E. J. (1991). Social information processing deficits of aggressive children: Present findings and implications for social skills training. *Clinical Psychology Review, 11,* 621–644.

Alvarez-Sanders, C., & Reyes, L. S. (1994). *Capital offender group program.* Giddings, TX: Giddings State Home and School of the Texas Youth Commission.

Arbuthnot, J., & Gordon, D. A. (1986). Behavioral and cognitive effects of a moral reasoning development intervention for high-risk behavior-disordered adolescents. *Journal of Consulting and Clinical Psychology, 85,* 1275–1301.

Atwood, R. O., & Osgood, D. W. (1987). Cooperation in group treatment programs for incarcerated adolescents. *Journal of Applied Social Psychology, 17,* 969–989.

Azar, S. T., Robinson, D. R., Hekimian, E., & Twentyman, C. T. (1984). Unrealistic expectations and problem-solving ability in maltreating and comparison mothers. *Journal of Consulting and Clinical Psychology, 52,* 687–691.

Babcock, R., & Sorenson, P. F. (1979). Matching treatment and management systems in correctional institutions. In J. F. McClure (Ed.), *Managing human services* (pp. 133–159). Davis, CA: International Dialogue Press.

Bales, R. F. (1958). Task roles and social roles in problem-solving groups. In E. E. Maccoby, T. M. Newcomb, & E. I. Hartley (Eds.), *Readings in social psychology* (3rd ed., pp. 437–447). New York: Holt.

Bandura, A. (1991). Social cognitive theory of moral thought and action. In W. M. Kurtines & J. L. Gewirtz (Eds.), *Handbook of moral behavior and development: Vol 1. Theory* (pp. 45–103). Hillsdale, NJ: Erlbaum.

Barlow, D. H., & Cerny, J. A. (1988). *Psychological treatment of panic.* New York: Guilford.

Barriga, A. Q., & Gibbs, J. C. (1995). *Measuring cognitive distortion in antisocial youth: Preliminary development and validation of the How I Think questionnaire.* Manuscript submitted for publication.

Barriga, A. Q., Harrold, J., Stinson, B. L., & Gibbs, J. C. (1995). *Cognitive distortions and mental health disorders in adolescence.* Unpublished manuscript, The Ohio State University, Columbus.

Basinger, K. S., Gibbs, J. C., & Fuller, D. (in press). Context and the measurement of moral judgment. *International Journal of Behavioral Development.*

Baumeister, R. F. (1991). *Meanings of life.* New York: Guilford.

Bear, G. G., & Richards, H. C. (1981). Moral reasoning and conduct problems in the classroom. *Journal of Educational Psychology, 73,* 644–670.

Beck, A. T. (1976). *Cognitive therapy and the emotional disorders.* New York: International Universities.

Beck, A. T., & Freeman, A. (1990). *Cognitive therapy of personality disorders.* New York: Guilford.

Berk, L. E. (1994). *Child development* (3rd ed.). Boston: Allyn & Bacon.

Bivens, J. A., & Berk, L. E. (1990). A longitudinal study of the development of elementary school children's private speech. *Merrill-Palmer Quarterly, 36,* 443–463.

Blasi, A. (1980). Bridging moral cognition and moral action: A critical review of the literature. *Psychological Bulletin, 88,* 1–45.

Blasi, A., & Oresick, R. J. (1986). Affect, cognition, and self in developmental psychology. In D. J. Bearison & H. Zimiles (Eds.), *Thought and emotion: Developmental perspectives* (pp. 147–166). Hillsdale, NJ: Erlbaum.

Brendtro, L. K., & Ness, A. E. (1982). Perspectives on peer group treatment: The use and abuse of Guided Group Interaction/Positive Peer Culture. *Children and Youth Services Review, 4,* 307–324.

Brendtro, L. K., Ness, A. E., & Nicolaou, A. W. (1983). Peer group treatment: Its use and misuse. In L. K. Brendtro & A. E. Ness (Eds.), *Re-educating troubled youth: Environments for teaching and treatment* (pp. 203–231). Hawthorne, NY: Aldine.

Brendtro, L. K., & Wasmund, W. C. (1989). The Positive Peer Culture model. In R. Lyman, S. Prentice-Dunn, & S. Gabel (Eds.), *Residential treatment of emotionally disturbed children* (pp. 81–93). New York: Plenum.

California Department of the Youth Authority. (1994). *Victim awareness/community safety: Student's and teacher's manuals* (rev. ed.). Sacramento: Author.

Campagna, A. F., & Harter, S. (1975). Moral judgment in sociopathic and normal children. *Journal of Personality and Social Psychology, 31,* 199–205.

Carducci, D. J. (1980). Positive Peer Culture and assertiveness training: Complementary modalities for dealing with disturbed and disturbing adolescents in the classroom. *Behavioral Disorders, 5,* 156–162.

Carducci, D. J., & Carducci, J. B. (1984). *The caring classroom: A guide for teachers troubled by the difficult student and classroom disruption.* New York: Bull.

Case, R. (1991). *The mind's staircase: Exploring the conceptual underpinnings of children's thought and knowledge.* Hillsdale, NJ: Erlbaum.

Caspi, A., Henri, B., McGee, R. O., Moffit, T. E., & Silva, P. A. (1995). Temperamental origins of child and adolescent behavior problems: From age 3 to age 15. *Child Development, 66,* 55–68.

Caspi, A., & Silva, P. A. (1995). Temperamental qualities at age 3 predict personality traits in young adulthood: Longitudinal evidence from a birth cohort. *Child Development, 66,* 486–498.

Chalmers, J. B., & Townsend, M. A. R. (1990). The effects of training in social perspective taking on socially malajusted girls. *Child Development, 61,* 178–190.

Chandler, M. (1973). Egocentrism and antisocial behavior: The assessment and training of social perspective-taking skills. *Developmental Psychology, 9,* 326–332.

Chandler, M., & Moran, T. (1990). Psychopathy and moral development: A comparative study of delinquent and nondelinquent youth. *Development & Psychopathology, 2,* 227–246.

Coats, K. I. (1979). Cognitive self-instructional training approach for reducing disruptive behavior of young children. *Psychological Reports, 44,* 122–134.

Coie, J. D., Dodge, K. A., Terry, R., & Wright, V. (1991). The role of aggression in peer relations: An analysis of aggression episodes in boys' play groups. *Child Development, 62,* 812–816.

Colby, A., & Kohlberg, L. (1987). *The measurement of moral judgment: Theoretical foundations and research validation* (Vol. 1). Cambridge, England: Cambridge University Press.

Colby, A., Kohlberg, L., Gibbs, J. C., & Lieberman, M. (1983). A longitudinal study of moral judgment. *Monographs of the Society for Research in Child Development, 48*(1–2, Serial No. 200).

Colby, A., Kohlberg, L., Speicher, B., Hewer, A., Candee, D., Gibbs, J., & Power, C. (1987). *The measurement of moral judgment* (Vol. 2). Cambridge, England: Cambridge University Press.

Colby, A., & Speicher, B. (1973). *Dilemmas for applied use.* Unpublished manuscript, Harvard University, Cambridge, MA.

Conquest, R. (1986). *The harvest of sorrow: Soviet collectivization and the terror-famine.* New York: Oxford University Press.

Damon, W. (1977). *The social world of the child.* San Francisco: Jossey-Bass.

Damon, W. (1988). *The moral child: Nurturing children's natural moral growth.* New York: Free Press.

Damon, W. (1995). *Greater expectations: Overcoming the culture of indulgence in America's homes and schools.* New York: Free Press.

Deluty, R.H. (1979). Children's Action Tendency Scale: A self-report measure of aggressiveness, assertiveness, and submissiveness in children. *Journal of Consulting and Clinical Psychology, 47,* 1061–1071.

Dishion, T.J., Loeber, R., Stouthamer-Loeber, M., & Patterson, G. R. (1984). Skill deficits and male adolescent delinquency. *Journal of Abnormal Child Psychology, 12,* 37–54.

Dodge, K.A. (1980). Social cognition and children's aggressive behavior. *Child Development, 51,* 162–170.

Dodge, K.A. (1991). The structure and function of reactive and proactive aggression. In D.J. Pepler & K. H. Rubin (Eds.), *The development and treatment of aggression* (pp. 201–218). Hillsdale, NJ: Erlbaum.

Dodge, K.A. (1993). Social-cognitive mechanisms in the development of conduct disorder and depression. *Annual Reviews in Psychology, 44,* 559–584.

Dodge, K.A., Bates, J. E., & Pettit, G.S. (1990). Mechanisms in the cycle of violence. *Science, 250,* 1678–1685.

Dodge, K.A., & Coie, J. D. (1987). Social information-processing factors in reactive and proactive aggression in children's peer groups. *Journal of Personality and Social Psychology, 53,* 1146–1158.

Dodge, K.A., Price, J. M., Bachorowski, J.A., & Newman, J. P. (1990). Hostile attributional biases in severely aggressive adolescents. *Journal of Abnormal Psychology, 99,* 385–392.

Dubow, E. R., & Tisak, B.J. (1989). School and neighborhood friendship patterns of blacks and whites in early adolescence. *Child Development, 60,* 1412–1423.

Duguid, S. (1981). Moral development, justice, and democracy in the prison. *Canadian Journal of Criminology, 23,* 147–163.

Edwards, C. P. (1975). Social complexity and moral development: A Kenyan study. *Ethos, 3,* 505–527.

Edwards, C. P. (1982). Moral development in comparative cultural perspective. In D.A. Wagner & H. Stevenson (Eds.), *Cultural perspectives on child development* (pp. 248–279). San Francisco: W. H. Freeman.

Ellis, A. (1977). Rational-emotive therapy: Research data that support the clinical and personality hypothesis of RET and other modes of cognitive-behavior therapy. *Counseling Psychologist, 7,* 2–42.

Fader, D. (1976). *Hooked on books.* New York: Berkley.

Feindler, E. L. (1991). Cognitive strategies in anger control interventions for children and adolescents. In P. C. Kendall (Ed.), *Child and adolescent therapy: Cognitive-behavioral procedures* (pp. 66–97). New York: Guilford.

Feindler, E. L., & Ecton, R. R. (1986). *Adolescent anger control: Cognitive-behavioral techniques.* New York: Pergamon.

Flavell, J. H., Miller, P. H., & Miller, S.A. (1993). *Cognitive development* (3rd ed.). Englewood Cliffs, NJ: Prentice-Hall.

Fort Worth's hiring of gang leaders stirs uproar. (1994, May 4). *Columbus Dispatch.*

Freedman, B. J. (1974). *An analysis of social behavioral skill deficits in delinquent and nondelinquent adolescent boys.* Unpublished doctoral dissertation, University of Wisconsin, Madison.

Freedman, B. J., Rosenthal, L., Donahoe, C. P., Schlundt, D. G., & McFall, R. M. (1978). A social behavioral analysis of skills deficits in delinquent and nondelinquent adolescent boys. *Journal of Consulting and Clinical Psychology, 46,* 1148–1462.

Gaffney, L. R., & McFall, R. M. (1981). A comparison of social skills in delinquent and nondelinquent adolescent girls using a behavioral role-playing inventory. *Journal of Consulting and Clinical Psychology, 49,* 959–967.

Garrett, C. (1985). Effects of residential treatment on adjudicated delinquents: A meta-analysis. *Journal of Research in Crime and Delinquency, 22,* 287–308.

Gavaghan, M. P., Arnold, K. D., & Gibbs, J. C. (1983). Moral judgment in delinquents and nondelinquents: Recognition versus production measures. *Journal of Psychology, 114,* 267–274.

Gibbs, J. C. (1987). Social processes in delinquency: The need to facilitate empathy as well as sociomoral reasoning. In W. M. Kurtines & J. L. Gewirtz (Eds.), *Moral development through social interaction* (pp. 301–321). New York: Wiley-Interscience.

Gibbs, J. C. (1991). Sociomoral developmental delay and cognitive distortion: Implications for the treatment of antisocial youth. In W. M. Kurtines & J. L. Gewirtz (Eds.), *Handbook of moral behavior and development: Vol 3. Application* (pp. 95–110). Hillsdale, NJ: Erlbaum.

Gibbs, J. C. (1993). Moral-cognitive interventions. In A. P. Goldstein & C. R. Huff (Eds.), *The gang intervention handbook* (pp. 159–185). Champaign, IL: Research Press.

Gibbs, J. C. (1994). Fairness and empathy as the foundation for universal moral education. *Comenius, 14,* 12–23.

Gibbs, J. C. (1995). The cognitive developmental perspective. In W. M. Kurtines & J. L. Gewirtz (Eds.), *Moral development: An introduction* (pp. 29–48). Boston: Allyn & Bacon.

Gibbs, J. C., Arnold, K. D., Ahlborn, H. H., & Cheesman, F. L. (1984). Facilitation of sociomoral reasoning in delinquents. *Journal of Consulting and Clinical Psychology, 52,* 37–45.

Gibbs, J. C., Barriga, A. Q., & Potter, G. (1995). *The How I Think questionnaire.* Unpublished manuscript, The Ohio State University, Columbus.

Gibbs, J. C., Basinger, K. S., & Fuller, D. (1992). *Moral maturity: Measuring the development of sociomoral reflection.* Hillsdale, NJ: Erlbaum.

Gibbs, J. C., & Potter, G. (1987, April). *Identify it/own it/replace it: Helping youth help one another.* Paper presented at the meeting of the Commission on Interprofessional Education and Practice, Columbus, OH.

Gibbs, J. C., & Potter, G. (1991, April). *Aggression Replacement Training in the context of Positive Peer Culture.* Paper presented at the meeting of the Ohio Council for Children with Behavioral Disorders, Columbus, OH.

Gibbs, J. C., & Potter, G. (1992). *A typology of criminogenic cognitive distortions.* Unpublished manuscript, The Ohio State University, Columbus.

Glasser, W. (1965). *Reality therapy: A new approach to psychiatry.* New York: Harper and Row.

Gold, M. (1970). *Delinquent behavior in an American city.* Belmont, CA: Brooks/Cole.

Goldstein, A. P. (1988). *The Prepare curriculum.* Champaign, IL: Research Press.

Goldstein, A. P. (1991a). Gang intervention: A historical review. In A. P. Goldstein & C. R. Huff (Eds.), *Delinquent gangs: A psychological perspective* (pp. 21–51). Champaign, IL: Research Press.

Goldstein, A. P. (1991b). Gang intervention: Issues and opportunities. In A. P. Goldstein & C. R. Huff (Eds.), *Delinquent gangs: A psychological perspective* (pp. 477–493). Champaign, IL: Research Press.

Goldstein, A. P. (1993). Interpersonal skills training interventions. In A. P. Goldstein & C.R. Huff (Eds.), *The gang intervention handbook* (pp. 87–157). Champaign, IL: Research Press.

Goldstein, A. P., & Glick, B. (1987). *Aggression Replacement Training: A comprehensive intervention for aggressive youth.* Champaign, IL: Research Press.

Goldstein, A. P., Glick, B., Irwin, M. J., Pask-McCartney, C., & Rubama, I. (1989). *Reducing delinquency: Intervention in the community.* New York: Pergamon.

Goldstein, A. P., Harootunian, B., & Conoley, J. C. (1994). *Student aggression: Prevention, management, and replacement training.* New York: Guilford.

Goldstein, A. P., Sprafkin, R. P., Gershaw, N. J., & Klein, P. (1980). *Skillstreaming the adolescent: A stuctured learning approach to teaching prosocial skills.* Champaign, IL: Research Press.

Gottfredson, G. D. (1987). Peer group interventions to reduce the risk of delinquent behavior: A selective review and a new evaluation. *Criminology, 25,* 671–714.

Green, R., & Murray, E. (1973). Instigation to aggression as a function of self-disclosure and threat to self-esteem. *Journal of Consulting and Clinical Psychology, 40,* 440–443.

Gregg, V., Gibbs, J. C., & Basinger, K. S. (1994). Patterns of delay in male and female delinquents' moral judgment. *Merrill-Palmer Quarterly, 40,* 538–553.

Greyson, B. (1993). Near-death experiences and antisuicidal attitudes. *Omega, 26,* 81–89.

Groth, A. N., & Birnsbaum, J. J. (1979). *Men who rape.* New York: Plenum.

Guerra, N., & Slaby, R. G. (1990). Cognitive mediators of aggression in adolescent offenders: Part 2. Intervention. *Developmental Psychology, 26,* 269–277.

Guidance Associates. (1976). *Relationship and values: Sound-filmstrip series.* Pleasantville, NY: Author.

Harstad, C.D. (1976). Guided group interaction: Positive Peer Culture. *Child Care Quarterly, 5,* 109–120.

Hartig, M., & Kanfer, E. H. (1973). The role of verbal self-instruction in children's resistance to temptation. *Journal of Personality and Social Psychology, 25*, 259–267.

Hartup, W. W., & van Lieshout, C. F. M. (1995). Personality development in social context. *Annual Review of Psychology, 46*, 655–687.

Hastings, J. M., & Typpo, M. H. (1984). *An elephant in the living room: The children's book.* Center City, MN: Hazelden.

Heaven, P. C. (1990). Factor structure of irrational family beliefs among adolescents. *Australian Journal of Marriage and the Family, 11*, 11–18.

Henggeler, S. W. (1989). *Delinquency in adolescence.* Newbury Park, CA: Sage.

Henggeler, S. W. (1994). *Treatment manual for family preservation using multisystemic therapy.* Charleston: Medical University of South Carolina, South Carolina Health and Human Services Commission.

Hickey, J. E., & Scharf, P. L. (1980). *Toward a just correctional system.* San Francisco: Jossey-Bass.

Higgins, A. (1995). Educating for justice and community: Lawrence Kohlberg's vision of moral education. In W. M. Kurtines & J. L. Gewirtz (Eds.), *Moral development: An introduction* (pp. 49–81). Boston: Allyn & Bacon.

Hildebran, D., & Pithers, W. D. (1989). Enhancing offender empathy for sexual-abuse victims. In D. R. Laws (Eds.), *Relapse prevention with sex offenders* (pp. 236–243). New York: Guilford.

Hilton, N. Z. (1993). Childhood sexual victimization and lack of empathy in child molesters: Explanation or excuse? *International Journal of Offender Therapy and Comparative Criminology, 27*, 287–296.

Hoffman, M. L. (1978). Empathy, its development and prosocial implications. In C. B. Keasey (Ed.), *Nebraska symposium on motivation* (Vol. 25, pp. 169–217). Lincoln: University of Nebraska Press.

Hoffman, M .L. (1981). Is altruism part of human nature? *Journal of Personality and Social Psychology, 40*, 121–137.

Holden, G. W., & Ritchie, K. L. (1991). Linking extreme marital discord, child rearing, and child behavior problems: Evidence from battered women. *Child Development, 62*, 311–327.

Hollin, C. R. (1990). Social skills training with delinquents: A look at the evidence and some recommendations for practice. *British Journal of Social Work, 20*, 483–493.

Hunter, N., & Kelly, C. K. (1986). Examination of the validity of the Adolescent Problems Inventory among incarcerated juvenile delinquents. *Journal of Consulting and Clinical Psychology, 54*, 301–302.

Hurley, D. (1988, January). Getting help from helping. *Psychology Today*, pp. 63–67.

Izard, C. E., Hembree, E. A., & Huebner, R. R. (1987). Infants' emotional expressions in acute pain. *Developmental Psychology, 23*, 105–113.

Jakubowski, P., & Lange, A. J. (1978). *The assertive option: Your rights and responsibilities*. Champaign, IL: Research Press.

Jennings, W. S., Kilkenny, R., & Kohlberg, L. (1983). Moral development theory and practice for youthful and adult offenders. In W. S. Laufer & J. M. Day (Eds.), *Personality theory, moral development and criminal behavior* (pp. 281–355). Lexington, MA: Lexington Books.

Johnson, D. W., Johnson, R., & Maruyama, G. (1983). Interdependence and interpersonal attraction among heterogeneous and homogeneous individuals. *Review of Educational Research, 53*, 5–54.

Jones, M. (1953). *The therapeutic community*. New York: Basic.

Kahn, T. J., & Chambers, H. J. (1991). Assessing reoffense risk with juvenile sexual offenders. *Child Welfare, 70*, 333–345.

Kahn, T. J., & Lafond, M. A. (1988). Treatment of the adolescent sexual offender. *Child and Adolescent Social Work, 5*, 135–148.

Kaufman, H., & Feshbach, S. (1963). The influence of antiaggressive communications upon the response to provocation. *Journal of Personality, 31*, 428–444.

Kazdin, A. E. (1988). *Child psychotherapy: Developing and identifying effective treatments*. New York: Pergamon.

Kazdin, A. E. (1994). Child maladjustment and psychotherapy: Troubles from within [Review of internalizing disorders in children and adolescents]. *Contemporary Psychology, 39*, 298–299.

Kazdin, A. E. (1995). *Conduct disorders in childhood and adolescence* (2nd ed). Newbury Park, CA: Sage.

Kazdin, A. E., Bass, C., Siegel, T., & Thomas, C. (1989). Cognitive-behavioral therapy and relationship therapy in the treatment of children referred for antisocial behavior. *Journal of Consulting and Clinical Psychology, 57*, 522–535.

Kelman, H. C., & Baron, R. M. (1968). Determinants of modes of resolving inconsistency dilemmas: A functional analysis. In R. P. Abelson, E. Aronson, W. J. McGuire, T. M. Newcomb, M. Rosenberg, & P. H. Tannenbaum (Eds.), *Theories of cognitive consistency: A sourcebook* (pp. 670–683). Chicago: Rand McNally.

Kenardy, J., Evans, L., & Oei, T. P. (1989). Cognitions and heart rate in panic disorders during everyday activity. *Journal of Anxiety Disorders, 3*, 33–43.

Kendall, P. C. (1991). Guiding theory for therapy with children and adolescents. In P. C. Kendall (Ed.), *Child and adolescent therapy: Cognitive-behavioral procedures* (pp. 3–24). New York: Guilford.

Kierulff, S. (1988). Sheep in the midst of wolves: Personal-responsibility therapy with criminal personalities. *Professional psychology: Research and Practice, 19*, 436–440.

Kohlberg, L. (1971). From is to ought: How to commit the naturalistic fallacy and get away with it in the study of moral development. In T. Mischel (Ed.), *Cognitive development and epistemology* (pp. 151–235). New York: Academic.

Kohlberg, L. (1984). *Essays on moral development: The psychology of moral development*. San Francisco: Harper and Row.

Kohlberg, L., & Higgins, A. (1987). School democracy and social interaction. In W. M. Kurtines & J. L. Gewirtz (Eds.), Moral development through social interaction (pp. 102–128). New York: Wiley-Interscience.

Kopp, C. B. (1982). Antecedents of self-regulation: A developmental perspective. *Developmental Psychology, 18,* 199–214.

Krauss, C. (1994, July 3). Women doing crime, women doing time. *The New York Times,* p. 3.

Kunen, J. S. (1989, May). Madness in the heart of the city. *People,* pp. 107–111.

Leeman, L. W. (1991). *Evaluation of a multi-component treatment program for juvenile delinquents.* Unpublished master's thesis, The Ohio State University, Columbus.

Leeman, L. W., Gibbs, J. C., & Fuller, D. (1993). Evaluation of a multi-component group treatment program for juvenile delinquents. *Aggressive Behavior, 19,* 281–292.

Lickona, T. (1983). *Raising good children.* Toronto: Bantam.

Lickona, T. (1991). *Educating for character: How our schools can teach respect and responsibility.* New York: Bantam.

Little, V. L., & Kendall, P. C. (1979). Cognitive-behavioral interventions with delinquents: Problem-solving, role-taking, and self-control. In P. C. Kendall & S. D. Hollon (Eds.), *Cognitive-behavioral interventions: Theory, research, and procedures* (pp. 81–115). New York: Academic.

Litwack, S. E. (1976). *The use of the helper therapy principle to increase therapeutic effectiveness and reduce therapeutic resistance: Structured learning therapy with resistant adolescents.* Unpublished doctoral dissertation, Syracuse University, Syracuse, NY.

Lochman, J. E., Burch, P. R., Curry, J. F., & Lampron, L. B. (1984). Treatment and generalization effects of cognitive-behavioral and goal setting interventions with aggressive boys. *Journal of Consulting and Clinical Psychology, 52,* 915–916.

Lochman, J. E., Nelson, W. M. III, & Sims, J. P. (1981). A cognitive behaviors program for use with aggressive children. *Journal of Clinical Child Psychology, 13,* 527–538.

Lochman, J. E., Wayland, K. K., & White, K. J. (1993). Social goals: Relationship to adolescent adjustment and to social problem-solving. *Journal of Abnormal Child Psychology, 21,* 135–151.

Lochman, J. E., White, K. J., & Wayland, K. K. (1991). Cognitive-behavioral assessment and treatment with aggressive children. In P. C. Kendall (Ed.), *Child and adolescent therapy: cognitive-behavioral procedures* (pp. 25–65). New York: Guilford.

Long, S. J., & Sherer, M. (1985). Social skills training with juvenile offenders. *Child & Family Behavior Therapy, 6,* 1–11.

Luborsky, L., & DeRubeis, R. J. (1984). The use of psychotherapy treatment manuals: A small revolution in psychotherapy research style. *Clinical Psychology Review, 4,* 5–14.

Lundahl, C. R. (1993). The near-death experience: A theoretical summarization. *Journal of Near-Death Studies, 12*, 105–118.

Luria, A. R. (1961). *The role of speech in the regulation of normal and abnormal behavior.* New York: Pergamon.

Lytton, H. (1977). Correlates of compliance and the rudiments of consciences in two-year-old boys. *Canadian Journal of Behavioral Sciences, 9*, 242–251.

Lytton, H. (1980). *Parent-child interaction: The socialization process observed in twin and singleton families.* New York: Plenum.

Lytton, H., & Zwirner, W. (1975). Compliance and its controlling stimuli observed in a natural setting. *Developmental Psychology, 11*, 769–779.

Maccoby, E. E. (1980). *Social development: Psychological growth and the parent-child relationship.* New York: Harcourt Brace Jovanovich.

Magnusson, D. (in press). The patterning of antisocial behavior and autonomic reactivity. In D. M. Stoff & R. B. Cairns (Eds.), *The neurobiology of clinical aggression.* Hillsdale, NJ: Erlbaum.

Mallick, S. K., & McCandless, B. R. (1966). A study of catharsis of aggression. *Journal of Personality and Social Psychology, 4*, 591–596.

Martin, F. P., & Osgood, D. W. (1987). Autonomy as a source of prosocial influence among incarcerated adolescents. *Journal of Applied Social Psychology, 17*, 97–108.

Mason, M. G., & Gibbs, J. C. (1993a). Role-taking opportunities and the transition to advanced moral judgment. *Moral Education Forum, 18*, 1–12.

Mason, M. G., & Gibbs, J. C. (1993b). Social perspective-taking and moral judgment among college students. *Journal of Adolescent Research, 8*, 109–123.

May, J. R., & Johnson, H. J. (1973). Physiological activity to internally elicited arousal and inhibitory thoughts. *Journal of Abnormal Psychology, 82*, 239–245.

McCorkle, L., Elias, A., & Bixby, F. L. (1958). *The Highfields story.* New York: Holt.

McCubbin, H., Kapp, S. A., & Thompson, A. I. (1993). Monitoring family system functioning, family, and adolescent coping in the context of residential treatment: Implications for program management, practice innovation, and research. *Child and Youth Services, 16*, 165–173.

McCullough, J. P., Huntsinger, G. M., & Nay, W. R. (1977). Self-control treatment of aggression in a sixteen-year-old male. *Journal of Consulting and Clinical Psychology, 45*, 322–331.

McFall, R. M. (1982). A review and reformulation of the concept of social skills. *Behavioral Assessment, 4*, 1–33.

McGinnis, E., & Goldstein, A. P. (1984). *Skillstreaming the elementary school child: A guide for teaching prosocial skills.* Champaign, IL: Research Press.

Meichenbaum, D. H. (1977). *Cognitive-behavior modification: An integrative approach.* New York: Plenum.

Meichenbaum, D. H., Gilmore, B., & Fedoravicius, A. (1971). Group insight vs. group desensitization in treating speech anxiety. *Journal of Consulting and Clinical Psychology, 36*, 410–421.

Mendelson, E. F., Quinn, M., Dutton, S., & Seewonarain, K. (1988). A community treatment service for sex offenders: An account at two years. *Bulletin of the Royal College of Psychiatrists,* 416–421.

Meyers, D. W. (1982). *Moral dilemmas at Scioto Village.* Unpublished manuscript, Ohio Department of Youth Services, Columbus.

Miller, P. A., & Eisenberg, N. (1988). The relation of empathy to aggressive and externalizing/antisocial behavior. *Psychological Bulletin, 103,* 324–344.

Mischel, W. (1974). Processes in delay of gratification. In L. Berkowitz (Ed.), *Advances in experimental social psychology* (pp. 249–292). New York: Academic.

Mischel, W. (1983). The role of knowledge and ideation in the development of delay capacity. In L. S. Liben (Ed.), *Piaget and the foundations of knowledge* (pp. 201–229). Hillsdale, NJ: Erlbaum.

Mischel, H. N., & Mischel, W. (1983). The development of children's knowledge of self-control strategies. *Child Development, 54,* 603–619.

Monahan, J., & O'Leary, K. D. (1971). Effects of self-instruction on rule-breaking behavior. *Psychological Reports, 29,* 1059–1066.

Moon, J. R., & Eisler, R. M. (1983). Anger control: An experimental comparison of three behavioral treatments. *Behavior Therapy, 14,* 493–505.

Murphy, W. D. (1990). Assessment and modification of cognitive distortions in sex offenders. In W. L. Marshall, D. R. Laws, & H. E. Barbaree (Eds.), *Handbook of sexual assault: Issues, theories, and treatment of the offender* (pp. 331–342). New York: Plenum.

National Institute on Drug Abuse. (1993). *Recovery training and self-help: Relapse prevention and aftercare for drug addicts* (NIDA Publication No. 93–3521). Rockville, MD: National Institute on Drug Abuse.

Nelson, J. R., Smith, D. J., & Dodd, J. (1990). The moral reasoning of juvenile delinquents: A meta-analysis. *Journal of Abnormal Child Psychology, 18,* 231–239.

Niles, W. J. (1986). Effects of a moral development discussion group on delinquent and predelinquent boys. *Journal of Counseling Psychology, 33,* 45–51.

Novaco, R. W. (1975). *Anger control: The development and evaluation of an experimental treatment.* Lexington, MA: Lexington Books.

Offer, D., Marohn, R. C., & Ostrov, E. (1979). *The psychological world of the juvenile delinquent.* New York: Basic.

Ohio Department of Youth Services. (1990). *Victim awareness: A comprehensive and integrated program.* Columbus: Author.

Osgood, D. W., Gruber, E., Archer, M. A., & Newcomb, T. M. (1985). Autonomy for inmates: Counterculture or cooptation? *Criminal Justice and Behavior, 12,* 71–89.

Page, R. A. (1981). Longitudinal evidence for the sequentiality of Kohlberg's stages of moral judgment in adolescent males. *Journal of Genetic Psychology, 139,* 3–9.

Paradissis, E. J. (1987). *Social skills assessment of conduct-disordered and adjust-ment-disordered adolescent females.* Unpublished master's thesis, The Ohio State University, Columbus.

Piaget, J. (1965). *Moral judgment of the child* (M. Gabain, Trans.). New York: Free Press. (Original work published 1932)

Platt, J. J., & Spivack, G. (1973). Studies in problem-solving thinking of psychiatric patients: Patient-control differences and factorial structure of problem-solving thinking. *Proceedings of the 81st Annual Convention of the American Psychological Association, 8,* 461–462.

Platt, J. J., Spivack, G., Altman, N., Altman, D., & Peizer, S. B. (1974). Adolescent problem-solving thinking. *Journal of Consulting and Clinical Psychology, 42,* 787–793.

Polsky, H. W. (1962). *Cottage Six: The social system of delinquent boys in residential treatment.* New York: Wiley.

Popkin, M. H. (1983). *Active parenting handbook.* Atlanta, GA: Active Parenting, Inc.

Potter, G., & Luse, G. (1988). *State of Ohio Department of Youth Services institutional complex. Title: Treatment teams.* Unpublished manuscript, Columbus, OH.

Power, C., Higgins, A., & Kohlberg, L. (1989). *Lawrence Kohlberg's approach to moral education.* New York: Columbia University Press.

Prothrow-Stith, D. (1987). *Violence prevention curriculum for adolescents.* Newton, MA: Education Development Center.

Quay, H. C. (Ed.). (1987). Patterns of delinquent behavior. In H. C. Quay, *Handbook of juvenile delinquency* (pp. 118–138). New York: Wiley.

Redl, F., & Wineman, D. (1951). *Children who hate.* Glencoe, IL: Free Press.

Redl, F., & Wineman, D. (1957). *The aggressive child.* New York: Free Press.

Rimm, D. C., & Litvak, S. B. (1969). Self-verbalization and emotional arousal. *Journal of Abnormal Psychology, 74,* 181–187.

Ring, K. (1993). Further evidence for veridical perception during near-death experiences. *Journal of Near-Death Studies, 11,* 223–229.

Robin, A. L., Armel, S., & O'Leary, K. D. (1975). The effects of self-instruction on writing deficiencies. *Behavior Therapy, 6,* 178–187.

Robin, A. L., & Roehling, P. (1986). Development and validation of the Family Beliefs Inventory: A measure of unrealistic beliefs among parents and adolescents. *Journal of Consulting and Clinical Psychology, 54,* 693–697.

Rodriguez, M. L., Mischel, W., & Shoda, Y. (1989). Cognitive and personality variables in the delay of gratification of older children at risk. *Journal of Personality and Social Psychology, 57,* 358–367.

Rose, S. D., & Edleson, J. L. (1987). *Working with children and adolescents in groups: A multimethod approach.* San Francisco: Jossey-Bass.

Rose, S. M. (1991). Defining a therapeutic selfhood for delinquent youth: A covert participant observation of a juvenile correction facility. *Child & Youth Care Forum, 20,* 255–268.

Rubin, K. H., & Krasnor, L. R. (1985). Social-cognitive and social behavioral perspectives on problem-solving. In M. Perlmutter (Ed.), *Minnesota symposia on child psychology* (Vol. 18, pp. 1–68). Hillsdale, NJ: Erlbaum.

Russell, P. L., & Brandsma, J. M. (1974). A theoretical and empirical integration of the rational-emotive and classical conditioning theories. *Journal of Consulting and Clinical Psychology, 42,* 389–397.

Sabom, M. B. (1982). *Recollections of death: A medical investigation.* New York: Harper and Row.

Samenow, S. E. (1984). *Inside the criminal mind.* New York: Random House.

Samenow, S. E. (1989). *Before it's too late.* New York: Random House.

Samenow, S. E. (1993, February). *Understanding and treating the criminal mind.* Workshop presented in cooperation with the Ohio Department of Rehabilitation and Correction, Columbus.

Sampson, R. J., & Laub, J. H. (1994). Urban poverty and the family context of delinquency: A new look at structure and process in a classic study. *Child Development, 65,* 523–540.

Schlichter, K. J., & Horan, J. J. (1981). Effects of stress inoculation on the anger and aggression management skills of institutionalized juvenile delinquents. *Cognitive Therapy and Research, 5,* 359–365.

Schnell, S. V. (1986). *Delinquents with mature moral reasoning: A comparison with delayed delinquents and mature nondelinquents.* Unpublished doctoral dissertation, The Ohio State University, Columbus.

Schuman, E. (Producer). (1994). *Commitment to change: Overcoming errors in thinking* [Videotape/Workbooks]. Carpinteria, PA: FMS Productions, Inc.

Sears, R. R., Maccoby, E. E., & Levin, H. (1957). *Patterns of child rearing.* Evanston, IL: Row, Peterson.

Selman, R. L., & Shultz, L. H. (1990). *Making a friend in youth: Developmental theory and pair therapy.* Chicago: University of Chicago Press.

Shockley, K. C. (1987). *Moral judgment, assertive social skills, and female adolescent birth control behavior in a middle class community.* Unpublished doctoral dissertation, The Ohio State University, Columbus.

Simonian, S. J. (1987). *Social skills in institutionalized male delinquents: A factor analytic investigation of the Inventory of Asolescent Problems–Short Form.* Unpublished doctoral dissertation, The Ohio State University, Columbus.

Simonian, S. J., Tarnowski, K. J., & Gibbs, J. C. (1991). Social skills and antisocial conduct of delinquents. *Child Psychiatry and Human Development, 22,* 17–22.

Slaby, R. G., & Guerra, N. G. (1988). Cognitive mediators of aggression in adolescent offenders: Part 1. Assessment. *Developmental Psychology, 24,* 580–588.

Slavin, R. (1990). *Cooperative learning: Theory, research, and practice.* Englewood Cliffs, NJ: Prentice Hall.

Snarey, J. (1985). The cross-cultural universality of social-moral development: A critical review of Kohlbergian research. *Psychological Bulletin, 97,* 202–232.

Snyder, J. J., & White, M. J. (1979). The use of cognitive self-instructions in treatment of behaviorally disturbed adolescents. *Behavior Therapy, 10,* 227–235.

Spivack, G., & Shure, M. B. (1974). *Social adjustment of young children: A cognitive approach to solving real life problems.* San Francisco: Jossey-Bass.

Spivack, G., & Shure, M. B. (1989). Interpersonal Cognitive Problem Solving (ICPS): A competence-building primary prevention program. *Prevention in Human Services, 6,* 151–178.

Steele, C. M. (1988). The psychology of self-affirmation: Sustaining the integrity of the self. In L. Berkowitz (Ed.), *Advances in experimental social psychology* (pp. 261–302). New York: Academic.

Stein, M., & Davis, J. K. (1982). *Therapies for adolescents: Current treatment for problem behaviors.* San Francisco: Jossey-Bass.

Stenberg, C., Campos, J., & Emde, R. (1983). The facial expression of anger in seven-month-old infants. *Child Development, 54,* 178–184.

Stephens, T. M., & Arnold, K. D. (1992). *Social behavior assessment inventory.* Odessa, FL: Psychological Assessment Resources.

Stone, M. (1989, August 14). What really happened in Central Park. *New York,* pp. 30–43.

Strodtbeck, F. Y. (1955). Husband-wife interaction over revealed differences. In A. P. Hare, E. F. Borgatta, & R. F. Bales (Eds.), *Small groups: Studies in social interaction* (pp. 464–472). New York: Knopf.

Sykes, G. M., & Matza, D. (1957). Techniques of neutralization: A theory of delinquency. *American Sociological Review, 22,* 664–670.

Texas Youth Commission. (1987). *Aggression control skills module.* Austin, TX: Author.

Timerman, J. (1981). *Prisoner without a name, cell without a number.* New York: Knopf.

Trevethan, S. D., & Walker, L. J. (1989). Hypothetical versus real-life moral reasoning among psychopathic and delinquent youth. *Development and Psychopathology, 1,* 91–103.

Tuckman, B. W., & Jensen, M. A. C. (1977). Stages of small group development revisited. *Group and Organization, 2,* 419–427.

Vorrath, H. H., & Brendtro, L. K. (1974). *Positive Peer Culture* (1st ed.). Chicago, IL: Aldine.

Vorrath, H. H., & Brendtro, L. K. (1985). *Positive Peer Culture* (2nd ed.). Hawthorne, NY: Aldine.

Vuchinich, S., Bank, L., & Patterson, G. R. (1992). Parenting, peers, and the stability of antisocial behavior in preadolescent boys. *Developmental Psychology, 28,* 510–521.

Vygotsky, L. S. (1987). Thinking and speech. In R. W. Rieber & A. S. Carton (Eds.), N. Minick (Trans.), *The collected works of L. S. Vygotsky: Vol. 1. Problems of general psychology* (pp. 37–285). New York: Plenum. (Original work published 1934)

Walker, L. J. (1988). Moral reasoning. In R. Vasta (Ed.), *Annals of child development* (Vol. 5, pp. 33–78). Greenwich, CT: JAI.

Walker, L. J. (1989). A longitudinal study of moral reasoning. *Child Development, 60,* 157–166.

Warren, R., Zgourides, G., & Englert, M. (1990). Relationships between catastrophic cognitions and body sensations in anxiety disordered, mixed diagnosis, and normal subjects. *Behaviour Research and Therapy, 28,* 355–357.

Wasmund, W. C. (1988). The social climates of peer group and other residential programs. *Child and Youth Care Quarterly, 17,* 146–155.

Wilson, J. Q. (1983). *Thinking about crime.* New York: Basic.

Wilson, J. Q., & Herrnstein, R. J. (1985). *Crime and human nature.* New York: Simon and Schuster.

Woodbury, R. (1993, October 11). Taming the killers. *Time,* pp. 58–59.

Wuthnow, R. (1994). *Sharing the journey: Support groups and America's new quest for community.* New York: Free Press.

Yalom, I. D. (1985). *The theory and practice of group psychotherapy* (3rd ed.). New York: Basic.

Yochelson, S., & Samenow, S. E. (1976). *The criminal personality: Vol 1. A profile for change.* New York: Jason Aronson.

Yochelson, S., & Samenow, S. E. (1977). *The criminal personality: Vol. 2. The change process.* New York: Jason Aronson.

Yochelson, S., & Samenow, S. E. (1986). *The criminal personality: Vol. 3. The drug user.* Northvale, NJ: Jason Aronson.

Name Index

Abel, G. G., 269

Abramson, L. Y., 115

Achenbach, T. M., 115

Agee, Vicki L.: advocate of family therapy, 265, 266; advocate of service projects, 40; checking technique, 26; combining PPC with equipping, 9; confronting technique, 25; crime reenactment role-playing, 276, 277–278; guidelines for mutual help meetings, 10; observation of empathic predisposition, 109; parent-child reconciliation, 266; "pat and swat technique," 38; positive youth culture, 264; role-reversal procedures, 92; starting a youth group, 225; study of juvenile sex offenders, 113; team unity, 250; treatment of severely antisocial adolescents, 4, 7

Ahlborn, H. H., 51, 52

Akhtar, N., 166

Altman, D., 167

Altman, N., 167

Alvarez-Sanders, C., 277, 279

Arbuthnot, J., 51, 53–54

Archer, M. A., 4

Armel, S., 107

Arnold, K. D., 48, 51, 52, 260

Atwood, R. O., 5

Azar, S. T., 265

Babcock, R., 237

Bachorowski, J. A., 110–111, 259

Bales, R. F., 224

Bandura, A., 110

Bank, L., 240

Barlow, D. H., 107

Baron, R. M., 109

Barriga, A. Q.: accountability, 240; How I Think (HIT) questionnaire, 226, 254, 282; observation of Assuming the Worst distortion, 111; observation of internalizing disorders in female adolescents, 259; observation of Mis-labeling distortion, 113

Basinger, K. S.: classification of moral development, 43; observation of moral development delays, 48, 50, 54, 239, 257; positive potential for reha-bilitating antisocial youths, 239; Sociomoral Reflection Measure–Short Form, 50, 65, 226, 254, 282

Bass, C., 54

Bates, J. E., 111

Baumeister, R. F., 114

Bear, G. G., 48

Beck, A. T., 108, 114, 115, 268

Becker, J. V., 269

Berk, L. E., 105

Birnsbaum, J. J., 113

Bivens, J. A., 105

Bixby, F. Lowell, 4

Blasi, A., 48, 109

Bradley, E. J., 166

Brandsma, J. M., 106

Brendtro, Larry K.: advocate of community service projects, 40; advocate of family therapy, 265; advocate of sharing life stories, 28; "ask-don't-tell" method, 29–30, 31; classification of leadership styles, 223; confronting technique, 26; development of PPC, 4, 11; evaluation of mutual help programs, 6; group-oriented approach, 116; guidelines for group membership, 226, 260; guide-lines for group size, 10; guidelines for participatory management, 244, 252; limitations of group setting, 39; obser-vation of development of self-esteem, 5, 211; observation of thinking errors, 14; observation of treatment of chil-dren, 260–261; opposition to hybrid programs, 9; PPC problem names, 11; "predicting possible outcomes" tech-nique, 32; "punch and burp" technique, 37–38; redirection of negative leader, 35, 36; relabeling techniques, 27; reversing technique, 24; stages of group development, 22, 23; starting youth groups, 225

Burch, P. R., 107

Campagna, A. F., 48

Campos, J., 104

Candee, D., 45

anger management, 107, 120; assessment tests, 254; development of Prepare Curriculum, 167; empathic encouragement, 39; equipping of children, 260; guidelines for meeting rules, 230–231; guidelines for participatory management, 247; guidelines for program description, 242; guidelines for staff, 241; mutual help programs in educational settings, 271; program evaluation, 281–282; role-playing, 38; short-term treatment, 264; spiritual development, 41; youth-to-youth service programs, 274
Gordon, D. A., 51, 53–54
Gottfredson, G. D., 5
Green, R., 107
Gregg, V., 48, 50, 54, 239, 257
Greyson, B., 96
Groth, A. N., 113
Gruber, E., 4
Guerra, N., 106, 111, 113, 115

Harootunian, B., 274
Harrison, Deborah, 231
Harrold, J., 259
Harstad, C. D., 5, 6, 24
Harter, S., 48
Hartig, M., 107
Hartup, W. W., 239
Hastings, J. M., 231
Heaven, P. C., 265
Hekimian, E., 265
Hembree, E. A., 104
Henggeler, S. W., 109, 172, 239, 240, 265
Henri, B., 239
Herrnstein, R. J., 113
Hewer, A., 45
Hickey, J. E., 4, 51
Higgins, A., 51, 52, 53
Hildebran, D., 279
Hilton, N. Z., 279
Hoffman, M. L., 49, 109, 239
Holden, G. W., 239
Hollin, C. R., 54, 172
Horan, J. J., 107
Huebner, R. R., 104
Hunter, N., 171
Huntsinger, G. M., 107
Hurley, D., 3

Irwin, M. J., 265–266
Izard, C. E., 104

Jakubowski, P., 171
Jennings, W. S., 48
Jensen, M. A. C., 22
Johnson, D. W., 273
Johnson, H. J., 106
Johnson, R., 273
Jones, Maxwell, 4

Kahn, T. J., 113, 115–116, 269
Kanfer, E. H., 107
Kapp, S. A., 265
Kaufman, H., 107
Kazdin, A. E., 54, 115, 281–282
Kelly, C. K., 171
Kelman, H. C., 109
Kenardy, J., 106
Kendall, P. C., 106–107, 115, 167
Kierulff, S., 240
Kilkenny, R., 48
Klein, P., 173, 230
Kohlberg, L., 43–45, 48, 51, 52, 53
Kopp, C. B., 104
Krasnor, L. R., 106, 166
Krauss, C., 260
Kunen, J. S., 112, 113

Lafond, M. A., 115–116, 269
Lampron, L. B., 107
Lange, A. J., 171
Laub, J. H., 239
Leeman, L. W.: EQUIP program evaluation, 17, 19, 52, 172, 270, 274, 282; recidivism rates, 274
Levin, H., 105
Lickona, T.: advocate of family therapy, 266–267; advocate of program adaptability, 283; "ask-don't-tell" method, 29, 31, 32; cooperative learning theory, 271, 272; guidelines for participatory management, 247; observation of moral development delays, 43, 48, 49; youth-to-youth service programs, 273
Lieberman, M., 45
Little, V. L., 106–107, 167
Litvak, S. B., 106
Litwack, S. E., 34
Lochman, J. E., 107, 111
Loeber, R., 171

Watson, Marilyn, 271
Wayland, K. K., 107, 111
White, K. J., 107, 111
White, M. J., 107
Wilson, J. Q., 93, 113
Wineman, David, 24, 50, 104, 109, 110, 112, 225, 240; accountability, 240; observation of Blaming Others distortion, 112; observation of deficiencies in self-control, 104–105; observation of Self-Centered distortion, 50, 109, 110; reversing technique, 24; starting a youth group, 225
Woodbury, R., 279
Wright, V., 112
Wuthnow, R., 3

Yalom, I. D., 10, 29, 270
Yochelson, S.: advocate of community service projects, 40; advocate of sharing life stories, 28; description of cognitive disorders, 108, 275; description of the criminal personality, 261; egocentrically biased sense of entitlement, 8; empathy with victims, 157; group-oriented approach, 116; observation of abuse of confrontation, 6; observation of development of self-respect, 5; phenomenologic reporting, 33; qualified approval, 37; redirection of the negative leader, 224; reversing technique, 25; spiritual development, 41; TOP technique, 161; treatment used, 261–263

Zgourides, G., 106
Zwirner, W., 105

Subject Index

Administrators: equipping of staff by, 247–250; orientation to EQUIP by, 226–230; role of, 242, 243, 244–247

Adolescent Problems Inventory (API), 171

Aggravates Others Problem, 12, 172, 221

Aggression, management of: by relabeling, 120–123; through social skills, 165–167. *See also* Anger management

Aggression Replacement Training (ART), 167, 257, 265–266

Aggression Replacement Training (Goldstein & Glick), 173

Al-Anon, 4

Alcoholics Anonymous (AA), 3, 160, 280

Alcohol or Drug Problem, 12, 122

Alcohol problems: definition of, 12, 222; problem situations concerning, 99–100. *See also* Rehabilitation programs

Alonzo's Problem Situation, 55, 80–82, 219, 220

AMBC (anatomy of anger), 124–126, 129, 148

Anger: anatomy of, 124–126, 129, 148–149; easy arousal to, 12, 120, 167, 213, 221; negative consequences of, 148–150; provocation in others, 154–155, 157, 171–172. *See also* Anger management

Anger management: benefits of, 122, 163; and cognitive disorders, 107–116; constructive consequences of, 148–150, 151, 166; deficiencies in, 104–107; evaluating and relabeling anger/aggression in, 120–123; for female adolescents, 259; learning tools for, 17, 116–117, 119–164; Novaco's program for, 116; relaxation techniques for, 139–142, 143, 165–166, 206; self-evaluation of, 127–128, 151–152; and self-report anger scale, 116; through mind and body control, 124–128; through self-talk, 105–107, 124, 126–128, 129, 139, 142, 143–147, 166, 206; weekly sequence of, 213

Anger management/thinking error correction course, 119–164, 213

Antisocial behavior. *See* Antisocial youths

Antisocial Peer Influence, 172

Antisocial youths: accountability of, 239–240, 267, 272; assessment of, 226, 254, 272, 282; primary cognitive distortions of, 8–9; secondary cognitive distortions of, 9; social skill deficiencies of, 7–8; sociomoral developmental delays of, 8, 43, 48; as treatment population, 238–240

Antonio's Problem Situation, 101–102, 219

Anxiety, 114

Approval, qualified, 37

"Ask, Don't Tell" methodology, 29–32, 34, 223

Assessment, of group members, 226, 254, 272, 282

Assuming the Worst distortion: definition of, 9, 13, 14, 110–111; examples of, 88, 207, 208, 222; among female adolescents, 259

Authority Problem, 12, 167, 221

Big Brother/Big Sister program, 273

Blaming Others distortion: definition of, 9, 13, 14, 111–113; examples of, 79, 81, 98, 160, 192, 220; reversing, 23–24, 153–156

California Department of the Youth Authority, 275, 277

Caring Classroom, The (Carducci & Carducci), 271–273

Caring for Someone Who Is Sad or Upset (social skill), 166, 173, 187–189, 212

Charlene's Problem Situation, 65

Cheating, 65, 101–102

Checking ("check yourself") technique, 26, 143, 220

Child molestation, 269–270

Children, adapting EQUIP program for, 260–261

Classrooms. *See* Educational settings

Clown—or Clowns?—in the Ring diagrams, 122, 123

Coaches: asking questions, 29–31, 34; definition of, 9; primary role of, 29, 222–224; redirecting negative leaders by, 25–27

351

About the Authors

John C. Gibbs, Ph.D. (Harvard University, 1972), is professor of developmental psychology at The Ohio State University. He is a member of the State of Ohio Governor's Council on Juvenile Justice and a faculty associate of The Ohio State University Criminal Justice Research Center. His work has concerned developmental theory, assessment of social cognition and moral judgment development, and interventions with conduct-disordered adolescents. He is first author (with Karen Basinger and Dick Fuller) of *Moral Maturity: Measuring the Development of Sociomoral Reflection* and coauthor (with Lawrence Kohlberg) of the second volume of *The Measurement of Moral Judgment*.

Granville Bud Potter, M.Ed. (Bowling Green State University, 1975), is Regional Administrator for the Ohio Department of Youth Services. Potter has 27 years of experience within institutions and the parole division of the Ohio Department of Youth Services. He is President Elect of the Ohio Correctional and Court Services Association. Much of his professional experience has involved the use of a peer-group modality.

Arnold P. Goldstein, Ph.D. (Pennsylvania State University, 1959), is founder and director of the Center for Research on Aggression, affiliated with Syracuse University. He has directed the New York State Task Force on Juvenile Gangs and is on the Council of Representatives of the International Society for Research on Aggression. His many books include *Aggression Replacement Training: A Comprehensive Intervention for Aggressive Youth, The Prepare Curriculum: Teaching Prosocial Competencies,* and *Delinquents on Delinquency*.